AN **APOSTLE** OF THE **NORTH**

William Carpenter Bompas

AN APOSTLE OF THE NORTH

Memoirs of the Right Reverend
William Carpenter Bompas

H.A. Cody

Introduction by
William R. Morrison
and Kenneth S. Coates

Western Canada Reprint Series

 The University of Alberta Press

Published by

The University of Alberta Press
Ring House 2
Edmonton, Alberta, Canada T6G 2E1

This edition copyright © The University of Alberta Press 2002

An Apostle of the North by H.A. Cody was originally published in 1908 by
Seeley & Co. Limited, London, Great Britain. This facsimile edition reproduces
the original text from the 1908 edition.

ISBN 0–88864–400–0
ISSN 0820-9561;7

National Library of Canada Cataloguing in Publication Data

Cody, H. A. (Hiram Alfred), 1872-1948
    An apostle of the north

    (Western Canada reprint series, ISSN 0820-9561 ; 7)
    Includes bibliographical references and index.
    ISBN 0-88864-400-0

    1. Bompas, William Carpenter, 1834-1906. 2. Church of
England—Canada—Bishops—Biography. 3. Bishops—Canada,
Northern—Biography. 4. Missionaries—Canada, Northern—Biography.
5. Indians of North America—Canada, Northern—Missions.
6. Northwest, Canadian—Biography. I. Title. II. Series.
BV2813.B6C62 2003   283'.092   C2002-910935-3

The University of Alberta Press is committed to protecting our natural environment. As part
of our efforts, this book is printed on Enviro Antique: it contains 100% post-consumer recycled
fibres and is acid- and chlorine-free.

Printed and bound in Canada by AGMV Marquis, Sherbrooke, Quebec.

The University of Alberta Press gratefully acknowledges the support received for its publishing
program from The Canada Council for the Arts. In addition, we also gratefully acknowledge
the financial support of the Government of Canada through the Book Publishing Industry
Development Program for our publishing activities.

CONTENTS

AN APOSTLE OF THE NORTH
Memoirs of the Right Reverend William Carpenter Bompas

PREFACE

FIRST PUBLISHED IN 1908, *AN APOSTLE OF THE NORTH* portrayed the life of William Carpenter Bompas (1834–1906) a key figure in the history of the Anglican Church in northern Canada. It speaks to our times of an era in Canada long past, when missionaries to indigenous people were revered, not reviled, and when the First Nations of the Canadian north were generally viewed as primitives, living in pagan ignorance. It is in tone and subject a period piece, and as such is an important document in our country's history.

The author of this biography, Hiram A. Cody (1872–1948) was born in New Brunswick, and, as a young Anglican priest, responded to a call from the Yukon to "take up the Indian work" at Whitehorse.[1] Arriving in the Yukon with his wife[2] in the fall of 1904, he served until the last days of 1909, then returned to his native province to serve a parish and then live in retirement until his death. He knew Bompas personally for the last two years of the bishop's life and was acquainted with many other well-known Yukon personalities, including Robert Service, who, though apparently agnostic, served as a sidesman in Cody's church.

Cody's approach to writing on church topics was permeated with a religiosity common to the late Victorian and Edwardian eras. Once, during a trip out of the Yukon, he visited the bishop at Carcross, and noted in his diary that

The river was calm & beautiful. At 8 pm we all knelt for prayers, the Bp. & Mrs. Bompas, and the Indian children & one white teacher. I looked at those two venerable ones kneeling there, then out at the river so peaceful & then up at the night Mtns. whose peaks were lost from view, and thought how true a picture of these two revered ones, their lives so full of peace, and yet so strong in faith rising to Heaven.[3]

Revered is certainly the right word, for *An Apostle of the North* is suffused with reverence for its subject.

Hiram Cody was at the bishop's funeral in the Yukon, and it was he who took the photograph of the coffin being rowed from the church to the cemetery that appears in the book. The biography was begun shortly after the bishop's death, and Cody was able to draw on the memories of Selina Bompas (1830-1917), the bishop's wife, and his only surviving brother (Henry, the London lawyer, by then a judge) for details of the bishop's life. He also used letters which he got from both widow and brother, and in turn submitted his manuscript to them for approval, so his book is very much an authorized biography. Ted Jones's biography of Cody gives considerable detail about how he wrote it and found a publisher, the contract (Cody got 15%, of which he gave a third to the diocese of Yukon), the selling price ($2.50), the number printed and sold (2000 printed in 1908, 1700 sold that year), his royalties ($334.48 from the English edition), and selections from a scrapbook in which Cody pasted 75 notices from newspapers about the book (he paid $5 to a New York clipping service for these). Selina Bompas seems not to have been entirely satisfied with the book, however, for Bishop Isaac O. Stringer, travelling in Ontario, wrote to Cody in September 1908,

I saw Mrs. Bompas in Montreal and I think she was able to clear her mind on one or two matters that troubled her. She would be glad to see you and if you could stop off for a day to see her I feel it would do her a world of good and disabuse her mind concerning any lingering idea she may have that the book is not all she had hoped. Poor soul she needs our sympathy and I hope you can manage to stop off even for a few hours.[4]

This was, however, only the beginning of Cody's literary career. He had already written some poetry and several articles for magazines, and was at work on a novel, *The Frontiersman: A Tale of the Yukon*. Published in 1910, it was well received, and stimulated him to write more. Eventually he wrote 24 similar books, ending in 1937 with *Storm King Banner*. Representative titles, which give an idea of the tone, are *Rod of the Lone Patrol* (1916), *Glen of the High North* (1920), and *Jess of the Rebel Trail* (1921). Like Pierre Berton, he did one a year, and they always sold well. The royalties from these books, though not large by today's standards, were substantial in comparison to his salary, which in 1911 was $1,000 a year. In that year he made $700 from the sale of his books, and one year in the 1920s he made over $3,000. By 1920 he had sold over 100,000 books in the United States alone.

Although the name of H.A. Cody is virtually unknown today, he was well known in his own time, writing books in the style of the more famous author Ralph Connor. He also continued to write articles for church and other magazines. He had a sufficient reputation in literary circles to be elected the vice-president for New Brunswick of the Canadian Authors' Association at its founding convention in Montreal in 1921. Here to his great pleasure, he mingled with Bliss Carman, Sir Arthur Currie, and other luminaries.

By the end of the 1930s, however, the type of novel he wrote was going out of fashion. Stories about honest, fearless men battling the perils of the frontier, often in a spirit of muscular Christianity, were giving way to books on more urban and sophisticated themes, and at the end of his writing career Cody was dismayed to have a manuscript rejected by a publisher on the grounds that there was no market for it. By the end of his life all of his books were out of print. He retired from the ministry in 1942, and began his autobiography, but suffered a stroke and was unable to finish it. He died in Saint John in 1948.

Our goal in republishing *An Apostle of the North*, originally published in 1908 by Musson in Toronto and by Seeley and Company Limited in London, is not to gild the reputation of William Carpenter Bompas, nor is it to savage his memory. Rather it is to humanize him, to see him as a human being, who carried on his shoulders the deep spirituality of his own faith, the assumptions of his background, and the cultural aggressiveness of the Victorian age—all this while facing the challenges of adaptation to a very difficult climate and terrain. Certainly missionaries are symbols of religious, cultural, and social history, and must be put in the context of their times. But they are also people, individuals whose lives reflect the combination of what the historian Donald Creighton called "character and circumstance," qualities that are the essence of historical biography. Bompas certainly had plenty of character; he was quirky and eccentric, in many ways rather an odd type even for his time. But he was an important figure in the history of the church in Canada, and in the history of the North. He had a significant impact not only on the role of the Anglican Church in the region, but on the pattern of aboriginal-newcomer relations, as well as on the history of the Canadian government in the North. Bompas's story needs to be given wider circulation, if only because it challenges both contemporary First Nations and Canadians in general to confront the full complexity of the history of relations between aboriginal people and the Church. In the process, perhaps we can find a better informed place for the men and women of the Christian Church who came north in the 19th and early 20th centuries, determined to plant the Cross in the "Land of the Midnight Sun."

Readers have a right to know our beliefs and prejudices in reissuing this historic work. Perhaps they can be inferred from what is written here, but for greater clarity we will make a declaration of our attitudes. One of us is politically rather liberal (neither of us, however, is Liberal), the other more conservative. One of us was brought up as a member of the United Church of Canada, then drifted into an agnosticism (cynics would say that this is not a long trip) coloured by a respect for religion as an institution. The other was brought up Anglican, then has attended the United Church from time to time, and is theologically open-minded. One is passionately fond of tradition and high culture, particularly in music, and would be a high church Anglican except for lack of faith; the other is pretty much tone deaf to the beaux arts. Neither of us has an agenda concerning religion, at least as far as self-analysis can tell us, either to glorify missionaries or to excoriate them.

We have been pursuing the idea of writing a biography of Bompas for about ten years. When we began to write in the late 1980s about the Yukon, we repeatedly came into contact with his record, especially his forceful letters to government and church officials, which provided insight into the early years of European activity in the far northwest. Intrigued, and believing that *An Apostle of the North* was a museum piece both in tone and in approach, we decided to write a new biography. We consulted a number of sources in widely different locations: the Anglican Church records in the Yukon Territorial Archives, the Ecclesiastical Archives of the Province of Rupertsland (in Winnipeg), the archives of the Diocese of London (UK), the archives of the Church of England at Lambeth Palace in London, the Bompas collection in Montreal's McCord Museum, and the voluminous files of the Church Missionary Society, which are available on microfilm.

But after a good deal of digging, we ran into a serious difficulty. First, we were unable to discover any substantial cache of private papers, which are essential for a biography based on a close analysis and understanding of the subject's character. Archival documents and published accounts tell much about Bompas the missionary, but not as much as we had hoped about Bompas the man. For instance, he was married in what looks very much like a marriage of convenience, to Charlotte Selina Bompas, his cousin, a lady well into the unenviable Victorian state of spinsterhood when she became a bishop's wife. We know that Bompas was not easy to be married to—he tended to put duty to his church well ahead of duty to his spouse—but about the details of their marriage, we know almost nothing. But this was not the main difficulty we encountered when we decided to write a conventional biography, for eccentricity in a subject is an asset to a biographer. The problem was this: although his many letters can be found in the files of the Church Missionary Society, the Anglican Church of Canada, the Canadian government, the Mounted Police, and other places, these letters are not personal. A few letters to his brother George have been deposited in the McCord Museum in Montreal. But even these letters are not particularly revealing of himself; if he had an inner life that was different from his public face, he did not talk about it. A conventional biography seemed therefore impossible, and we decided that a reprint of H.A. Cody's work would be more valuable, accompanied by a long introduction from our modern perspectives to Bompas and the world of Victorian missionary work in which he spent his life.

Notes

1. Ted Jones, *All the Days of His Life: A Biography of Archdeacon H.A. Cody* (Saint John NB: New Brunswick Museum, 1981), 81.
2. He married Jessie M. Flewelling (1884–1967), and they had five children.
3. Jones, 102.
4. Jones, 154.

ACKNOWLEDGEMENTS

THIS PROJECT HAS BEEN HELPED IMMEASURABLY BY A number of people to whom we are deeply indebted. Rabia Chung, a graduate student at the University of Northern British Columbia, performed the heroic task of reading the microfilm copy of the correspondence files of the Church Missionary Society over the entire period of Bompas's service. There were hundreds of letters, and Ms Chung copied and annotated all of them—a truly gargantuan task. Our research has taken us, over the past two decades, to the Yukon Archives in Whitehorse, the National Archives in Ottawa, the Archives of the Anglican Church of Canada in Toronto, the Archives of the Ecclesiastical Province of Rupertsland and the Hudson's Bay Company Archives (both housed in the Provincial Archives of Manitoba), and in the United Kingdom to the Diocese of London archives and the Lambeth Palace archives. Without exception, we have been welcomed and helped by our professional colleagues in the archival profession, whose stewardship of the historical record and whose support for historical scholarship remains steadfast.

We received financial assistance from the Northern Research Fund at Yukon College, and a personal donation from the Jackman Foundation of Toronto. This project would not have been completed without this timely assistance. We are grateful to Mary Mahoney-Robson of The University of Alberta Press for her encouragement, and to the Press itself for agreeing to re-issue this long out of print work. Thanks to the Ven. Peter Zimmer, Rector of the church of St. Michael and All Angels in Prince George, B.C., for reading the introduction, and advising us on some points of Church doctrine and procedure. We benefited, in the tradition of peer-reviewed scholarship, from the two anonymous scholars who read the manuscript for the University of Alberta Press and provided extremely helpful comment.

Thanks also to the University of Saskatchewan and the University of Northern British Columbia for grants to assist in publication of this work. Additional funding for this new edition of *An Apostle of the North* has come from The Western Canadiana Publications Project as part of its Western Canada Reprint Series.

Two of our professional colleagues, Keith Thor Carlson from the University of Saskatchewan and Kerry Abel from Carleton University read the manuscript with great care and offered us a great deal of good advice. We trust that all those who reviewed the drafts of this work recognize the degree to which we have relied on their sage advice. All faults and errors here are ours.

Our most heartfelt thanks go to Anne Maxwell of Halifax, N.S., a great-niece of the Bishop, who has kept the family history alive in this country, has encouraged us with advice and much information, and has been heroically patient with the many delays the project has encountered.

We write, too, in grateful thanks to our families for their indulgence, support and largely unacknowledged contributes to our work over the years. To Carin and Linda, we offer special thanks for encouragement and tolerance. We continue to treasure the company and accomplishments of our children—Hana, Marlon, Laura, Mark, Bradley, Catherine, John, Claire and Ruth.

GLOSSARY

For those unfamiliar with the terminology of the Church of England, the following definitions may be helpful.[1]

archbishop: the chief **bishop** in an episcopal church who has authority over a **province**. An archbishop has precedence over other bishops and **dioceses**.

bishop: the senior order of ministry—bishop, **priest, deacon**; the chief minister in the episcopally ordered church who is usually in charge of a **diocese**.

priest: an ordained member of the clergy empowered to celebrate the Eucharist (that is, Holy Communion), hear confessions, and pronounce the absolution of sins.

deacon: from the Greek *diakonos* meaning servant, used to refer to the lowest Order in the Christian ministry, below the **priest** and **bishop**. The term is for men (and now women) who may undertake the tasks assigned to **priests** except presiding at Holy Communion and hearing confessions.

diocese: the area or district under the pastoral and administrative care of a bishop, normally consisting of a number of parishes.

curate: An ordained clergyman without a benefice (income from a parish) of his own, who acts as a paid assistant to a rector or vicar, usually as a step towards gaining his own living.

province: a group of **dioceses** under the care of an **archbishop**. England is divided into two Provinces: the Province of Canterbury is the Southern Province; the Province of York is the Northern Province. Bompas's diocese was part of the Province of Rupertsland, with its headquarters in Winnipeg.

rector: An ordained clergyman receiving a living (income) from a parish.

Church Missionary Society: The CMS is a voluntary association of people rooted in the Anglican Communion who are united in obedience to Christ's command to fulfill his Great Commission. They strive to share the love of God with people of all races and to gather them into the fellowship of Christ's Church. That means that all members of CMS try to participate actively in Christian mission wherever they are, in their home country or overseas.

Founded in 1799, CMS has attracted upwards of nine thousand men and women to serve as mission partners during its 200-year history. Today there are about 150 mission partners in 26 countries in Africa, Asia, Europe and the Middle East. A budget of £5.75 million a year is needed to maintain and expand this work.[2]

The Society for Promoting Christian Knowledge: Founded in 1698, the primary concern of the Society's founders was to "counteract the growth of vice and immorality," which they ascribed to "gross ignorance of the principles of the Christian religion." The main ways in which they felt the situation could be tackled were through encouraging education and through producing and distributing Christian literature. Through the work of SPCK, they hoped to build up a more learned clergy and to find ways of communicating the basic principles of the Christian faith to a wider audience, both in Britain and overseas.[3]

The Society for the Propagation of the Gospel: The Society for the Propagation of the Gospel was founded in 1701 to "minister to Her Majesty's subjects in plantations, colonies and factories beyond the seas including native peoples, slaves and settlers."[4]

Notes

1. Adapted from "Litchfield Cathedral."
   http://www.lichfield-cathedral.org/glossary.htm, 22 January 2002.
2. http://www.cms-uk.org/about.htm, 22 January 2002.
3. http://www.spck.org.uk/about-us/history.html, 22 January 2002.
4. http://www.uspg.org.uk/hist.html, 22 January 2002.

W.C. BOMPAS

AN APOSTLE OF THE NORTH

THERE ARE MANY PHOTOGRAPHIC IMAGES OF THE GOLD
Rush, most of them full of life, showing miners, packers, Mounted
Policemen, dancers, and the like. Few of the images show age or
death, yet one remains from the early 20th century that shows not
only the death of a famous Yukoner, but the death of a way of life
that the rush swept aside. It is a picture of a group of men—First
Nations men—standing reverently around a small boat. In the boat
lies a coffin, draped with a pall,[1] bearing the body of William
Carpenter Bompas, first Anglican bishop of the Yukon and for forty
years a missionary to the indigenous people of northwestern
Canada. The photograph would have been taken within a day or two
of the bishop's death on June 9th, 1906. His congregation, almost all
of them First Nations, had gathered for his funeral in the church he
had built, then lowered his coffin in a boat, and rowed it across the
softly-flowing Nares River to the cemetery near the small Klondike-
era settlement of Carcross.[2]

The Carcross cemetery, filled mostly with bodies that Bompas
had buried, sat in an idyllic location. The graves were a mixture of
western-style headstones and the small spirit interment lodges of the
local First Nations, and accepted by Bompas. To the west lay the
snow-covered peaks of the coastal mountains, to the east was Lake
Bennett, whose shores had for centuries been home to the Tagish
people and starting point of the river journey for the tens of thousands of men and women who had headed for the gold fields in the
spring of 1898. Standing among the trees and moss of the cemetery,

the funeral party stood round the open grave, while Isaac O. Stringer,[3] soon to be the new bishop of the Yukon, read the service of committal from the *Book of Common Prayer*, and the bishop's body was lowered into its final resting place.

The location of the grave was a link between past and future. On traditional indigenous land, it overlooked the main transportation route from the Yukon to the "outside," within sight of the river route, and within sound of the trains that ran from Whitehorse to tidewater at Skagway, Alaska. Sam Steele, the famous Mounted Police officer, had come that way, as did the dancehall queen Diamond Lil, and Martha Black, doyenne of the Yukon and second woman to be elected to the Canadian House of Commons (1935). Frederick Schwatka, a U.S. Army Lieutenant, William Ogilvie, the government surveyor, George Carmack and Dawson Charlie, the discoverers of gold—all had been there. Sam McGee and Dangerous Dan McGrew would have come to the Klondike the same way, had they been real people instead of creations of Robert Service's imagination, but Service passed the grave a year or two later. Bompas, however, had been in the region longer than any of these people; he had come with the fur traders, stayed throughout the early mining period and the turbulence of the great gold rush, and lived to see the beginning of the Territory's decline. At the time of his death he had been in the Yukon longer than any other nonaboriginal person.

THE MISSIONARY IMPULSE

As the third millenium of the Christian era begins, the word "missionary" does not have the connotations it did when William Carpenter Bompas began his clerical career in the late 1850s. Then the word suggested a man or woman of self-sacrifice, dedicated to spreading the gospel of Christ to the "heathen," (and the word would not have been put in quotation marks then; there was no squeamishness about calling indigenous people heathen in the 19th century) in far-off places. Missionaries were heroes in that era;

David Livingstone is perhaps the best example, but there were many others famous in their day, giving their lives to bring light to places and people of presumed darkness, to bring words of comfort to the "lesser breeds without the law," as Kipling put it. Missionaries provided the humane rationale for British imperialism: one did not acquire colonies merely to exploit their inhabitants, but also to civilize them and bring them the word of God.

What does the word "missionary" suggest today? To one segment of society, that of evangelical Christianity, its meaning has not changed since Bompas's day, and men and women from the Mormon, Pentecostal, and other faiths still serve their churches in foreign lands. But for the majority of the general public the word has assumed different meanings. It suggests, to many, a rigid, interfering person with archaic moral standards, the kind portrayed in James Michener's novel *Hawaii*, forcing the native women to cover their breasts with cotton shifts in the name of decency, the sort of person the Australians call a "wowser"—a prude, a killjoy. Worse, in Canada, missionaries past and present have come to be regarded by many as agents of social genocide and worse still, as pedophiles.

If one feels this way about missionaries (and we do not necessarily), why study them, other than merely to condemn them and all their works? A simple answer is that they were an important part of the history of First Nations in this country, of the history of the relations between First Nations and others, of the remoter regions of Canada, and of the North in particular. A blanket condemnation, such as constantly appears in the mainstream press today, serves to obscure more than it reveals. In the first place, it is simplistic and absurd to criticize the entire missionary initiative as bad, and to assert that Christian outreach was inherently and entirely evil and destructive. Even if one agrees, and the fact can hardly be denied, that missionaries included among their number some abusers and some whose appetite for power approached megalomania, and that their enterprise, by our standards, was arrogant and ethnocentric, the relationship between First Nations people in Canada and the Christian churches has been too close, too complex, too mutually-supportive to be glibly dismissed simply as one more case of European colonial oppression of indigenous people.

Yet, oddly, one of the greatest sources of criticism of the missionaries is the churches. As those who sponsored the missionaries—the Roman Catholics, the Anglicans, and the United Church of Canada in particular—struggle to come to terms with the tragedies that did occur, especially in the residential schools, they seem to make no effort at all to emphasize the positive aspects of the missionary era. They say nothing, at least in public, about the virtues of what once they called the "missionary saints" who carried the Cross to the First Nations of Canada. One would have to be able to see into the minds of church leaders to know why this is the case; perhaps it stems from genuine embarrassment and remorse, perhaps from the fact that the leaders of the churches tend to be politically left-leaning (and belief in the victimization of First Nations people is an article of faith on the political left), perhaps from the fact that some church leaders no longer believe what their 19th-century predecessors believed: that the traditional Christian beliefs are more valid than indigenous beliefs and ought to replace them. For whatever reason, the history of the missionary enterprise, once fodder for sermons, the focus of church women's organizations, and a staple of Sunday school lessons until two generations ago, has now become an embarrassment; the tales that once inspired such dedication now gathering dust on the bookshelves of Canada's churches. In some places, it must be said, they are still venerated, even by Anglicans. An internet site[4] urges people to remember the missionaries in their prayers, and speaks of Bompas with reverence, if not with accuracy:

> Early Christian missions can be summed up by recounting the story of one couple: William and Lena Bompas. Raised in high society in England, they gave it all up to answer the call of God to serve Him in the remote reaches of Canada's Yukon Territory. They withstood hardships and bravely spread the Gospel. Late in the 19th century, Klondike fever brought

thousands to the Yukon. With them came a handful of dedicated Christians, determined not for gold, but for treasure that lasts—souls.

The Christian churches in Canada, and in particular the three "old-line" denominations–Roman Catholic, Anglican, and United (formerly Methodist, Congregationalist, and Presbyterian)–have been vilified in the past few years for their involvement in residential school education. Recently, one denomination approached the Innu of Labrador to extend a formal apology and to begin a relationship different from that of the past. The Innu rejected the offer of apology, giving the frank and brutal explanation that when they thought of the role of the church in their past, the picture that arose was that of a missionary forcing a young aboriginal boy to perform oral sex. No apology would do, and only time would make things better. Broader efforts to heal the wounds and to reach some rapprochement between Christian churches and First Nations in general were rebuffed by Matthew Coon Come, Grand Chief of the Assembly of First Nations. Coon Come warned church leaders that words of apology were not enough for the 90 percent of the aboriginal people of Canada who considered themselves Christian. Coon Come's advice was that the church leaders should show action, not words, that they should visit First Nations communities to confront the effects of the damages their predecessors had wrought. He called on the leaders to show understanding if their efforts were received with bitterness and frustration. Apologies would never be enough, and the process would not be quick. Some church leaders, such as Vancouver Island's Roman Catholic Bishop DeRoo, were quick to move in the direction Coon Come advised, and the results of such initiatives have been largely welcomed and rewarding for all concerned.

Contemporary debates, particularly those surrounding the issue of residential schooling and the alleged cultural imperialism of aggressive Christianity, make it impossible to reach conclusions in a manner that will please everyone. For critics, indigenous and nonindigenous, the missionaries exemplify the worst excesses of European colonialism, along with a process of deliberate cultural destruction. Supporters of the Christian missionary enterprise emphasize, in contrast, the compassion, devotion, and sacrifice, even as they admit and apologise for the excesses that occurred. Between these views there is no middle ground, and for those (like us) who try to find one, the footing can be slippery indeed.

In such an atmosphere one must open with some trepidation the question of the role of missionaries in this country. Their role has changed. While the Roman Catholic and United Church missionaries still work with Canadian First Nations communities, contemporary missionaries tend to spread the gospel in other countries, to those who have never heard of Christ (or, as in the case of some American fundamentalist groups, to Roman Catholics in Latin America and the Philippines, who in their eyes are the next thing to heathens). And among the remaining traditional missionaries, such as the Oblate Order, their work is more concerned with promoting community health through a very "Vatican II" definition of spiritual well-being than with religious conversion. After all, if 90 percent of aboriginal people in this country think of themselves as nominally Christian, the "good word" as a new thing has presumably been sufficiently spread, and since responsibility for educating aboriginal people has been turned over to the state, the missionary era in Canada has come to an end. When everyone has at least heard about the Christian God, there is no need for proselytizing. Certainly, however, there are still "missionaries" in the Canadian North, particularly members of evangelical denominations, whose work involves persuading the aboriginal people to join their churches. But this almost always involves leaving the church to which they already belong, and thus is more in the nature of denominational poaching than bringing the Christian faith to those who do not already have it.

Until recently, most historians of missionaries in Canada have focused on the role of Christian evangelists in the transformation of indigenous cultures through the processes of contact. A large and growing number of scholars have taken a different approach.

John Webster Grant, Jean (Usher) Friesen, Kerry Abel, Margaret Whitehead, Jacqueline Gresko, Clarence Bolt, Martha McCarthy, Myra Rutherdale, and Raymond Huel[5] who have written on missionaries working with First Nations and Ruth Whitehead, Margaret Prang, and others who have studied Canadian missionaries working overseas have emphasized the personal, spiritual and theological qualities of the men and women who worked often as much on behalf of Native communities as for the Christian churches. In their work, they draw on the voluminous correspondence files, journals, diaries and memoirs of the vanguard of Christianity. Some missionaries left much more personal records than did William Carpenter Bompas, permitting their biographers to explore the nuances of thought and action in ways that are not possible with Bompas.

THE BIOGRAPHICAL TRADITION

For much of the 19th and 20th century, the missionary experience spawned a flood of biographies and autobiographies of missionaries from and in Canada. Many of these books, including Cody's *An Apostle of the North*, attracted a great deal of attention in their day. In more recent times, the lives of Canadian missionaries like Robert McClure have continued to find a ready audience. The principal student of this culturally rich body of Canadian literature is Terrence Craig. His *The Missionary Lives: A Study of Canadian Missionary Biography and Autobiography*[6] provides a thoughtful analysis of the intellectual and cultural insights to be gleaned from this vast library. As Craig writes of this material:

> The fascination of the missionary, supported by the mythic infrastructure of archetypal caricature on the one hand and the hero-worship of the faithful on the other hand, is an undeniably persistent feature of this writing, one that survives its "dating" of form and content, and one that has perhaps survived its own

purpose. As part of Canadian literature, representative of many Canadians' interests in the past century and still a vital if reduced presence, mission writing deserves acknowledgement, which it has not had.[7]

Craig makes a compelling case that historical and literary scholars should use missionary autobiography and biography as a means of exploring cultural, social, religious, and other realities in Canadian history. More than any other analyst, he argues forcefully that the very nature of books such as *An Apostle of the North*—hagiographic, uncritical, celebratory, spiritually and culturally directed—provides access to aspects of Canadian society that have often been ignored. In a point particularly relevant to Cody's biography of Bompas—which was an Anglican standard for many years—Craig asserts "I would argue that many Canadians have learned more about the Arctic through their churches than through their schools."[8] Connecting this experience to contemporary church life, he notes that overseas mission work and the writing about that work continues to provide many Canadians with their primary introduction to the people, societies and issues of distant lands. To know more about the major books and personalities of the missionary world, then, is to gain important insights into how non-Natives in earlier generations viewed Canada, First Nations, the North and the Christian church.

Craig, who refers to Cody's biography and some of William Carpenter Bompas's writings at several points in his analysis, seeks to resurrect interest in missionary writings, much as we do with the reprinting of Bompas's biography. Craig could well be speaking specifically of Cody's biography of Bompas when he observes, "Their biographies and autobiographies assert their extremism in deceptively subtle and attractive tones, and linger in the present as archaisms of a past when life offered clear certainties that were worth giving one's life for. Perhaps this nostalgia for an idealized past and a romantic literature that supports it, explains their persistence in contemporary life."[9] Bishop William Carpenter Bompas continues to generate a strong response, both from those who laud his accomplishments and celebrate his life and others who would see him as an agent of cultural imperialism and spiritual destruction. The reality is that Bompas's life contained elements of both "realities"—and many others as well. Bompas was a complex man, with a deep and complicated relationship with the First Nations, and a stand-offish approach to the nonaboriginal population. Cody's book is better at capturing the zeitgeist of the missionary age, and the mentalities of aggressive Christianity, than it is at exploring the nuances of Bompas's lived experience and lingering impact. By making this book available to a broader audience again, we hope to stimulate interest in both the lives of northern missionaries and to encourage greater understanding of the impact of Christian evangelists and their nonaboriginal companions on the First Nations in the Canadian North.

The missionary era, in its classic sense, is over in this country, having ended around 1950, and it seems to have left a bad historical taste in most people's mouths. But this does not mean the study of the missionary era should be confined within narrow critical boundaries. Certainly there is no reason to write another hagiographical biography of Bompas and his ilk, if for no other reason than it has already been done, as *An Apostle of the North* bears witness. But in the same way there is no reason to write polemics against missionaries that portray them as unalloyed evil; such polemics are really hagiography pointed in a different direction. Moreover, the kind of writing that portrays indigenous people as simple victims of newcomers ignores the important factor of "agency," specifically that First Nations people had a certain measure of control and influence over the newcomers; the power did not flow only in one direction.[10] As the life of Bompas illustrates, there is much social complexity in the missionary experience, as well as drama, cultural interplay, and general historical interest. On a personal level, missionaries are interesting and complex people, as one would expect, given the impulses that drove them to places that were to them wild and remote. It is fascinating to examine and dissect their character and motivations.

Relations between First Nations and missionaries were always more complex than the contemporary rhetoric of victimology suggests. Missionaries were not necessarily wicked agents of cultural genocide, simultaneously disparaging if not exterminating the way of life of adults, while abusing the minds and bodies of their children. Some missionaries in fact had a deep and mutually supportive relationship with their aboriginal congregations, establishing close and mutually supportive friendships that endured for a lifetime and shaped communities for generations. Others were insensitive to the point of megalomania, turning their churches into little Englands, exercising the kind of brutal cultural superiority that gave the whole enterprise a bad name. Missionaries were competent and foolish, deeply spiritual and shallow, Eurocentrists who denigrated indigenous culture and Rousseauian mystics who glorified the "noble savage." Some, through insights and careful writing, left an enduring record of the inner workings of the aboriginal spiritual and cultural world. Others disparagingly treated First Nations as almost sub-human creatures whose culture was worthless and whose personal habits were disgusting. It must also be remembered that they often served as buffers against the jagged edge of colonial expansion, as intermediaries between First Nations and the more brutal forces of the newcomers: whiskey traders, resource exploiters, even Indian agents. Certainly Bompas performed an important service in this regard.

THE BISHOP AND THE NORTH

Visitors to the North today, if they know where to look or whom to ask, can still find the bishop's grave. Traces of him linger. A school in Fort Simpson is named after him, and there is a Bompas Street in Inuvik. His name is recorded and part of his story told on an historic marker outside the newer Anglican cathedral in Whitehorse, an unpretentious building close by the old log church, which was built during Bompas's last years. Looking at either building it is hard to believe that they are the headquarters of an Anglican diocese, filling

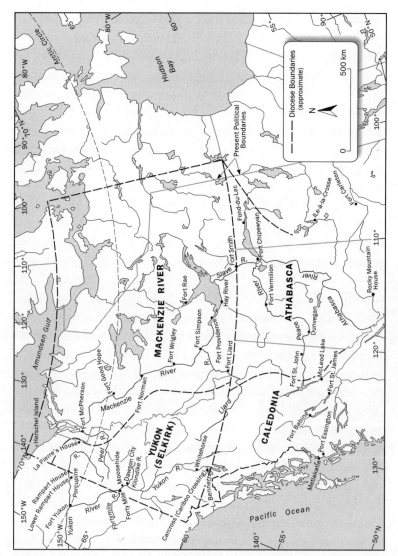

The Canadian Northwest, c. 1900.

the same clerical functions as huge English gothic structures such as Salisbury or Winchester cathedrals.[11] Southerners need to modify their understanding of such trappings of Yukon Anglicanism as the bishop's "throne," the cathedral chapter, and the rest, but the building is a cathedral all the same. There are occasional references to Bompas in pamphlets published by the government historic sites service and in museum displays. But memory of him is blurred and forgotten, and nothing in the Yukon is named after him, for this is not an age when Canadians celebrate religious heroes, or mark the contributions of those who "opened" (we must now put the word in quotation marks) the Canadian North for European settlement.

In his day, however, Bompas was a giant among Yukoners, the first nonaboriginal person to dedicate his life and work to the region, and certainly the first to do so for reasons other than personal financial gain. While others came north to exploit the country for money or fame, then quickly left, Bompas positively refused offers and entreaties in his middle years to leave the region and live a more comfortable life in the south. Instead he made his life into old age along the rivers and lakes of the Yukon, amidst the indigenous people he would have considered his friends. His work proved critical in the unfolding of the history of the region. Without his urgent appeals to and his harassment of Canadian officials, the government (in the persons of the North-West Mounted Police) would not have been in the Klondike before the gold rush occurred, and the history of the region could have been very different. Even leaving aside his religious work, he ought to be remembered for this fact alone. But in a secular age, when a declining minority of Canadians attend church regularly,[12] too much faith can be a liability to a political career. When missionary work is viewed as at best quaint and at worst genocidal, Canadians will not be much interested in their religious past, particularly as it applies to First Nations people.

Bompas was a difficult man, cantankerous, stubborn, and more than a little eccentric. Father Grouard, a Roman Catholic missionary priest, wrote of Bompas "the man is a mystery to me. If he is quite sincere, he is almost a saint. If not—he is truly a devil."[13] He was not a man people warmed to on a personal level, though those who knew him praised his devotion, energy, determination, and deep commitment to the welfare of First Nations people. He took his duties seriously, and wrote many reports. He spoke out often and strongly about perceived wrongs and injustices. But in his many official letters he almost never talked about himself, about his feelings, his fears and hopes, his ambitions. He had acquaintances and colleagues, but seemingly no friends or confidants to whom he could unburden himself, except for his relatives, and there are not many letters to them extant. As a man, then, he remains somewhat of a mystery.

But is there a mystery? Perhaps the public man was also the private man. He was devoted to his calling. How much enjoyment he received from it is hard to tell, and he probably never thought of it in those terms. He seems to have found satisfaction in performing what he knew to be his duty. His crankiness stemmed not from anti-social or misanthropic impulses but from his anger at injustice, particularly towards First Nations people. He appears not to have been ambitious in the conventional sense, and he disdained the ceremony and prestige of being a bishop. It was not false modesty that impelled him to do so but an intense sense of duty, one imposed by God, which he was single-minded in pursuing. His theology also prevented him from playing the role of bishop; born a Bapist, a denomination that had no bishops, he had no inborn love of hierarchy; as a strict evangelical, he viewed the office of bishop as a vestige of what he would have called "popery."

How then does one recount the life of such a man? A biography without access to private and personal material would be less than adequate. H.M. Cody, also a missionary in the Yukon, and also a writer of Canadian fiction in the early 20th century, wrote his biography just after Bompas's death in 1906, and was able to gather some information on his early life, presumably from his widow and from members of the Bompas family in England. Cody had the advantage of knowing Bompas personally. His book is hagiography in the formal sense of the word—to our eyes almost absurdly so, for the awe and reverence with which Cody treats his subject makes it difficult sometimes to remember that the man he is writing about is a mere mortal. The book tells the life of a man Cody saw as a wilderness saint. This was the way Bompas was seen by his church at home and abroad—a man who sacrificed himself for his Christian duty, a model of Christian citizenship and devotion. To say that Cody's book is old-fashioned in its approach is not to denigrate it; it provides insights into Bompas's life and works, and if it were not for this book, it is doubtful if we would know anything at all about the subject's early life.

No scholar would today write a book like this one, and none but a religious publisher would issue it. The language seems quaint to our ears, and excessively reverent. The tone is so old-fashioned as to be almost charming, were it not so antithetical to the politically correct discourse of our own era. It is rife with stereotypes and tinged with Victorian racism. Cody sought to praise Bompas, not analyze him, and the bishop's life is clearly meant to be a model for Christian service and living. Nor would one ever read this book for ethnographic insights; there is much about First Nations people, but the tone is unkind and full of moral superiority and Christian paternalism. To point out its shortcomings, however, is not to deny its value and contributions. It is a wonderful illustration of the thinking that attracted missionaries to the North in the second half of the 19th century. The ideas and phrases that make us wince were commonplace up to the middle of the 20th century. But this is where its value lies: not in analysis, but in the fact that it is a contemporary account, written in the period it describes, by a man who was a witness to the events it narrates. It puts Bompas in the midst of his contemporaries—the First Nations, fur traders, miners, government and church officials—and describes how the missionary's life fit (and, in Bompas's case, often did not fit) with a rapidly changing northern society.

An Apostle of the North is a work of its time, not ours, celebrating the values of the "muscular Christianity" of the late 19th century[14]—that combination of faith, fresh air, and exercise which brought a healthy physical and spiritual life into wholesome unity. It is really a tract, a long sermon that portrays its subject as a model of Christian virtue and fortitude, in which rhetoric mingles with fact. Readers will find passages that provoke and perhaps anger them, because of the assumptions and values that underlie Cody's account. The book portrays First Nations people through the lens of Victorian racial assumptions, though the harsher edges of these assumptions have been softened by Cody's first-hand experiences in the North. It must be remembered that Bompas, despite his personal oddities, was in many ways a typical missionary of his era. His life might be compared with that of, say, Wilfred Grenfell, the medical missionary to the Labrador coast in the 1890s, the era's leading muscular Christian in Canada, and a contemporary of Bompas. Though Grenfell's personality was quite different (think of a combination of Rudyard Kipling and *Tom Brown's Schooldays*), his energetic devotion to bringing Christian light to the darkness was much the same, and his view of the cultural inferiority of aboriginal people mirrored that of Bompas.

We hope that this reissue of Cody's book will stimulate a new consideration of the relationship between the churches and the indigenous people of Canada. Alongside the clear evidence of abuse there needs to be appreciation of the complexity that characterized the missionary enterprise, and this means appreciating the fact that there were partnerships and friendships as well as victimization and colonization. There needs to be some appreciation of something that is rarely mentioned in current discussions of the missionary era: specifically that First Nations aligned themselves with Christianity not only because of European cultural domination, or paternalism, or because indigenous culture was in crisis, but also because they found something compelling in the teachings of Christianity. The fact that to say this in our era is likely to stimulate a hurricane of criticism from First Nations apologists does not mean it is not true.

There is no simple guide through the cultural and spiritual maze of the relations between missionaries and indigenous people; certainly not Bompas or Cody, who saw the issue mostly from one perspective and were not given to self-questioning. Furthermore, the First Nations groups with whom Bompas interacted were not members of a single culture. They included such diverse groups as Dene, Gwich'in, Inuit, Han, Tutchone, Southern Tutchone, and Inland Tlingit. Like all peoples, they included a variety of individuals with different interests, expectations, and spiritual experiences. Personal and group reactions to missionaries varied according to local conditions and circumstances, the personalities and attitudes of missionaries, and nature of non-Native intrusions into an area, and many other factors.

Somewhere in this complex social, cultural, and spiritual relationship lie the threads that bind the past to the present, threads that explain the deep attachment of many northern First Nations people to the Anglican Church, and that illustrate the impact of the curious mixture of compassion, paternalism, Christian theology, British values, and cultural blindness that Bompas and his colleagues brought to the far northwest. Somewhere in the history of northern mission work there are explanations for the powerful social, spiritual, and personal forces that drew Bompas and others from comfortable British and Canadian lives into the cold, dark, and difficult life of the region. And somewhere in the life and times of these earnest people are the illustrations of the changing temper of the times, which sapped the vitality of the northern mission fields and transformed and then damaged the Church in the region. More than anything, Bompas's life in the North should offer insights into the compelling force of religion and faith, one of the most pervasive forces in human experience, capable of transforming people, creating conflict, spreading hope, motivating entire nations, and, as the history of the recent past has shown, making horrible and damaging mistakes.

WILLIAM CARPENTER BOMPAS

Who was William Carpenter Bompas? Cody's book gives the basic facts, to which it is possible only to add details and comment. In the first place, he had an unusual name. If the bishop escaped persecution at school because of his name—unkind variations on it come to mind—he was either a good fighter, or children were kinder in the 1840s—and there is no reason to believe that either was the case. Some families have the variation "Bumpus," which must be a worse burden. Other variants also exist. It was likely French originally, "Bonpas," and family legend has it that it resulted from a royal quip about a "good step." The most likely historical source of the name is Bonpàs, a small commune near Perpignan in the south of France, which is now spelled "Bompas." The tourist guide says that the town was first mentioned in 1153, but was then called Malpàs, that is the "bad passage," owing to the fact that it was a difficult ford over a stream on an ancient road. The name was changed to Bonpàs, that is, "good passage," either because a bridge was built, or for the same reason that Leif Ericsson called his icy discovery Greenland—for publicity purposes. Another village of the same name exists near Avignon, and the name may have come from there. There are few things duller than other people's genealogy, but on the subject of odd names it can be noted that the bishop's father-in-law, who was also his uncle, began life as Joseph Cox Bompas, but when he was adopted by his mother's cousins, changed his name to Joseph Cox Cox.

The Bompas family came to England, probably as Huguenots, in the mid-16th century, landing at Bristol,[15] and the bishop's branch of the family lived at Bredon, in Worcestershire, where there are twenty-two birth, death, and marriage records in the parish register under the name Bumpass between 1563 and 1600. The bishop's father, Charles Carpenter Bompas (1791–1844), was a Baptist, and a prominent barrister who practiced first in Bristol and then in London. He was a Serjeant-at-law, which meant that he was the leading barrister of his area, which in his case was the Western Circuit Court. Family tradition holds that he was used as a model by

Charles Dickens for the minor character "Serjeant Buzfuz" in the novel *The Pickwick Papers*. His religion prevented him from securing the judgeship that he might otherwise have received.

C.C. Bompas had five sons, of whom the bishop was the fourth, and three daughters. The eldest son, Charles, was Assistant Secretary to the London Zoological Society, but died at 24; the second, George, was a solicitor who sent the bishop money to help with expenses in the North; the third, Joseph, emigrated to Canada and farmed; the fifth, Henry, was a successful lawyer and a County Court judge. Two sisters, Mary and Selina, were unmarried, and the third, Sophia, married a Unitarian minister.

Altogether it was a prosperous middle-class family into which William Carpenter Bompas was born on January 20th, 1834, in London, his early life marred only by the early death of his father. Left fatherless at the age of ten, William (it seems inconceivable that anyone ever called him "Bill")[16] was raised as a Baptist. The theology emphasized a personal relationship with God and the literal interpretation of the Bible, in contrast to the "high church" of formal Anglicanism, which emphasized authority and ritual. An example of Bompas's attitude to ritual appears in a letter he wrote to his assistant on the occasion of the death of Queen Victoria in 1901. The assistant had suggested a special commemorative service in Dawson City; Bompas demurred, on the grounds that it would seem too much like a Roman Catholic requiem mass.

He seems to have been a serious and solitary child, and the Baptist church was an important part of his life. At the age of sixteen, he accepted baptism and became a church member. Not much is known of his early life, but it seems not to have been a particularly happy one, despite the presence of his mother, Mary, and his many siblings. It was difficult for him to determine his role in Britain of the mid-19th century. Lacking in social graces, not particularly well-schooled, already showing the signs of the austerity that marked his later life, he was unsure of his calling. At first he tried law, the family profession, but he found that it did not satisfy him. In 1858 he left his job in a law office. He found the work uncongenial, his family was hard-pressed for money, and he had proposed marriage to his cousin Selina and had been refused. He seems to have had a nervous breakdown that involved a crisis of faith, but no details of it are known. In 1859 he accepted ordination as a deacon in the Church of England.

Why did William Bompas join the Church of England instead of remaining a Baptist, a faith with which he seemed spiritually more in harmony? Was it ambition? The Church of England was the spiritual arm of the British Empire, and an ambitious and well-connected clergyman might rise to be a bishop or even an archbishop. The Baptist church lacked such a hierarchy. But Bompas was not ambitious in that sense, and was in fact quite reluctant to accept a bishopric when one was offered to him. The Established Church had the great cathedrals, the regalia, the support of the government, but again that was not Bompas's style. His religion was based on faith, not ritual. Kerry Abel summed up his theological orientation:

> He was determinedly idealistic about the promise of salvation through the realization of sin and the acceptance of true faith. He felt church rituals such as crosses, candles, incense and processions were insults to God. Practices like confession, veneration of the Virgin Mary, prayers for the dead, or the formation of religious communities were medieval inventions which had to be swept aside in order to return to the purity of the early church. Ministers had no power to pardon sin or act as mediators between God and man; their sole duty was to preach the gospel as "servants" of the laity rather than its masters.... Apostolic succession was an invention of "Tractarians"[17] ...Even towards the end of his life, Bompas still perceived himself as an "old fashioned evangelical."...Those evangelical convictions were at the root of his early reluctance to establish schools or model farms in his diocese. He chose his mission agents

according to their support for the evangelical doctrines
rather than their educational or personal suitability for
the work.[18]

Bompas lacked the money and connections that would have helped
him in a clerical career. But he did not care. Fortunately for him, the
Church had a large spiritual umbrella, able to accommodate low
church believers who were not far from Baptists, and also the high
church members of the Oxford Movement, who were not much
different from Roman Catholics. No answer can be given to the
question of why he left the Baptists; perhaps it was genuine spiritual
conviction, perhaps he had been influenced by a charismatic
preacher, perhaps the job prospects looked better.

Whatever the reason, he had joined the church and chosen a
career. But his early years were difficult. Most of the Church of
England clergy held university degrees; that Bompas had none held
him back, and meant that he had to be ordained a deacon through
special dispensation. As a deacon he could administer the sacraments
but not consecrate them; it was a position halfway to the priesthood.
Lacking money and connections, he accepted the curacy at the
parish of Sutton-on-the-Marsh, Lincolnshire, a post he held from
1859 to 1862, serving afterwards briefly in Nottinghamshire. A
curate was an assistant to a parish priest, paid a salary. Most priests
began as curates, as a sort of apprenticeship. Those who had the
influence to be appointed to a "living" or the money to buy one (as
military commissions were bought) then became the rectors of
parishes, living off endowments and other revenues, but a man such
as Bompas, without money or connections, might stay a curate all
his life. Sometimes the curate did all the work while the priest lived
elsewhere and collected the parish revenues. The curate was a figure
of Victorian fiction and melodrama, usually young, impoverished,
and socially anxious. A famous cartoon in the humour magazine
Punch[19] shows a timid curate having breakfast with his bishop, eating
a boiled egg. The bishop says "I'm afraid you've got a bad egg,
Mr. Jones," to which the curate, desperate not to give offence,

replies, "Oh no, my Lord, I assure you that parts of it are excellent." The cartoon was so popular that the phrases "curate's egg" and "good in parts" passed into the language. There was a sharp edge to the joke, however: curates could live servile lives, something that would not have appealed to Bompas.

A way out of this situation was foreign missionary work, something that in any case appealed to his wish to serve. When he applied, on more than one occasion, to the Church Missionary Society for a foreign posting, however, he was rejected. This was a surprise, since unlike its wealthier and more highbrow cousin, the Society for the Propagation of the Gospel in Foreign Parts, the Church Missionary Society represented the low church end of the Anglican spectrum. The CMS accepted men with lower educational qualifications, often sending them to less prestigious mission fields. To be turned down in this way seemed to sentence Bompas to a life of ill-paid parish work. Why he was rejected is unclear, but it may have been that the CMS thought he was too old at nearly thirty to learn new languages, or perhaps it was his dour and ascetic personality. He lacked the warmth and outgoing nature that could have won converts among the "heathen." Put plainly, he was unimpressive, seemingly destined for a life of professional disappointment and dissatisfaction, a failure in the eyes of his family and of himself.

Luckily for him, however, circumstances arose that improved his prospects. In the mid 1860s the Church Missionary Society was seeking recruits for one of its most unattractive mission fields—the northwest of British North America. To the British, the land was vast, cold, and full of perils. The indigenous population was few in number and roamed widely over the huge sub-Arctic wilderness. A handful of European fur traders and missionaries represented "civilization" in the wilderness of the northwestern part of the continent. A small number of CMS missionaries and a handful of Roman Catholic nuns and priests were engaged in a struggle to win the hearts and minds of the indigenous population—a "race for souls" that was hotly contested. It was impossible to conduct a mission in the region based on ministering to a settled community, since most of the First Nations spent much of the year travelling between hunting, trapping, and fishing sites; this mobility made converting them to Christianity much more difficult. But the struggle with the Catholics was a goal in itself.

Relations between the missionaries of the two denominations were civil on the surface, but the hostility was evident in private correspondence. On his way to the northwest in the early winter of 1865, Bompas made a typical observation about the rivalry:

> [Archdeacon Hunter] converted 2 or 3 Papists to Protestantism & I suppose raised the jealousy of the Romanists who have been pouring in priests ever since. There are now nearly a priest to every fort. At one of their missions about a day from this there are now residing a Bishop 3 Priests 4 Lay Brothers & 4 servants & sisters of mercy are expected next summer. All these are with much difficulty kept from starving & the Company can hardly bring in needful supplies for them. Now it so happens that there are no Indians near the Mission Station in question so that the object of it all does not very plainly appear.[20]

Anxious to get a leg up on the ever-aggressive Roman Catholics, Bishop David Anderson of Rupertsland had sent Robert McDonald (1829–1913) down the Mackenzie River in 1853. McDonald was no expert theologian, but he was one of the North's most accomplished missionaries. He moved into the Fort McPherson/Rat River area near the mouth of the Mackenzie River and ventured across the mountains into the upper Yukon River basin. McDonald was successful in establishing relations with the Gwich'in. He blended local knowledge, excellent personal relations with First Nations people, a sensible, compassionate Christianity, and immense practicality. McDonald set down roots among the aboriginal people in the region, and his labours continue to bear fruit a century and a half after his arrival in the area. The Anglican Church enjoys its strongest northern following in McDonald's mission field, for the first CMS missionary in the area did an excellent job of building the church into Gwich'in society and culture.

In 1865, McDonald fell seriously ill. At the least, he would have to leave the field to recuperate; many believed that he was soon to be called to be with his Lord. Bishop Anderson faced an immediate problem, the potential loss of a valued friend and accomplished mission worker. The Roman Catholic Church was nipping at the Anglican's heels in the Mackenzie Valley and was poised to move into any vacuum left by McDonald's illness, departure, or death.

While praying for McDonald's recovery, Anderson urgently sought a replacement. Mission workers were difficult to find in Canada. As a result, most of the western and northern clerics, Anglicans and Roman Catholics alike, came from England or France. Anderson's appeals brought no volunteers. On a speaking tour in England in May 1865, Bishop Anderson preached about the need in the far northwest mission field and called on his audiences to pray for an answer to the church's appeal. In one of his audiences sat a thirty-one year old curate, a man of uncertain destiny and accomplishments. To a deeply spiritual man seeking a role in the church and searching for a message from God, Anderson's words struck deep into the soul. While others in the audience pledged money, prayers and continuing support, Bompas offered himself.

This time, the Church Missionary Society accepted his offer. The posting was no sinecure. It was ill-paid, extremely remote, in one of the most difficult and forbidding territories in the world. Repeating a scene witnessed hundreds of times throughout the 19th century, Bompas leapt from the obscurity of a small British parish into the unknown and uncertain world of overseas mission work. Others were called to do the church's work in China, Japan, the South Pacific Islands or the challenging fields in Africa. Bompas had been drawn to volunteer to carry the Anglican message into the hunting and fishing camps of the First Nations people of the British North American sub-Arctic. Within a month of hearing Anderson speak in England, Bompas accepted the call and was ordained a priest; by the end of June, he was in Rupert's Land. When Bishop Robert Machray, Anderson's replacement, put his seal of approval on William Carpenter Bompas, he unleashed a vigorous and determined missionary on the aboriginal people of the far northwest.

There are few comments from his contemporaries about the new missionary. At this stage, he lacked the stature and reputation of his predecessor. He left correspondents, rather than friends, in his wake, and he made few attempts to develop friendships with the fur traders in Rupert's Land. Many of the Hudson's Bay Company employees, in fact, failed to measure up to Bompas's exacting standards, and often had to bear the brunt of his demands and expectations. He was earnest, liberated from his sense of failure, and filled with enthusiasm for his great new venture. He felt called to the mission field, and believed that God had selected him, specifically, for the purpose of bringing Christianity to the aboriginal people in the Canadian North.

Bompas's colleagues almost immediately realized his resolve and determination. After his ordination as a priest, Bompas set out for his mission station, ignoring the long-standing pattern of waiting for the regular Hudson's Bay Company fur brigades to carry the preachers and their supplies to the far northwest. By August he was at Red River, now Winnipeg, Manitoba. Then, setting off on his own, Bompas travelled alone, joining fur boats and ignoring warnings to remain in place lest he be trapped on the trail by winter. With Metis guides, Bompas pressed on, travelling more than 3,000 km under difficult conditions in under five months. The man was evidently physically tougher than he seemed, and his hike across a vast expanse of northern British North America became the stuff of legend. Where did he find the strength and physical stamina for such a trip? There was nothing in his life before 1865 to suggest he was particularly physically strong, let alone athletic. The journey from Red River to the Mackenzie River would have taxed a seasoned explorer, and this was only the first of many trips through rough country that he was to make over the decades. Evidently he had unsuspected reserves of inner strength. From the beginning, his missionary colleagues knew that they had a most unusual man in their midst.

The new priest arrived at Fort Simpson on Christmas Day, 1865, to the amazement of the Rev. Mr. Kirkby, the resident missionary, who had no idea that he was coming. A letter Bompas wrote his brother the following March gave his first impressions of the northwest. Of course the winter and the extreme cold were of great interest, as was the food, which was mostly fish, moose, and rabbit. He was immediately concerned with his Native charges:

> The condition of Indian tribes in this vicinity is indeed pitiable. They have lost their hardihood & independence through contacts with the Europeans & have as yet obtained nothing to counterbalance this loss. They are many of them afflicted with disease caught I fear through contact with Europeans. Their fondness for flimsy European dress instead of their own skins & furs is not for the best. Through idleness or otherwise they mostly neither use tent nor dwelling of any sort to live in in winter, but only an open camp....This is formed only by scraping away the snow in a circle, and laying pine brush or small branches on the ground for a carpet with other branches put round as a hedge or fence. In the centre of this they crouch over the small fire which they make by bringing the ends of a few long poles together in opposing directions....They leave their little children in camp when they go out, huddled together one over the other in the corner like young cubs or kittens to keep themselves warm.
>
> With such habits you may imagine the intellect is not of a very high order and one wonders sometimes how they are ever to be reached. We must try, & not only say but feel too. With man this is impossible but not with God for with God all things are possible.[21]

These attitudes were typical of the 19th-century imperialist. Bompas had been in the country only a few months, and was already speaking authoritatively about people he had just met. He noted their method of winter living, which to him seemed primitive, concluded that they were of subnormal intelligence, but vowed to soldier on to save their souls with God's help. From the perspective of 150 years his attitude is more than a little depressing, not to say offensive, but it was the standard approach to the "heathen" in that era.

When Bompas arrived in the Mackenzie Valley at the end of 1865, he became a member of a tiny fraternity of English-speakers in the region, almost all of them employees of the Hudson's Bay Company, staffing the fur trade posts that stretched from the Red River to the upper Yukon basin. At each post, a chief factor managed a few British (often Scottish) employees and a larger number of Metis—employees of mixed ancestry. Most of the British employees had signed five-year contracts, with the aim of rising through the ranks of the company. To do this was more difficult for the Metis, though some managed it. Most of them spent their lives in the tough labour of manning the canoe brigades and packing supplies and furs back and forth over portages and mountain passes.

In the early 19th century, heated competition between the Hudson's Bay Company and Montreal-based fur traders, particularly the North West Company, had given the fur trade a tremendous spirit and energy, and sparked a race for furs that had spread the industry across the continent in two generations. The merger in 1821 of the two major rivals, carried out under the firm control of Governor George Simpson (1787–1860), brought order to the industry, and resulted in the closing of many redundant posts and the layoff of hundreds of employees. Simpson supervised a rapid expansion of operations into the Mackenzie and Peace River regions, and, in the late 1840s, into what is now Yukon Territory. In the 1860s the company had passed its time of greatest strength; independent traders had successfully challenged its monopoly of the fur trade, and outsiders were beginning to settle and farm in its territory. Within a decade, in 1870, it would surrender its control over Rupert's Land, but for the time being it was still a powerful force. It was de facto the government of all of western and northern British North America (except for British Columbia), and it dominated the continent's economy from Lake of the Woods to the Pacific Ocean. The Oregon Boundary Settlement of 1846 had cut the company off from its operations south of the 49th parallel in the west, and the British Columbia gold rushes of the 1850s and 1860s were undercutting its operations on the Pacific coast.

On the southern prairies the company was vulnerable in this era. Its critics had complained for years that it had failed to colonize the vast agricultural lands of the region, as its charter had required it to do. The company claimed that the prairies were unsuited to settlement, but expeditions sent from the east, particularly that headed by Henry Youle Hind in 1857–1858, spoke glowingly of the vast open spaces waiting for cultivation, lands that could support hundreds of thousands of settlers. With the Americans busily exploiting the lands to the south, the British government and politicians in Ottawa openly criticized the Hudson's Bay Company's control of the region as anachronistic and dangerous to British-Canadian power in North America. In the 1860s the good agricultural land in Ontario and especially Quebec was almost all under cultivation. Where were the children of these farmers to find new land? To the distress of the authorities, the answer as often as not was the United States. The departure of young Canadians across the border was one of the great problems for what was shortly to become the Dominion of Canada. In order to survive, Canada would have to grow, and the only place for agricultural growth was Rupert's Land. Removal of the Hudson's Bay Company's influence and power was thus an important part of Canadian national policy at the time of Confederation in 1867.

The Hudson's Bay Company eventually accepted this situation and made the best of it. When they surrendered formal control over Rupert's Land to the British and then the Canadian governments in 1869–1870 they were well paid in cash, and in land, which they later sold, forming the base of their 20th century role as a major force in the retail department store sector.

North of the 60th parallel, however, the company was still supreme in the 1860s. The area was rich in furs of high quality, and the First Nations participated willingly in the fur trade. Relations between the indigenous people and the company were generally good, since it was not in the company's interests to abuse them. Relations between the company and missionaries were, however, more ambivalent. As part of an effort to placate critics, Governor Simpson, who headed the company from 1820 until his death in 1860, ordered company officers to cooperate with missionaries. They were not obvious allies. The fur traders needed the First Nations people to be mobile, working the traplines and bringing the furs to the posts for trade. The missionaries, however, generally hoped that the aboriginal people would settle down and turn to agriculture under the watchful and benevolent eye of the Church. A further difficulty was that while the company's sympathies lay with the Church of England, they could not ignore the presence of Roman Catholic missionaries, most of whom were French-speaking. The Catholics, particularly the Oblates of Mary Immaculate, had worked hard among the Metis and First Nations of the Red River district, and expected to continue their work in the Mackenzie valley. Most of them, unlike Bompas, did not want to set out for the North on their own, and they naturally expected the Hudson's Bay Company to provide logistical support.

The Hudson's Bay Company's public policy was to show no favouritism to either faith, even though privately most of its officers were Protestants, typically Scottish Presbyterians, who had no love for "Romish" priests. Simpson ordered that all missionaries should be accommodated—that they should be permitted to buy goods from company stores, to stay temporarily in company buildings, and, most important, to join existing canoe brigades. Without such permission, most of them would have found it nearly impossible to reach the far northwest.

The struggle for souls north of the 60th parallel was a friendly or at worst a civil one, at least on the surface. Roman Catholics and Anglicans could not openly attack each other; to do so would have irritated the Hudson's Bay Company, on which they depended, and would have aroused unfavourable comment in the settled parts of Canada, and in Britain. It would also presumably have been un-Christian, though this consideration did not prevent constant private sniping. The denominations could not afford to mount full-scale campaigns in any case; the best they could manage was to send a few missionaries into huge regions populated by small and highly mobile First Nations populations. In private correspondence, however, the missionaries made it clear how much they loathed each other's beliefs, if not each other's persons. The Anglicans railed endlessly about Papist errors and ambitions, and Romish practices. Catholic priests were no less harsh in their condemnation of the soft theology of the Church of England, and made it clear to First Nations people that damnation awaited those who embraced the heresies of Anglicanism. Clerical rivals often found themselves sharing company canoe brigades and post facilities, vying for the attention and favour of the officers, and struggling for the loyalty of the same groups of First Nations people. It was enough to try the patience of a saint, even a wilderness saint.

It mattered very much in the long run, theologically speaking, which denomination was first past the post. It is easy to tell who won the race in which region, for the First Nations are still, at least nominally, faithful to the church that first won their allegiance: generally the Roman Catholics in the Mackenzie Valley, and the Anglicans in the Yukon. In this race, the Anglicans were favoured by the officials, but the Catholics had the better team. Their great advantage was that their clergy were not free agents, in the way the Anglican clergy were. Roman Catholic priests and nuns could be sent anywhere they were needed, and for however long was required. The result was that the typical Catholic missionaries would come from France or Belgium as young men or women, and would spend their entire working lives in the Mackenzie Valley, perhaps as much as forty or fifty years. They would learn the local language, would travel with the people to fishing and hunting camps, learning their way of life. They would become closely identified with their flock, integrated into their society in a way that did not happen with Anglicans. Within the Church of England, the missionary calling was less permanent. Missionaries had to be recruited, and there was no obligation on them to remain in the North. If they were good at what they did, they would get job offers in more attractive locations in the south. God's call to Anglican missions tended to be less permanent than to Catholics, and turnover among those called to the far northwest tended to be high—though this was not of course the case with Bompas. This meant that some missionaries did not stay long enough to learn the language and to come to know their charges through talking to them.

Before and after the missionaries arrived, the Hudson's Bay Company posts in the far northwest were cramped and sometimes difficult places to live. Food shortages were not uncommon, and periods of near-starvation not unheard of. The small log buildings housed a rigid hierarchy. Company officers had better quarters and food, and dreamed of progression through company ranks. Their days were filled with bureaucratic routine, the maintenance of account books, journals, and personal and company correspondence. Some spent time in scientific pursuits, especially after Robert Kennicott (1835–1866) travelled through the region in 1859–1862 to persuade them to send specimens of flora and fauna to the Smithsonian Institution. The labourers lived in barracks, subsisting on fish and dried meat, clearly socially subordinate to their superiors. For long periods, especially during the winter, there was little to be done beyond cutting firewood and repairing equipment. The officers, who were British, or English-speaking mixed bloods, were mostly Anglicans; the workers, who tended to be Metis, were Roman Catholics. It was a tough, and sometimes boring and tense life.

The missionaries added a new ingredient to this mix. Their arrival, as with any new face, was a cause for celebration, unless food was running low, which was sometimes the case in the winter. The Anglican missionaries were almost always middle or upper-middle class, and socialized comfortably with the company's officers.

The Roman Catholic missionaries were more socially varied, and found their communicants in the barracks. This also helped them solidify their relations with First Nations people, since it was the Metis who were most likely to have personal relationships with the local indigenous people. Earlier in the century, company traders often took "country wives" while in the field, often then "turning off" (as they put it) these women to another employee when they left the fur trade region. But when George Simpson brought his wife Frances to the Red River in the 1830s, the racial politics of company social relations were altered forever.[22] Thereafter, men hoping to rise through the ranks were warned to avoid entanglements with Native women. By the time the missionaries arrived in the Mackenzie Valley, it was less likely that the company's officers would have Native partners; if they did, they were either secretive about it, or they maintained them at the cost of future promotion. The Anglicans, therefore, had more support from and personal contact with the company's officers than the Catholics did, but they had less access to the broader fur trade society.

There was not much about the young Bompas—he was 31 when he arrived at Fort Simpson on Christmas Day 1865—that would have predicted a brilliant missionary career. He had no special training; unlike David Livingstone, he was not a medical doctor, nor did he have any scientific or linguistic training. He had no knowledge of the region and its inhabitants, except what he had picked up on his journey north. A man of the British middle classes, he was a townsman with few practical skills. He lacked the social graces expected of an Anglican clergyman, and he also lacked a wife, a "helpmeet" as the Victorians liked to call them, a woman to assist him on his great northern adventure, to share the burdens of missionary field work, and to provide an alternative to the sexual temptations that might befall a young man in the wilderness. He was pious and inflexible in his beliefs, critical of those who strayed from the biblical path. Not for him the more easy tolerance of human moral frailty exhibited by the upper classes of high church Anglicanism. He would not have been popular at the dinner table at

Fort Simpson, save for the fact that he was educated and brought news from Home.

No sooner had he arrived than his plans derailed. Missionary Robert McDonald did not die, but to the delight of all made an unexpected and full recovery. Bompas had lost his congregation, for McDonald returned to the religious trenches to hold the line against the Papists. Bompas had one strength, however, that the Church could now put to use. He was zealous, and moreover was indefatigable. The CMS made him an itinerant preacher and sent him off into the wilderness to carry the Gospel to the farthest corners of what was in 1874 to become the diocese of Athabasca, of which the Mackenzie Valley was a part. His energy was prodigious. It must have been a tremendous jolt for him to be a curate in a rural English parish one month, and just a few months later be trudging from Red River to Fort Simpson. He must have had considerable and unsuspected reserves of physical and mental toughness.

Bompas had found his calling. He was not interested in the landscape, the climate, the animals, or the other attractions of the region; other traders, explorers and missionaries wrote eloquently of these things, but not Bompas. His book *Northern Lights on the Bible* (1893) uses the North as a series of not particularly felicitous metaphors to illustrate the Christian faith; it is not a lively read. But fortunately for him, he found delight in the First Nations, in their lives and in their culture. He found that he first pitied them, and then loved them. This was not to say that he considered them his equals, except as creatures before God. As God's children they were equal to the son of a Sergeant-at-law, but as British citizens they had much to learn; on one occasion he called them the "lowest of the low of all people," degraded in habits and in their way of life. But that was why he loved them. Modern readers may find this a strange contradiction, but it was central to the missionaries' world view in that era. The missionary impulse was about more than souls: it was the intellectual rationalization for imperialism. If the British had thought the "natives" were their equals, they could not have cleared their consciences to take over their lands and rule them. Their justification for doing so was in part to bring them to God and to civilization.

But perhaps he loved them more in the abstract than as individuals, for even as they welcomed him into their camps and tents, they seemed to tolerate rather than celebrate his presence. He found them welcoming; of an 1872 visit to the Dene in the Mackenzie Valley he wrote, "Each day spent in the Indian camps was like as Sunday as the Indians were clustered around me from early morning till night learning prayers, hymns, and Scripture lessons."[23] But he perhaps mistook friendliness for Christian enthusiasm, for his visits had only transitory impact. The Roman Catholics were the victors in that region.

What Bompas became over the years, either willingly or in spite of himself, was a northerner, a man in and of the north, who increasingly during his career came to think of the south as "outside," to use the term still current in the Yukon. He was not the kind of northerner who mined for gold, except, as in a letter quoted by Cody, "digging the mines of God's holy Word."[24] He was a northerner mostly because he identified himself with the region and with its people, defending them against outsiders, unwilling to leave them and his beloved homeland. His quirkiness—a trait shared by many northerners—only added to this new identity.

Austere and reserved, Bompas was not given to affectionate or human gestures. He travelled constantly to meet the Dene (the First Nations of the Mackenzie Valley) where they lived, tireless in his quest to carry the Gospel to them. They welcomed him, fed and sheltered him, listened to him, and participated in the services he held. What they did not do, however—as First Nations in other parts of the continent had done to certain trusted and favoured missionaries—was to put their lives under his control. Much more than he wished, they continued to live off the land, and generally spent only a few days each year in his presence.

Bompas's misgivings about the capabilities of indigenous peoples brought him into opposition to one of the Church Missionary Society's most cherished hopes: the "Native Church" policy. The idea was that Native people would be trained as catechists,[25] then as deacons, and eventually ordained as priests, so that they could minister to their people and set an example to them. Over the years, and for a number of reasons, Bompas came to doubt and finally oppose this policy. In the first place, he concluded after some years in the North that the First Nations themselves did not want their own people as catechists and priests: "This is the view of the Indians themselves," he wrote in 1882, "who do not much value one of their own countrymen as teacher for they have not sufficient trust in their attainments and they seem to view Christianity as a message from the White man's God."[26] The second reason sprang from his low view of indigenous culture:

> Although he found the Dene generally "inoffensive and submissive," they were in a sad state of "decay and degeneration." After several years in the field, he came to the conclusion that preaching the gospel was insufficient to save their souls. European missionaries were preferable, he argued, because they "can hope to raise the Natives to a higher grade of intelligence and civilization which they cannot do for each other..."[27]

Bompas's strict definition of what constituted true Christian faith caused another difficulty. While others, the Oblates among them, were quite willing to baptize First Nations at any sign of nominal acceptance of Christianity, Bompas insisted on evidence that they understood and had internalized the message of the Gospels—that they were "true" Christians. This meant that he had fewer converts, and this in turn had practical implications. The Canadian government, which after Confederation assumed responsibility for aboriginal people, naturally considered baptized First Nations people as belonging to the denomination that had baptized them. Numbers of converts influenced the amounts that Ottawa gave to the churches to support church-provided education, medical care, and other services. Since the missions always operated on a shoestring, this money was vitally important to them. While theologically defensible, this attitude handicapped Bompas in the race for souls. Another handicap was his low church distaste for ritual. The Oblates found that ceremony appealed to the Dene, and they made full use of it in their services.

Bompas, ever the man of the Spirit, was not as interested in the practical aspects of missionary activity. While other missionaries devoted their time and energy founding schools and hospitals, and otherwise endearing themselves to First Nations and involving themselves with their daily lives, Bompas concentrated on religion. He believed strongly in the power of the Gospel and the presence of God in the lives of individuals. He lived for the experience of seeing his flock undergo conversion, and believed that, through his work and his witnessing, he could bring them to a better understanding of God and His word. This did not always bear fruit, certainly not at first. The Dene were polite and accommodating, on a personal level, but their lack of enthusiasm for Bompas's religious message was palpable.

This is not to say that Bompas's early career was marked by failure; rather, it was simply not marked by the large number of conversions that the church hoped for. One thing he did as well as any missionary in the North, however, was travel. His 1865 journey to the Mackenzie River district became the stuff of northern and missionary legend, repeated often (but not by Bompas) as testimony to the determination of Anglican missionaries in the field. He had to travel constantly in the early years; since the aboriginal people would not come to him, he had to go to them. His visits to the Dene of the Mackenzie were apparently well-received, sparking joy in the heart of the weary missionary.

As an itinerant missionary, Bompas was often on the move. In 1868 he crossed the Richardson Mountains into the present Yukon Territory and visited Fort Youcon, as it was then spelled, which had been built on the Yukon River well within what had the year before become the American territory of Alaska. From this small outpost he travelled along the Yukon and Porcupine rivers and, in a series of notable expeditions, carried the Gospel as far as the Inuit camps along the Arctic Coast. How did the young curate from rural England transform himself into an Arctic traveller whose energy and stamina compared well to that of any explorer of his era? We simply do not know; Bompas was anything but a self-publicist, simply going where he believed he needed to go, without fuss or complaint. Had he possessed the public relations instincts of a Robert Peary, to take an extreme example, he might have become famous outside the church as an explorer. But he had no interest in this kind of fame. From the beginning of his mission, he determined to make it his life's work. An early letter to his family in England, written one hopes partly tongue in cheek (though it is hard to find humour in Bompas's writings) makes this clear:

> Though sometimes this has been a source of pain to me to recall bygone scenes & associations yet I am thankful to say I feel now sufficiently reconciled to my present lot not to feel much [illegible] when I receive your letters from beyond [the] sea & I find I can read them without "looking back" in the sense that those are forbidden to do who have put their hand to the gospel plough. Only one thing I must forbid you all, & that is ever to speak to me of returning & circumscribing my Missionary labour otherwise it may cause me to burn your letters or refuse to receive more. I say this because Sophia has already transgressed in this respect.[28]

Until the Klondike gold rush of the mid-1890s Bompas devoted significant parts of each year to visiting his aboriginal communicants in their camps. Some missionaries wrote extensively about such travels, but Bompas did not. Comments such as "I have also visited at their camps the whole of the Loucheux [Gwitch'in] Indians connected with this post"[29] are masterpieces of understatement, masking the fact that much of this travelling occurred in winter, involving snowshoe treks of hundreds of miles in sub-zero temperature and Arctic darkness. His largely undocumented journeys, many undertaken alone, represent a remarkable record of northern travel. Several of his trips, had they been better recorded, would stand as major feats of Arctic exploration and travel. In 1872, he went overland from the Porcupine River in the northern Mackenzie valley, meeting with "a tribe of Esquimaus encamped on the sea coast about 2[oo] or 300 miles west of Mackenzie River," that is, in the region of the Yukon-Alaskan Arctic coast.[30] It was a long journey, harsh and dangerous, and he was the first European to make it on foot. Because he did not draw maps or publicise his exploits, they were not well known, but this does not contract the fact that he was an extraordinarily determined man, possessed of surprisingly great stamina and physical ability.

Very little is known from the First Nations perspective of the indigenous response to Bompas's early activities. He reported back to England that he had been enthusiastically received wherever he went, but it is hard to know if this was because he was a novelty or for some other reason. He worked hard to learn the aboriginal languages, and was eventually able to make himself understood by most of the groups in the region, though it is not known how deep his grasp of each language was, or whether it permitted him to explain complex theological concepts to them. That he translated several works into indigenous languages suggests that his knowledge was fairly extensive. He conducted basic religious services: some apt readings from the Bible, some hymns, which he found the First Nations people enjoyed singing, though he found them unmusical, and some homilies, to which they listened politely. What they really thought of him and his message in those early days is impossible to say, as there appears to be little or no memory of him in the oral history of the region.

One important part of his job—the organizational imperatives of the Church Missionary Society and the Church of England in general—he found uncongenial, and he avoided it as much as he could. He did not ask much from the CMS or the Church, beyond basic financial support, and he took little interest in their institutional affairs. He did report regularly to the CMS, as he was required to do, and he provided articles for church publications about his activities. But he was not interested in raising money, flattering potential donors, or publicising the work of his northern mission. Unlike most of his colleagues, Bompas did not look forward to sabbaticals in southern Canada or in Britain, visiting church officials, lecturing, being lionized, and generally spreading word of his work. He saw this aspect of his role as worldly and a hindrance to his religious duty, and he recognized that he was not very good at it. Not for him the role of charming cleric drinking tea with the wives of the upper-middle classes in England, making their hearts beat faster with tales of fortitude with a view to a generous dona-tion for his mission. He preferred a self-imposed exile in the North.

The Church, however, eventually intruded upon him. In 1873, eight years after his arrival at Fort Simpson, Bompas learned that the enormous diocese of Rupertsland was to be divided, and a new diocese of Athabasca created, centred on the Mackenzie River valley. To his dismay, he found that he was to be nominated as its first bishop, a coup for any cleric not yet forty. He was not interested in being a bishop, which involved administrative duties he found uncongenial, and which interfered with what he considered his real spiritual work. Alarmed, he returned to England to argue against his appointment, but in vain. The growing success of the Roman Catholic Church in the region convinced the leaders of the Church of England that the Mackenzie Valley needed an Anglican diocese, and Bompas was the man who knew the region best. On May 3, 1874, he entered St. Mary's Church in London as William Carpenter Bompas and left it with the right to sign his name William Athabasca. What a strange and unexpected turn of events this was for a man who had been an unhappy and unimpressive curate with few career prospects in the Church of England. Now he was the Bishop of Athabasca, dressed (one assumes, but perhaps for the only time) in cope and mitre—people who knew church etiquette (and did not know his dislike of ceremony) addressed him as "My Lord." He did not leave the North again for thirty years, and then only once, to attend a Provincial Synod in Winnipeg in 1904 following the death of Archbishop Machray, a duty that as the senior bishop in the Province[31] he could not avoid.

There was another change in his life that occurred during this trip. It was awkward for an Anglican missionary not to have a wife; it was unthinkable, as the Church made clear to him, for a bishop to be a bachelor. A wife was needed to oversee the "women's" part of his mission; the mission schools and hospitals needed a female presence, and a wife would be a role model to First Nations women as Bompas was supposed to be for the men. Bompas dealt with this demand with his usual energy; less than a week after his consecration he returned to church to be married. He knew the bride well, for she was his first cousin, Charlotte Selina Cox, to whom he had apparently proposed (with what degree of ardour it is difficult to say) some twenty years earlier. By modern standards Bompas was not much of a catch. He was forty years old, a man driven by inner purpose, but lacking what we would consider charm; moreover, he was determined to return to a remote wilderness at the earliest possible moment. Why did Selina Cox marry him? The main reason was probably that she was devout, and the opportunity to participate in godly work appealed to her. Perhaps she thought it was her duty to do so. Possibly it was a consideration that she was older than he was. Born in 1830, she was 44 when she was married (she outlived him too, dying in 1917), and had few prospects other than caring for aging relatives and slipping quietly into genteel spinsterhood. Within days of the wedding, William and Selina Bompas were on a ship to Canada and to Fort Simpson.

Selina Bompas was a well educated woman, who had spent much of her childhood in Italy, where her father had gone to restore his health. She spoke Italian well, and "even as an old lady she always carried her Dante in her pocket."[32] She was well aware of what the role of a missionary's wife should be: to be a helpmate to her husband, but also to serve as a role model for Native women as an example of morality and virtue, both moral and domestic. Writing in the *Canadian Churchman* the year after her husband's death, she made this clear:

Dear sister-settlers amongst the Indians, there is a power given you from on high which is intended you should use among them or any other race with whom you may be placed—it is the power of *influence*....In your Christian households, in your modest demeanour, in your fair dealings with all let them see what they should seek to copy more than the jewels and costly attire which in their eyes are all that is needed to constitute a lady.[33]

She found particular satisfaction in caring for the Native children who were left at the mission because they were orphans, or for some other urgent reason. Caring for these children, especially the babies, was Christian work, and also seemed to fill a void in her life, and she on occasion referred to herself in her letters as "Mama Bompas." Writing in 1876 about an infant named Jennie she said "The dear babe is very delicate and has needed constant watching and care ever since she came to me a year ago. Still, she has been a great blessing and comfort to me, and I know not what I should have done on some of these long dreary nights without her little hand patting my face, and her bright little face cheering many an anxious hour."[34] Sadly, the child died the next year.

The implacable force under her kindness is made clear in an account she wrote in 1898 for a juvenile audience about how Native children adapted to the school at Carcross:

The first year of school is often very irksome to an Indian child. He will be as merry as a grig [a kind of elfin person; "merry as a grig" was an English catchphrase] at times, but if he catches sight of his father or any friend going hunting, the hunger for freedom comes upon him. He will start to run after the hunter, and if caught and sent back to school, he will cry and yell until the whole camp is roused, and tearful symphathizing mothers rush in to know who is dealing this harshly with their darling. The girls are equally resentful of restraint, and look upon a closed door or window as their natural enemy. These spasmodic fits of intolerance of confinement cease after a year or so; but we have to remember that fresh air is an Indian's most needed element; he was born and bred in the woods, and has early been used to such extremes of temperature as would make a white child shudder.[35]

The chilling phrases "hunger for freedom" and "fits of intolerance of confinement" show that she knew exactly how the children were reacting to the school; that she and the Bishop persisted in their policy shows, among other things, how strong was their belief that it was the best thing to do for them.

Since this is a modern account, we must ask the question that H.A. Cody forbore to ask: what was their married life like? The phrase "marriage of convenience" comes to mind, but it is difficult to say what their domestic life was like. Given her age, the fact that they had no children is not indicative. She certainly was loyal to him and to his work, and she fulfilled, though not very aggressively, the expected role of a bishop's wife; she succoured the sick and the distressed. At one point she adopted a Native child. She wrote a children's tale that was published in Britain.[36] However, she fell ill several times, of what disease is not known—perhaps she was sick of the North, or of the Bishop—and she spent a total of ten years at different times during their 42 years of marriage living in southern Canada and in England. One incident may be illustrative. She appealed to Bompas to come south and visit her; on one occasion she suggested that she was near death. He replied that God's work in the North took precedence over personal commitments. This suggests that it was, to say the least, not a passionate or even a particularly warm relationship. It was, however, a lasting one, as such a marriage was bound to be under those circumstances in that era.

By the time Bompas became a bishop, the northern mission field was beginning to change. The first shift occurred in 1867, when the

Americans purchased Alaska from the Russians. The Russian Empire had neglected the interior of Alaska, restricting their activities mostly to the coastline. The Americans were more aggressive, and in 1870 they told the Hudson's Bay Company to move Fort Youcon east across the international boundary (the 141st meridian). The Company complied, and the Americans who followed to take over the trade of the Yukon River valley were less scrupulous than the Company, bringing alcohol to the First Nations of the region and extending the social life of the posts into their communities in undesirable ways. At the same time, the first mining prospectors were crossing the Chilkoot Pass and arriving to look for gold in the Yukon River valley.

An important episode that occurred in the early part of Bompas's career concerned the charismatic missionary William Duncan (1832–1918), who is usually referred to as William Duncan of Metlakatla. Like Bompas, Duncan was born in England, but of much lower social status: he was illegitimate, and had been a tanner's apprentice and a travelling salesman when he volunteered for the CMS in 1854.[37] Like Bompas, Duncan was an evangelical who disliked ritual; unlike Bompas, Duncan passionately believed in the Native Church policy, and when he was sent to minister to the Tsimshian of northwest British Columbia, he put it into practice, establishing a model village at Metlakatla where Christian habits and the work ethic prevailed. The success of his mission, at least in economic terms, convinced Duncan that his approach was the best one, but his refusal to use Anglican rituals in his church services brought him into conflict with his bishop (in Victoria), a situation made worse when he supported the losing side in a famous struggle that took place in the 1870s in Victoria between the bishop and the dean of the cathedral there.

Relations between Duncan and the church authorities weakened further when he refused to offer Holy Communion to the Tsimshian on the grounds that they were spiritually "unpredictable." In 1877 the CMS asked Bompas to visit Metlakatla and report on the situation. Despite the fact that their religious views were quite similar in that they were both low church evangelicals, the two had little in common. Duncan had a great deal of charisma (and was in fact the most famous missionary in the Canada of his day) while Bompas had none, Duncan believed in the Native Church policy and Bompas did not, and Duncan was heading towards a kind of semi-secular mission community based on social and economic improvements while Bompas never wavered from the view that spiritual salvation was the most important thing for indigenous people.

Bompas's visit had little positive result, only convincing Duncan that the church hierarchy wanted to undermine his work. Eventually Duncan broke with the CMS, and in 1887, with some six hundred Tsimshian who chose to follow him, he moved to an island on the Alaska panhandle. There he exercised authority over the community of New Metlakatla until his death. He never married, nor did he ever accept ordination in the church. His estate was valued at $146,000, a remarkable sum for a missionary to acquire.

In 1891 Bompas's Diocese of Athabasca was divided in two, and Bompas again chose the more isolated portion, becoming the first Bishop of Selkirk (the diocese was later renamed the Diocese of Yukon). The centre of his new diocese was at Fortymile, on the Yukon River a few miles east of the international boundary, where there were already mission buildings, and a location, which to the Bishop's dismay, was fast becoming the centre of the new mining frontier in the region.

The missionaries and fur traders had benefitted from the extreme isolation of the far northwest. Bompas's Diocese of Athabasca (the Mackenzie Valley and the modern day Yukon) had been protected by distance from the intrusions of private fur traders, the northward thrust of the western American and Canadian gold mining frontier, and from the other advances of the development and settlement frontiers. The fur trade was comparatively benign, providing the First Nations with access to trade goods while permitting them to continue their traditional way of life with a minimum of disruptions. While the missionaries wished the First Nations would settle down, they were glad of the fact that the disruptive influence of miners, free traders, whiskey peddlers and others had been kept at a distance. Now the luxury of isolation was broken, particularly in the Yukon River valley, though the Mackenzie River valley would remain relatively untouched until the beginning of the 20th century.

By 1890 there were more than a thousand newcomers in the Yukon, either prospecting for gold or serving the prospectors. Bompas was alarmed by this change. He was appalled that the Canadian government had no official presence anywhere near the region, which was unregulated and unpoliced. A few officials had passed through the region, surveyors who had marked the point where the international boundary crossed the Yukon River and had given the country a glimpse of this far-off region. The incoming whites, Bompas believed, were hell-bent on destroying the First Nations, if not physically, then certainly morally. He made the link between Christianity and morality clear when he wrote that "to abandon them [the Indians] now that the place is overrun by miners would involve their destruction by more than a relapse to heathenism, namely in their being swallowed up in the miners' temptation to drink, gambling and immorality."[38] Bompas began to write letters to Ottawa, charging that the miners were debauching the First Nations with alcohol, and that the whalers who wintered on Herschel Island, off the Beaufort Sea coast of the Yukon, were doing the same thing to the Inuit. He demanded that the Canadian government send official representatives to the region, and when they ignored him, he wrote to church authorities and temperance societies to press his case. In one of his letters he made his priorities clear:

> My own interest lies principally in the preservation of the Indians who I fear will be finished in a few years unless Government protection is afforded them. Some of them manufacture liquor and it is supplied to them by Whites, and especially to the Indian women for the purposes of debauchery.[39]

The Canadian government did not welcome these appeals. In the 1890s they had more important concerns to attend to, especially the settlement of the Canadian prairies, which was the great goal of all governments for fifty years after 1870. But they could not ignore him, especially when others supported him. Government neglect of the North was a minor sore point with Canadian nationalists of that era, but for the government the fact that miners and traders were selling liquor to Indians and Eskimos was not an incentive to act, unless matters got out of hand and violence occurred, as had happened on the southern prairies in the early 1870s. What worried the authorities more, and what prodded them to act, was the realization that Americans were operating in a border region, that Canadian sovereignty was being ignored with impunity, and that potential revenues from customs and excise were not being collected.

In 1894 the federal government decided to act, and sent two members of the North West Mounted Police to the upper Yukon basin to reconnoitre and report on Bompas's charges. The senior member of the pair was Inspector Charles Constantine, an experienced officer with a realistic view of human nature. The abuse reported by Bompas—he had written of "nights of debauch"—seemed fairly tame to Constantine. Contrary to what the Bishop had charged, the police officer found the miners to be professional, fairly well controlled (they policed themselves), and actually anxious for the government to arrive, if only to protect their mining claims. Constantine agreed that a police presence was needed, but more to control the border and collect customs than to protect the First Nations from the miners. The federal government responded by sending a detachment of twenty members of the North-West Mounted Police to the Yukon in 1895.

This episode damaged Bompas's reputation with the government. Officials were used to receiving moral appeals from missionaries, and had long learned to discount them. The missionary agenda was clear enough—to keep indigenous people apart from newcomers, keep alcohol away from them, and to lobby for government help for schools and hospitals—and Ottawa knew how to deal with it, usually by ignoring it for as long as possible. Bompas was particularly urgent in his appeals, and in the long run he was proved right: the arrival of the miners signalled a sea-change in Yukon history that would eventually cause serious disruption to the lives of First Nations. But this was in the future, and his rhetoric overstepped the circumstances of his time, and was dismissed by the police and others who had experience with the indigenous people. He came to be viewed by the authorities as something of a sancti- monious crank, a sharp and unreasonable critic who did not appreciate the benefits of the advance of civilization. By this time he was writing rather morose letters to his relatives in England:

> You will not expect me to give you news from this side [he wrote in August 1895], and I think you are aware that I am becoming myself increasingly indifferent to passing events. The chief pleasure I find in life is the near prospect of its termination, and it is now a happi- ness that the nearness of this result is no longer as formerly a disappointing hope but an assured certainty. Still I find enough pleasure in Scripture study to occupy me while I remain on earth, and whether the same study will be continued in heaven we know not, only we read that these things the angels desire to explore.[40]

One can hardly imagine a world view or a personality more at odds with the kind of people who came to the Klondike during the gold rush. No wonder he was not popular with the newcomers. Inspector Constantine, in particular, did not like him, finding him too concerned with the First Nations' welfare. In January 1896 he complained to the Commissioner of the NWMP that

> Bishop Bompas is a disturbing element. He has no use for any person unless he is an Indian. Has the most utmost contempt for the whites generally and myself in

particular because I would not give an order to the Dr. to attend Indians, in fact to go over a couple of times a week to see if they were all right. The Indians are chiefly American ones, a lazy shiftless lot...[41]

Later that year, when Bompas tried to get the government to pay compensation to First Nations people who had been shifted from their lands around Dawson City, Constantine opposed the idea, writing "I don't propose to be bluffed by an arrogant Bishop who thinks the only people worth considering are a few dirty Indians too lazy to work, and who prefer starvation."[42] Nor did other government officials view Bompas and his cause with much enthusiasm. One wrote of him and missionaries in general: "My complaint with regard to the missionaries is that instead of teaching the Indians self-reliance and independence they aid most strongly in making them mendicants. I am daily in receipt of letters from Indians, written by a missionary, asking for all sorts of favours."[43]

Bompas, like most missionaries in the North, saw his role partly as being a defender of his charges, and in his case, increasingly so as the years went by. His appeals were touched with paternalism and self-righteousness, and they reflected nothing favourable about the miners, entrepreneurs and exploiters who flooded into the North in search of gold and instant wealth. His appeals on behalf of the First Nations carried more than a hint of self interest; his demands for compensation for loss of lands included the suggestion that assistance be provided in the form of government grants to Anglican church schools.

In August 1896 the great discovery of gold occurred on Bonanza Creek, sparking an international stampede to the Yukon, one that saw the First Nations people quickly reduced to a minority population in their own land. It was lucky that the police were already on the scene, and reinforcements were rushed north. Tens of thousands of would-be Klondikers swarmed over the mountain passes behind Skagway, Alaska and rafted down the Yukon River to Dawson City and the Klondike. First Nations people who lived near the gold fields pulled away and went to their traditional hunting and fishing territories. The Han were the nearest people to Dawson City, and some soon found themselves on a small reserve named "Moosehide," a few miles downstream from the gold rush boom town.

The Klondike gold rush was Bompas's worst nightmare. His aboriginal flock were about to be swamped by newcomers of the lowest kind. Those of his charges who were drawn by the lure of the boomtown—and some were—were doomed, he felt, to be ensnared by liquor and would end up dead or condemned to prostitution. He moved the seat of his diocese from Fortymile to the Moosehide reserve, where he could be surrounded by his charges, away from the miners. From Moosehide he could travel easily to visit his flock in distant regions, and he had the facilities—a church and a small school—that he needed to provide for the needs of his congregation. But then to his dismay the community of Dawson City was established, not far from Moosehide, and he found himself once more in the midst of the mining population.

He hardly knew how to deal with the gold rush. The miners who had arrived in the 1880s and early 1890s were bad enough. Now tens of thousands of miners, typically single males, many seeking alcohol and women, had transformed the country in a matter of months. He had never been comfortable with nonaboriginal people. Those who might have been his allies, the "establishment"—the government officials, the police officers, the leading citizens, the traders and the other missionaries who came north—found him to be abrupt, unrealistic, and distant. Another man would easily have assumed a position near the head of Yukon society, as men of the same rank did in Britain; after all, in the competitive arena of the socially ambitious upper ranks of Dawson City, a man who had the right to be addressed as "My Lord" had an enviable cachet. But Bompas was not interested in Dawson's society, not because it was artificial, though it was, but because he was not much interested in any aspect of nonaboriginal life. It is noteworthy that Bompas took no part at all in the social reform movements that emerged in Dawson City during and after the gold rush; he was not interested in prohibition or campaigns against prostitution. He had been in the North for thirty years when the rush occurred, and he was set in his ways. The task of ministering to the miners he left to others. He had to leave.

Securing permission from the Church Missionary Society, Bompas packed up and left for Carcross, in the southern Yukon, where he built a small church and a residential school. Here he could minister to the local First Nations and educate indigenous children from across his diocese. At Carcross, Bompas saw the gold rush flare and then fade; by the end of his life the rush was well over and the population of the Yukon was falling rapidly. Isaac O. Stringer, his fellow missionary and successor as Bishop of the Yukon, stayed in Dawson City. Stringer was a missionary to the Inuit, and a man famous for an ill-fated expedition across the Richardson Mountains that resulted in near starvation (he survived by boiling and eating his footgear; his biography is called *The Bishop Who Ate His Boots*). By all accounts he served well in Dawson City. Bompas preferred to stay in Carcross and minister to the First Nations. In 1905, in failing health, he resigned as Bishop and was replaced by Stringer, who came to Carcross. Bompas died the next year of a heart attack.

The most unkind thing one could say about William Carpenter Bompas is that he was what a sociologist once called a "marginal man," a term that describes someone who having failed at home, finds success on the margins of the civilized world.[44] Unable to fit in to or succeed in English society, he goes off and assumes a leading role elsewhere, one which the British considered to be less sophisticated. There is some truth to this depiction of the bishop. Bompas was somewhat of a misfit in England, socially awkward and unsure of himself. In the far northwest he found a function and a role that eluded him at home. His significance extends, however, beyond the details of his life. He was part of a great world effort to bring the

Christian gospel to non-Christian peoples, and he chose to play his part in one of the most unattractive parts of the world—unattractive, that is, to English missionaries, who preferred the mission fields of Africa and China, where souls to be saved were much more numerous. He volunteered to serve where others would not.

As one reads Cody's biography, it is important to keep in mind the many ways in which Bompas's life illustrates important themes in Canadian and world history. His career highlights and overlaps themes central to the history of the church in Canada and abroad, and to aboriginal-newcomer relations. Bompas participated in one of the great rushes for aboriginal souls, racing the Roman Catholic Church to claim the spiritual allegiance of the indigenous people of northern Canada. To be first was to gain control of the future, in this life and beyond, of the aboriginal population. Bompas kept up the pressure on the Catholics throughout his life, and in the Yukon he won the battle, shaping for generations the social and spiritual lives of the Territory's First Nations people.

In recent years, most of the attention focussed on indigenous-church relations has highlighted the negative and lingering effects of the residential school system, which Bompas founded in the Yukon. These schools, particularly as they operated after the Second World War, have been accused of destroying indigenous cultures and abusing children in various ways. In Bompas's time, however, they had different functions. One of the most important was the care and education of orphan children, a function that figured prominently in the early days of the schools at Fortymile and later Carcross. It is difficult to argue that this was a socially or culturally destructive activity.

It is true that Bompas and his successors tried to impart Christian knowledge, British mores, and Protestant discipline to his students, at the expense of values that he considered pagan, savage, and licentious. It is true that he considered "white" values and habits of far more worth than those his students had learned from their parents. There is no denying this, and saying that all Europeans thought that way in 1890 does not excuse it, though it certainly helps to explain it. It is true that he was rigid and self-righteous; he would have said that he was armed with the righteousness of Christ and the Bible. He thought he was doing the best for his charges.

Autres temps, autres moeurs. Over the past thirty years, as Christian missions and missionaries have increasingly come under attack by social critics and First Nations leaders, attention has shifted away from the role played by missionaries in aiding and defending the First Nations people to focus on their social agenda, and their cooperation with the state in a program of assimilation and acculturation. Some of these criticisms are undeniably valid, and the revelations of abuses at residential schools run by the churches on behalf of the government are painful to contemplate. A kind of justice is now being secured by those who have suffered abuse and are now winning substantial sums in court settlements. The punishment is not being borne by government alone; rather the penalty is falling upon the Anglican and other churches, which must pay a portion of the damages. As of this writing, one Anglican diocese (Cariboo, in British Columbia) has declared bankruptcy as a result of court-imposed damage settlements.

Amidst the revelations of the outrages perpetrated upon aboriginal people in the name of education it seems unfashionable to say anything positive about the missionary enterprise. But contemporary critics, to give a balanced picture, should not overlook the crucial role that missionaries played in protecting aboriginal people from the onslaught of newcomers, or trying to. At a time when few if any nonaboriginal people paid attention to the needs of First Nations people, missionaries such as Bompas worked tirelessly to represent their interests (as he saw them) to government. In the Yukon he lobbied for protection against the miners, demanded a reserve near Dawson City (the government was reluctant to assign them any land at all for fear gold might be discovered on it), insisted that the government respect hunting and trapping rights, and in other ways pressed Ottawa to uphold its obligations to protect the indigenous people of the region. The federal government found Bompas an irritant—they preferred to ignore the indigenous people, hoping they would simply stay out of the way of progress. But he knew how to write letters and how to orchestrate a campaign to prod government into action.

In an important study of the Beotucks of Newfoundland, historian L.F.S. Upton argued that they suffered not from too much contact, but from an absence of support.[45] Without missionaries to present their case and to protect them from predatory whites—or at least to try to—the Beotucks were vulnerable to isolation and indifference, factors that contributed to their extinction as a people. Perhaps, Upton argues, contact was not entirely a bad thing:

> The strategy of withdrawal may have prolonged the life of the Beotuck people, but the success of the Micmacs raises some question about its validity as a response to the white presence. Could it be that the Beotucks died because they did not have enough contact with the whites? There was no missionary to plead for their souls, no trader anxious to barter for their furs, no soldier to arm and use them as auxiliaries in his wars, no government to restrain the settlers. The presence of all these white intruders served to strength the Micmacs. Perhaps those same intruders could have saved the Beotucks from extinction.[46]

Bompas stood between his charges and the wider society that came to dominate the North. If he acted without consulting the First Nations—and his approach was strongly paternalistic—he nonetheless worked hard on their behalf. Not until the 1960s would northern First Nations again find such passionate advocates for aboriginal rights among the missionary corps.

Bompas was not the only Anglican missionary in the North, and one of his duties involved recruiting others to work with him. Since he refused to make tours to promote northern work (he had been recruited that way) or to raise money, the northern missions were not as well staffed or financed as they might have been under a more charismatic or affable leader. He did do a good deal of writing, and the church promoted his activities quite extensively. A few missionaries did come north, some to flee to the south or back to Britain after a winter or two. Bompas had an opinion on the kind of man needed, which is revealing of his social attitudes and of northern conditions:

> ...it is best not to try to send gentlefolks hither whether male or female, simply because these gentlefolks who undertake pioneer life in the far west, have to come down a peg in their position which is mostly painful to themselves and to those about them. Those of an inferior grade in going to the far west [he did not call it the North] generally rise a peg which is mostly pleasant to themselves and to their neighbours. It is less consequence to me whether he passed a College course or not.[47]

What Bompas wanted for his diocese, therefore, were the so-called marginal men. The church wrestled endlessly with the problem of drawing people to the arctic regions, for Asia, Africa, and the South Pacific were more attractive to British missionaries. Even Canadians were reluctant to serve in the North, though some, like Stringer, did volunteer; perhaps Toronto had enough winter for most Canadians.

The missionaries who served with Bompas had uneven careers. One of the most successful was Kenneth McDonald, who was based at Fort McPherson in the Mackenzie Delta, from where he travelled at least 2,000 km every year. V.C. Sim was based at Rampart House, and also travelled extensively, but he suffered from the rigours of service and died in 1885 after only four years in the country. T.H. Canham also ministered mostly to First Nations. J.W. Ellington ministered to the early mining community at Fortymile, where he established Buxton mission in 1887. He was so unpopular that the miners played practical jokes on him. He had a nervous breakdown and had to be taken back to England, where he soon died. I.O. Stringer began his northern career in the extreme north of the Yukon, at Herschel Island.

Bompas was dedicated to the core of his task, spreading the Gospel and preaching the word of God. Secondary tasks, attending to the niceties of church business, were of secondary importance, as doubtless they should have been. He dealt with the Church Missionary Society by writing letters and reports back to England. The Society in turn respected his zeal but wished he were more forthcoming and more interested in the greater good of the Church of England. He had the zealot's distaste for money, and since money was the water that brought the missions into bloom, his diocese was always somewhat parched. Faced with limited resources he made do; asked to devote more effort in promoting the Church in the south, he emphasized his dedication to his flock. In any case, the Church Missionary Society was on the verge of withdrawing from Canada, which they eventually did towards the end of Bompas's life, so they did not put as much pressure on him as they might have to take a greater role in promoting their work. The far northwest was the last great commitment of the CMS in Canada, and one that they were tiring of by the end of the 19th century. There were too few souls in too large an area, and it cost too much to serve them. With limited resources and personnel, the CMS felt that it was more cost-effective to save souls in China or elsewhere. Bompas did not resist the slow withdrawal of the CMS; he took it as a sign that they did not share his zeal, and simply soldiered on.

Bompas was never one for hierarchy and structure. The Anglican Church in the 19th century was a complex and variable institution. At one end stood the ceremonial formalities of the "high church." This branch hearkened back to the Reformation, maintaining the symbols and rituals of their Roman Catholic ancestor, and emphasizing the authority of the Archbishop of Canterbury. There were churches in England (as in Canada today) where incense was used, the psalms chanted in Latin, confession heard by the priest, and the services marked by genuflection and other signs of the Roman past. This was not Bompas's church. Born and raised a Baptist, he belonged to the low church, which placed more emphasis on personal experiences of faith and the authority of the congregation. His church sought to bring people closer to God and into a personal relationship with the Gospel and its teachings. This explains his reluctance to be named a bishop (Baptists did not have bishops), his failure to attend to the niceties of office (though he did wear the working bishop's dress of vest and gaiters), and his unpretentious, faith-based approach to missionary work.

Historians have been struggling for years to explain the spiritual relationship between indigenous peoples and missionaries. The current fashion is to present missionaries as agents of imperial state and culture, and certainly it is impossible to deny that this was part of their role, even if it was sometimes unconscious. But how does this explain the fact that many indigenous people became sincere and devoted Christians, and that their descendants remain so? Some studied and earned their way into the ranks of the clergy. Hundreds across the country became lay readers for their church. Long after the first wave of baptisms thousands of First Nations people remained active, practicing Christians. Why did a people with their own deeply spiritual tradition abandon it for the messages of the missionaries? Bompas's contemporaries attributed the conversions to the irresistible power of the Lord's word. Others credited the zeal and dedication of the missionaries. These two explanations will suffice for the devout, but for others the puzzle remains. Was John Webster Grant right when he said that Christianity represented a logical response to the onslaught of imported disease, rapid depopulation, and loss of faith in the traditional spiritual world of traditional interpreters, or shamans?[48]

Whatever the applicability of Grant's interpretation may be elsewhere, it does not hold up for Bompas's career. There was no connection between conversions to Anglicanism or Roman Catholicism in the Mackenzie and Yukon valleys and epidemics of disease or the other disruptions that caused the "moon of wintertime" that Grant describes. Rather, First Nations enthusiasm for missionaries (perhaps less so for Bompas himself) and their message seems to have been genuine. They were not tricked, shamed, or bribed into baptism or professions of faith, nor did they turn to Christianity in a desperate attempt to acquire the technological and economic power of the newcomers. Christianity, as Kerry Abel and others have argued, appealed to many northern First Nations people because of its message, its messengers, and its accordance with indigenous spirituality.

For some time, observers have seen Christianity and aboriginal world views as antithetical. Initially, this was presented as a clash between the "savage" and the "civilized" world, with the latter destined by history to win out. The assumption that governed much of the writing on missionaries was that acceptance of Christianity meant abandonment of indigenous beliefs. Bompas, however doctrinaire he might have been at the onset of his career, did not always insist on this, and over the years became more flexible in accepting the continuation of traditional practices alongside Christianity. There was, and still is, considerable synergy between Christian and aboriginal efforts to understand spirituality; adopting the former did not mean abandoning the latter. Many First Nations found Christianity socially attractive—the music, the community, the ceremony, and the social and spiritual guidance. Some rejected the teachings of the church on morals and personal behaviour; others accepted them. For many First Nations people, the new God offered by the missionaries, and the stories about Christ, fit well with their social and spiritual beliefs. The Gospel teachings about sharing, stewardship, and interdependence coincided in critical aspects with aboriginal concepts of the world.

Critics and supporters of the 19th century missionary enterprise in northern Canada can both find evidence for their case in the career of William Carpenter Bompas. His description of the lives of aboriginal people sounds harsh and even bigoted to our ears, for he did not see them as social or cultural equals. He did not wish to see indigenous culture flourish, even if, given the realities of northern life, he was prepared to tolerate its continued existence. He had a Christian and British zeal for education, and for the work and way of life of the industrial age. But at the same time he was a ferocious advocate for First Nations people, and he saved his harshest words for the miners and other newcomers who threatened to despoil the North and disrupt the lives of its people, and for government officials who did nothing to stop this disruption.

As Bompas knew, the missionary effort in the Canadian North was flawed as a process of social and cultural change. Throughout his career he relied on the help of a handful of men, some skilled and dedicated, some of doubtful talent and dedication, to minister to hundreds of First Nations people spread thinly over a vast and difficult land. Most people saw a missionary only infrequently, when they visited a mission station during a trading trip, or when an itinerant preacher reached their camp. The linguistic skills of the missionaries left much to be desired, and thus the effect of the sermons and homilies was uneven. Most First Nations people in Bompas's day spent almost all of the year in the hunting, gathering, and fishing grounds; they did not gather at the feet of the missionaries to absorb their teachings. When they did stay in one place for long periods, as at Fortymile and Moosehide, the attraction was often the mining camps, shops, and taverns, not the missionaries' sermons. That Christianity survived and even flourished is a testament to a few particularly skilled missionaries and especially the aboriginal lay readers and communicants who kept the flame alive in the North.

When Bompas and his colleagues arrived in the Canadian North, full of missionary zeal, bibles and crosses in hand, they did not create a spiritual world where none existed. Instead, they entered a highly spiritualized environment. What they did was to add to the complexity of the northern spiritual world, providing another means for celebrating and acknowledging spiritual authority. What emerged from this process—and Bompas played a crucial role in initiating it—was a merging of indigenous and newcomer spirituality and an acceptance on the part of

First Nations people of selected aspects of European faith, ritual, and culture.

It must be said of Bompas that his legacy was institutional rather than personal. He worked tirelessly, and sacrificed his life (and his wife's health) to his cause. But he did not create a following: Robert McDonald, one of his colleagues, left a much stronger personal legacy among the First Nations, while Bompas had no effect at all on non-Native northerners, who found him to be a cantankerous and self-righteous loner. The wider Anglican church hailed his fortitude, his formidable travels, and his devotion. He was an almost Jesuitical Anglican (though the comparison would have horrified him), disdainful of personal comforts and unconcerned about his personal life. He proved in the end to be too much of an ascetic for the North. But by his death, white-bearded and saintly in appearance, he had become a kind of icon of missionary self-sacrifice to Anglicans in Canada and in Britain.

By 1900, the Anglican Church of Canada was beginning to lose whatever interest it might have had in the northern mission field. The Church did not wish to abandon the work, but found it increasingly difficult to attract clergy to the North. Mission work there was a financial drain, a situation later made worse by a scandal in the late 1920s in which the treasurer of the Ecclesiastical Province of Rupertsland (which included the northern dioceses) absconded with most of the endowment of the archdiocese (and the pension funds of the faculty of the University of Manitoba as well). With waning zeal and empty pockets, the Church fell back on half measures to keep the parishes alive, and the Roman Catholics at bay. They recruited a small number of First Nations lay readers, catechists, and deacons, and relied on these inexpensive spiritual leaders to keep the faith alive in the absence of full-time clergy. They made an arrangement with the federal government whereby the Department of Indian Affairs paid theology students to provide short-term summer classes in Native communities, enabling them to bring a Christian message. The government eventually provided funding for the residential school at Carcross, where some students found a useful education, while others emerged scarred by bad food and strict discipline. More than a few died there, particularly of tuberculosis.

The Anglican church remains strong in the Canadian North, where Native deacons continue to keep its work alive, though as elsewhere it speaks more to the aged than to the young. Northern congregations in the smaller villages frequently mix aboriginal spiritual and cultural activities with Christian ones, and older Anglicans regularly read prayers and sing hymns in their own language. The Bible is available in indigenous languages, although most of the people can read English.

As the 21st century begins, the future of the Anglican church in northern Canada is unclear. The national church, the source of financial support for the northern churches, is reeling from the financial effects of the residential schools scandals. The Diocese of Cariboo went into bankruptcy at the end of 2001, and others are threatened, though an effort to lobby the federal government to cover legal costs may avert the crisis. Without such help, the national church may be crippled, something that will damage its northern operations.

Under these circumstances, it is not surprising that the historical memory of Bompas continues to fade, for the work for which he gave his life has been seriously discredited in the eyes of the modern public. He was a man of a very different age, representing values that Canadians have forgotten, or have chosen to discard. It is a pity he is not better known, for he represented an important part of our country's history. Nor was he some sort of stereotype bishop from fiction or the Monty Python show. He was a real person, with the convictions and quirks of a strong personality. His achievements were formidable, and he established a foundation for the long-term survival of the Church in the Canadian North. In an age when the work and value of Anglican and other missions are being called to account, and in many quarters sharply criticized, it is important that his record be remembered and that we consider again the lessons to be learned from his life and his approach to mission work.

Bompas was one of the last of the high profile northern adventurers, followed only by Robert Peary, Vilhjalmur Stefansson, and a few others, though his adventures were directed towards a different purpose. Those churchmen who came after him lacked his heroic distinction, which was based on the fact that he was a pioneer in the wilderness. He was very much a man of his age, a creation of the mid-Victorian imperial spirit. He embodied many of the most widely admired traits of that era: selflessness, modesty, dedication to Christian goals, hard work, and commitment to the betterment of "inferior" peoples. He attracted attention precisely because of these traits. But as the Victorian era faded and muscular Christianity became unfashionable, men such as Bompas became anachronisms, even figures of fun and scorn. Once a hero to the church and the public in general, he was forgotten after his death, except among the devout.

The early 20th century, a period characterized as the "onset of doubt," saw the Anglican and other churches (though not the evangelicals) questioning their missionary endeavours. One of the present authors remembers that as late as the mid-1950s part of his Sunday School offering (in the United Church) was earmarked for missionary work, though significantly, in India rather than northern Canada. By the 1960s and 1970s celebration of the missionary impulse had been abandoned, and by the 1980s it was being replaced with a certain sense of shame. When the government took over the residential schools, the church breathed a sigh of relief, for it had come to regret the cultural imperialism and paternalism of the missionary past. In the universities the missionaries became icons, not of self-sacrifice, but of intolerance and cultural genocide, and the new Marxist, post-modernist, and First Nations studies scholars were hardly likely to be sympathetic to them, even without the dismal revelations of abuse in the residential schools.

But as the life of William Carpenter Bompas shows, the historical situation of the missionaries was complex, not readily reducible to stereotypes. Indeed, if there was a stereotypical missionary, Bompas was not it. He was an unpromising young man, but grew to have some international fame. Difficult to the point of eccentricity, he nevertheless earned the deep respect of many. He was a church leader who often disagreed with his church and ignored their advice.

He held an important position in an expanding British-Canadian society that he mistrusted and disliked. His goal was to supplant aboriginal spirituality, but he succeeded by adopting the travel and survival techniques of the First Nations, who used his teachings as they saw fit. He quarrelled with his church, with local authorities, and with the Canadian government, but always with the welfare of his people in mind, as he saw it.

In his book, H.A. Cody tried to capture the essence of a man who let no one close to him, not even Cody, and if we could ask him one question, it would be why he wrote the book in the first place. Was it out of affection for Bompas, or was it because he wanted to memorialise a northern icon to publicize the missionary work of the church? Bompas would probably have scoffed at the idea of a biography, for he made little effort during his life to cultivate the reputation that would have been his for the asking. He kept no journal or diary; to have done so would have been an affront to his attitude towards his calling. While we end up knowing less about Bompas than we would have liked, in some ways it is good to confront his legacy without any of the self-promotion other figures give us. He was austere and single-minded, and it seems that his career marked the man; he had no secret life. Cody's book captures perfectly the zeal of the 19th century missionary, a world attitude largely absent in contemporary Canadian life, both north and south, and tells the story of a man called to do God's work, who found his future in the most unlikely of places.

Notes

1. A pall is a cloth, often velvet, which covers a coffin during funerals.
2. It was originally called Caribou Crossing; Bompas petitioned the government to change the name to avoid confusion with other similarly named places.
3. The O stood for nothing; like Harry S. Truman, he put it in to make his name more dignified. We have put one in for consistency.
4. www.canadianprayer.com, accessed November 2001.
5. See the bibliography for works by these authors.
6. T.A. Craig, *The Missionary Lives: A Study in Canadian Missionary Biography and Autobiography* (New York: Brill, 1997).
7. Craig, p. 134.
8. Craig, p. 2.
9. Craig, p. 137.
10. Kerry Abel writes about agency in "Of Two Minds: Dene Response to the Mackenzie Missions," in K.S. Coates and W.R. Morrison, eds., *Interpreting Canada's North: Selected Readings* (Toronto: Copp Clark Pitman, 1989).
11. The word "cathedral" comes from the Latin *cathedra*, or throne.
12. A survey of nearly 11,000 Canadians carried out for Statistics Canada in 1998 found that only 34 percent of Canadians aged 15 and over attended a religious service at least once a month. The figure for 1988 was 41 percent. *Christianweek Online*, 9 January 2001,www.christianweek.org/stories/vol14/no18/story2.html, accessed 17 January 2002.
13. K. Abel, "Bishop Bompas and the Canadian Church," in B.G. Ferguson, ed., *The Anglican Church and the World of Western Canada, 1820–1970* (Regina: Canadian Plains Research Center, 1991), p. 115.
14. See Clifford Putney, *Muscular Christianity: Manhood and Sports in Protestant America, 1880–1920* (Cambridge: Harvard University Press, 2001).
15. Family information is contained in R.A.B. Maxwell, ed., *Roots, Branches and Twigs: A Bompas Trilogy* (Tancook Island, NS: Little Daisy Press, 1990).
16. In the letters to his brother and sister (and even to his wife) he signs his name W.C. Bompas, and sometimes W. Carpenter Bompas, but never William C. Bompas.
17. A Tractarian was a supporter of the Oxford movement, which espoused the High Church principles advocated in the Oxford Tracts, published in the mid-19th century.
18. Abel, "Bishop Bompas and the Canadian Church," p. 114.
19. *Punch*, 9 November 1895.
20. Letter to his brother George, Long Island Fort, Mackenzie River, 6 December 1865, McCord Museum, Bompas Papers.

21. Letter to his brother George, 15 March 1866, McCord Museum, Bompas Papers. The passage concludes with a paraphrase of Matthew 18:26, Mark 10:27, and Luke 18:27.

22. See H.R. Driscoll, "'A Most Important Chain of Connections,' Marriage in the Hudson's Bay Company," in T. Binnema, G. Ens and R.C. Macleod, eds., *Rupert's Land To Canada* (Edmonton: The University of Alberta Press, 2001).

23. CMS papers, Bompas to CMS, 6 December 1872.

24. H.A. Cody, *An Apostle of the North* (London: Seely & Co. Limited, 1908), p. 280.

25. A catechist is a person who gives religious instruction particularly through catechism, or a series of questions and answers. In missionary work the term sometimes referred to a teacher of indigenous ancestry.

26. Quoted in Abel, "Bishop Bompas and the Canadian Church," p. 119.

27. Ibid.

28. Letter to his brother George, 16 June 1868, McCord Museum, Bompas Papers.

29. Bompas to Secretary of the CMS, 6 December 1872.

30. Ibid.

31. "Province" in the Anglican sense means a district consisting of several dioceses, under the jurisdiction of an archbishop. See Glossary, p. *XVI*.

32. S.A. Archer, ed., *Heroine of the North Pacific: Memoirs of Charlotte Selina Bompas (1830–1917)* (Toronto: Macmillan, 1929 [also London: Society for the Propagation of Christian Knowledge, 1929]), quoted in Myra Rutherdale, "Models of Grace and Boundaries of Culture: Women Missionaries on a Northern Frontier, 1860–1940," Ph.D. dissertation, York University, 1996, p. 137.

33. Selina Bompas, "Our Women of the North," *Canadian Churchman*, November 1907, p. 739, quoted in Rutherdale, p. 139.

34. Quoted in Rutherdale, p. 284.

35. Selina Bompas, "The Carcross School Children," in *The New Era*, July 1908, quoted in Rutherdale, p. 289–90.

36. Selina Bompas, *Owindia: A true tale of the Mackenzie River Indians, North-West America* (London: Wells Gardner, 1886).

37. The entry by Jean Friesen in the *Dictionary of Canadian Biography*, vol. XIV, is a good summary of his career. For a longer treatment, see Jean Usher [Friesen], *William Duncan of Metlakatla: A Victorian Missionary in British Columbia* (Ottawa: National Museum of Canada, 1974), on which this account is based.

38. CMS papers, Bompas to CMS, 4 May 1898.

39. Letter to the Minister of the Interior, 5 June 1894, National Archives of Canada, RG10, vol. 3906, file 105, 378.

40. Letter to his brother George, 26 August 1895, McCord Museum, Bompas Papers.

41. W.R. Morrison, *Showing the Flag: The Mounted Police and Canadian Sovereignty in the North, 1894–1925* (Vancouver: The University of British Columbia Press, 1985), p. 26.

42. Morrison, *Showing the Flag*, p. 59.

43. National Archives of Canada, RG10, vol. 4001, f. 207,418, Congdon to Pedley, 28 May 1903.

44. R.W. Dunning, "Ethnic Relations and the Marginal Man in Canada," in *Human Organization* 18 (1959), pp. 117–22.

45. L.F.S. Upton, "The Extermination of the Beotucks of Newfoundland," *Canadian Historical Review* 58, no. 2 (June 1977), pp. 133–53.

46. Upton, "The Extermination of the Beotucks," p. 153.

47. See K.S. Coates, "Send Only Those Who Rise a Peg: Anglican Clergy in the Yukon, 1858–1932," *Journal of the Canadian Church Historical Society* 28 (Summer 1986), pp. 3-18.

48. See John Webster Grant, *Moon of Wintertime: Missionaries and the Indians of Canada in Encounter since 1534* (Toronto: University of Toronto Press, 1984).

SELECTED BIBLIOGRAPHY

Works by William Carpenter Bompas and Charlotte Selina Bompas

Bompas, Charlotte Selina. *Owindia: A true tale of the Mackenzie River Indians, North-West America*. London: Wells Gardner, 1886.

———. "Our Women of the North," *Canadian Churchman*, November 1907.

———. "The Carcross School Children," *The New Era*, July 1908.

Bompas, William Carpenter. *Diocese of Mackenzie River*. London: Society for Promoting Christian Knowledge, 1888.

———. *Northern Lights on the Bible: Drawn from a Bishop's experience during twenty-five years in the great North-West*. London: J. Nisbet, n.d.

———. *The Symmetry of Scripture*. New York, 1896.

NOTE: The British Library Public Catalogue lists a number of translations of books by William Carpenter Bompas into the Slave, Chipewyan, and Beaver languages. These consist of the Bible, chiefly the gospels, and translations of the Book of Common Prayer, hymns, and other religious works. These are also listed in *Canadiana, 1867–1900* and the *National Union Catalogue*.

Secondary Sources

Abel, K. "Bishop Bompas and the Canadian Church." In B. Ferguson, ed., *The Anglican Church and the World of Western Canada, 1820–1970*. Regina: Canadian Plains Research Centre, 1991.

———. "Of Two Minds: Dene Response to the Mackenzie Missions." In K.S. Coates and W.R. Morrison, eds., *Interpreting Canada's North: Selected Readings*. Toronto: Copp Clark Pitman, 1989.

———. "William Carpenter Bompas." *Dictionary of Canadian Biography*, vol. XIII. [This entry contains a full list of Bompas's writings.]

Archer, S.A., ed. *A Heroine of the North: Memoirs of Charlotte Selina Bompas... With extracts from her journal and letters.* Toronto: Macmillan, 1929 and London: Society for the Propagation of Christian Knowledge, 1929.

Bolt, Clarence. *Thomas Crosby and the Tsimshian: Small Shoes for Feet Too Large.* Vancouver: University of British Columbia Press, 1992.

Boon, T.C.B. *The Anglican Church From the Bay to the Rockies: A History of the Ecclesiastical Province of Rupert's Land and its Dioceses from 1820 to 1950.* Toronto: Ryerson, 1962.

Coates, K.S. "Send Only Those Who Rise a Peg: Anglican Clergy in the Yukon, 1858–1932," *Canadian Church Historical Society Journal* 28: 1986, pp. 3-18.

Coates, K.S. and W.R. Morrison. *Land of the Midnight Sun: A History of the Yukon.* Edmonton: Hurtig, 1988.

Cody, H.A. *On Trail and Rapid by Dog-Sled & Canoe. The story of Bishop Bompas's life amongst the Red Indians and Eskimo told for boys and girls.* London: Seeley, 1911.

Craig, T.A. *The Missionary Lives: A Study in Canadian Missionary Biography and Autobiography.* New York: Brill, 1997.

Driscoll, Heather Rollason. "'A Most Important Chain of Connections,' Marriage in the Hudson's Bay Company." In Theodore Binnema, Gerhard Ens and R.C. Macleod, eds., *Rupert's Land To Canada*, pp. 81–107. Edmonton: The University of Alberta Press, 2001.

Dunning, R.W. "Ethnic Relations and the Marginal Man in Canada," in *Human Organization* 18 (1959), pp. 117–22.

Entwistle, Mary. *Tom Tiddler's Ground: An account of the missionary work of William and Charlotte Bompas in the Yukon.* London: Edinburgh House, 1942.

Friesen, Jean. "William Duncan," *Dictionary of Canadian Biography*, vol. XIV.

Grahame, Nigel. *Bishop Bompas of the Frozen North.* London: n.p., 1925.

Grant, J.W. *Moon of Wintertime: Missionaries and Indians of Canada in Encounter Since 1534.* Toronto: University of Toronto Press, 1984.

Gresko, J. "Missionary Acculturation Programs in British Columbia," *Etudes Oblates* 32, no. 3, 1973.

Huel, Raymond. *Western Oblate Studies 4: Proceedings of the Fourth Symposium on the History of the Oblates in Western Canada.* Edmonton: Western Canadian Publishers, 1996.

Jones, Ted. *All the Days of His Life: A Biography of Archdeacon H.A. Cody.* Saint John, NB: The New Brunswick Museum, 1981.

Maxwell, R.A.B., ed. *Roots, Branches and Twigs: A Bompas Trilogy.* Tancook Island, NS: Little Daisy Press, 1990.

McCarthy, Martha. *From the Great River to the Ends of the Earth: Oblate Missions to the Dene, 1847–1921.* Edmonton: The University of Alberta Press, 1995.

Morrison, W.R. *Showing the Flag: The Mounted Police and Canadian Sovereignty in the North, 1894–1925.* Vancouver: University of British Columbia Press, 1985.

Prang, Margaret. *A Heart at Leisure from Itself: Caroline Macdonald of Japan.* Vancouver: University of British Columbia Press, 1995.

Putney, Clifford. *Muscular Christianity: Manhood and Sports in Protestant America, 1880–1920.* Cambridge: Harvard University Press, 2001.

Rutherdale, Myra. "Models of Grace and Boundaries of Culture: Women Missionaries on a Northern Frontier, 1860–1940," Ph.D. dissertation, York University, 1996.

Stock, Eugene. *The History of the Church Missionary Society: Its Environment, its Men and its Work.* 4 vols. London: Church Missionary Society, 1899–1916.

Upton, L.F.S. "The Extermination of the Beotucks of Newfoundland," *Canadian Historical Review* 58, no. 2 (June 1977), pp. 133–53.

Usher, Jean [Friesen]. *William Duncan of Metlakatla: A Victorian Missionary in British Columbia.* Ottawa: National Museums of Canada, 1974.

Whitehead, Margaret. *Cariboo Mission: A History of the Oblates.* Victoria: Sono Nis Press, 1981.

AN APOSTLE OF THE NORTH

BISHOP BOMPAS
From a photograph taken in 1905

AN APOSTLE
OF THE NORTH

MEMOIRS

OF THE RIGHT REVEREND

WILLIAM CARPENTER BOMPAS, D.D.

First Bishop of Athabasca, 1874-1884
First Bishop of Mackenzie River, 1884-1891
First Bishop of Selkirk (Yukon), 1891-1906

BY

H. A. CODY, B.A.

Rector of Christ Church, Whitehorse, Y.T., Canada

WITH AN INTRODUCTION BY THE

MOST REV. S. P. MATHESON, D.D.

ARCHBISHOP OF RUPERT'S LAND

" The unexpressive man whose life expressed so much."

JAMES RUSSELL LOWELL.

" I know your great Bishop Bompas, and I tell you that the Apostles are living yet."

BISHOP WHIPPLE.

INTRODUCTION

It has been a great joy to me to learn that a life of my dear friend, Bishop Bompas, is being prepared for publication. Quite apart from the pleasure which the perusal of the record of his life will afford to a large circle of friends, it is, I consider, in the interests of missions that the Christian public should know something more of the heroic work of that great " Apostle of the North." That work was carried on in the seclusion of a prolonged isolation in the wilds of a land which was entirely shut out, except at rare intervals, from communication with the rest of the world. The Bishop loved to have it so. He had no care to speak to galleries or to come to the front. On the contrary, he retired before an approaching civilization, and when he saw it coming he retreated into " regions beyond."

His first episcopate covered what is now comprised in the districts of Athabasca, Mackenzie River, and Yukon. When the first subdivision took

INTRODUCTION

place, and the diocese of Athabasca was formed out of his jurisdiction in 1883, he selected, not the part most accessible to civilization, but the northern portion, and became Bishop of Mackenzie River. When, subsequently, another subdivision took place, he gave up Mackenzie River, retreated again farther North, and assumed charge of the distant Yukon.

This "hiding of self" was typical of the man. His life was "hid with Christ in God," and he hid the activities of it in an unselfish shrinking from the world's gaze. Some of us thought that in this latter he made a mistake, and he was frequently urged to give us the help and inspiration of his presence at our Synods once in three years at least. We longed to see and show "our hero." But it was of no avail. His unvarying answer was, "You can do without me at your meetings. My work is with my Indians."

As a consequence of this self-imposed isolation, the work of Bishop Bompas was little known to the general public outside of those who were near enough to see it. I rejoice, therefore, that we are to be privileged to have placed before us in this biography a short record of his work, and I pray that its story of simple devotion may appeal to some hearts, and draw from them, while the harvest still is great and the labourers few, the self-surrendering cry, " Here am I ; send me."

No matter how vivid the story is made, it will be hard to portray the real greatness of the man.   In order even measurably to appreciate William Carpenter Bompas and realize his personality, so simple and yet so great, it was necessary to see him and hear his self-effacing words.   After we write our best about him, we have to recognize the inadequacy of verbal description, and are constrained to exclaim, " Quantum mutatus ab illo!"

S. P. RUPERT'S LAND.

BISHOP'S COURT, WINNIPEG,
    January, 1908.

PREFACE

I⊤ has been the custom in all ages for people to ascribe to their heroes wonderful accomplishments and deeds of daring. The further removed in time and place, the greater the glamour.

There is something similar to this in reference to the life of Bishop Bompas. So long did he live apart from the bustle of civilization, and so little did he speak of his own achievements, that people have loved to weave around his life the garment of romance. Time, instead of lessening, has only increased this disposition, and some of the stories related have no foundation whatever.

In the following pages every endeavour has been made to adhere strictly to facts, and to record nothing that is not well authenticated.

The Bishop kept no journal of his many wanderings, and of his numerous hardships and dangers he seldom spoke. When he did refer to them it was with the utmost brevity, as in a letter to England,

PREFACE

dated November 23, 1876 : " I have been nearly frozen and nearly drowned this winter already." But all available sources of information have been placed at my disposal.

I wish to record my thanks for invaluable assistance received from Mrs. Bompas, whose journals have been of great service to me ; to His Honour, Judge Bompas, and to other members of the Bishop's family, for letters written by him and for information communicated ; to the Church Missionary Society for extracts from its records ; to the Right Rev. Bishop Stringer, the Ven. Archdeacon McDonald, the Ven. Archdeacon Collison, the Rev. John Hawksley, the Rev. William Spendlove, the Rev. R. J. Bowen, and many others, to whom I am much indebted.

Mr. Eugene Stock's " History of the Church Missionary Society " has been of great use to me, and also Dr. George Bryce's " Remarkable History of the Hudson Bay Company." My grateful thanks are due to the Society for Promoting Christian Knowledge for permission to quote from the Bishop's little book on " The Mackenzie River Diocese," and to Messrs. J. Nisbet and Co. for leave to make extracts from his " Northern Lights on the Bible."

PREFACE

The illustrations are almost all reproduced from photographs kindly lent by friends, and by the Society for the Propagation of the Gospel, the Church Missionary Society, and the Colonial and Continental Church Society.

This sketch of one of the Church's noblest missionaries is now sent forth, with the earnest prayer that

" The afterglow of his devoted life
Will lead men on to do and dare for Christ,
And win for Him through darkness, pain, and strife."

H. A. CODY.

" Christ Church Rectory,
  " Whitehorse, Y.T.,
      " January 11, 1908."

CONTENTS

CONTENTS

LIST OF ILLUSTRATIONS

LIST OF ILLUSTRATIONS

AN APOSTLE OF THE NORTH

CHAPTER I

THE VOLUNTEER

(1834-1865)

" Here am I ; send me."
ISA. vi. 8.

A MASTER was touching the living keys with subtle power in a crowded building on May 1, 1865, at St. Bride's, London, England. He had travelled a long way to attend the anniversary of the Church Missionary Society, and was preaching the sermon which was destined to bear so much fruit.

Bishop Anderson, late of Rupert's Land, was the bearer of a great message to the Church in England. He had much to tell of the vastness of Canada, and the great regions where the children of the wild lived and died without the knowledge of Christ. He told of a lonely mission-station on the mighty. Yukon River, where a soldier of the cross, the Rev. Robert McDonald, with health fast failing, was standing bravely at his post of duty till some one should relieve him. What thoughts must have surged through his mind as he looked on the many upturned faces before him! Who was there among those listeners willing to consecrate his life to the Master's work? Lifting up his voice, the Bishop uttered these words, which have become so memorable :

"Shall no one come forward to take up the standard of the Lord as it falls from his hands, and to occupy the ground ?"

The service ended, the clergy retired, and the congregation began to disperse. But there was one whose heart had been deeply touched by the speaker's words, and, walking at once into the vestry, a Lincolnshire curate, in the prime of life, offered to go to Canada to relieve the missionary at Fort Yukon.

William Carpenter Bompas, this young volunteer, was born at 11, Park Road, Regent's Park, London, on January 20, 1834. He was the fourth son of Charles Carpenter Bompas, Serjeant-at-Law, one of the most eminent advocates of his day, and leader of the Western Circuit, and of Mary Steele, daughter of Mr. Joseph Tomkins, of Broughton, Hants. Serjeant Bompas, it is said, was the original of Charles Dickens's celebrated character " Serjeant Buzfuz " in the " Pickwick Papers."

The Bompas family is of French extraction, and the name still exists in the West of France, but it is believed that in the seventeenth century members of the family owned land in Gloucestershire and

Worcestershire. We find the name spelled in different ways : Bonpar, Bonpart, and de Bonpas in Languedoc, Provence, and near Caen in Normandy, of which last one writer says, "They bear the coat of three lions rampant." There is a tradition that the motto "C'est un Bonpas" was given on the field of Crécy to an ancestor, who was knighted by Edward the Black Prince for his valour in the fight. A bystander remarked, "C'est un Bonpas," and the knight replied that he would take that for his motto. The great-grandfather of Bishop Bompas was lord of the manor of Longden Heath, in Worcestershire, and was descended from the Gwinnetts of Gloucestershire. There are records of an Edward Bompas who sailed, in 1623, in the ship *Fortune*, which followed the *Mayflower*, for America, and received a grant of land in the new country, where many of his descendants still reside. The family on the mother's side was partly Royalist and partly Puritan. One member is known to have been private secretary to Henrietta Maria, and was hanged by the Parliamentarians for aiding Charles I.; another, at one time, was secretary to Hampden.

On February 29, 1844, Serjeant Bompas died very suddenly, leaving a widow and eight children, five sons and three daughters, in poor circumstances. The eldest son, Charles, a lovable character, but of delicate constitution, died in 1847. The second son, George, who had been intended for the Bar, was articled to a firm of City solicitors,

with whom he worked for fifty-nine years, retiring
as senior partner in 1903, and died in May, 1905. To
his continued liberality the Dioceses of Mackenzie
River and Selkirk (Yukon) have been much indebted. Joseph, the third son, emigrated to Canada,
where he died. William and Henry, the two youngest
sons, were educated by Mr. Elliott, a distinguished
graduate of Cambridge University. Henry, after
obtaining a gold medal at the London University,
proceeded to St. John's College, Cambridge, where
he became Fifth Wrangler. After a short period
employed in tuition, he was called to the Bar, and
became, like his father, leader of the Western
Circuit. He continued to practise until 1896,
when he accepted the County Court Judgeship of
Bradford Circuit.

William, in early youth, showed most plainly
those characteristics which marked his whole life.
He was a shy boy, owing partly, no doubt, to
private tuition at home, which deprived him to a
large extent of the society of other boys. Cricket,
football, or such games, he did not play, his chief
pleasure being walking, and sketching churches and
other buildings that he encountered in his rambles.
Gardening he was fond of, and the knowledge thus
gained stood him in good stead years later when
planning for the mission-farms in his northern
diocese.

The influence of a religious home made a deep
and lasting impression upon him. His parents were
earnest Christians, belonging to the Baptist de-

nomination. Sunday was strictly observed, the father making it a firm rule never to read briefs or hold consultations on the Day of Rest. Bible reading, too, was carefully observed. Serjeant Bompas was a man of liberal views, allowed his children to indulge in harmless amusements, and occasionally permitted them to attend the theatre and to play cards, if not for money.

William from childhood was of a deeply religious nature, and at the age of sixteen was baptized by immersion, on a profession of his faith, by the Hon. and Rev. Baptist Noel. This step caused his mother great joy, and after her death the following was found among her many papers:

" *July* 7, 1850.—This day I would record the mercy which has rendered it one of peculiar blessing and happiness. The favour and presence of God has been manifested to us again during the past week, and I have enjoyed the best earthly happiness in seeing my dear and dutiful son W. devote himself unreservedly to the service of his Saviour. Having conscientiously decided on baptism by immersion, he was publicly baptized on the 5th by Mr. Baptist Noel, at his chapel in John Street, and was at the same time admitted as member of Mr. Stratten's church, and to-day I have had the privilege of partaking with him of that ordinance which I trust will be most profitable to us both."

At this time William was attending the small day-school kept by Mr. Elliott, and of him the latter wrote:

THE VOLUNTEER

" I never had a pupil who made such acquisitions
of knowledge in so short a time ; his attainments
in mathematics and classics are far beyond the
majority of youths at his age, and would warrant
anyone conversant with the state of education in
the Universities in predicting a brilliant career for
him, should he ever have that path open to him. I
think, however, that the development of his mind
is still more remarkable than the amount of his
knowledge."

But a University career was not practicable, and
William was therefore articled in 1852 to the same
firm of solicitors with whom his brother George
was working. At the expiration of his five years
of service he transferred himself to another City firm,
Messrs. Ashurst, Morris, and Company, with whom
he remained about two years. While here a catas-
trophe occurred in the failure of a great company,
involving ruin to unnumbered families. The harrow-
ing spectacle of the poorer shareholders who brought
their claims into court, having lost their all without
remedy, was a terrible strain upon the young man's
nervous system, which had been weakened by a
severe illness but a short time before. This,
together with strenuous labour, brought on a
second breakdown, and early in 1858 he was
forced to give up work altogether. He declared
that it took him three months to learn to do
nothing. During his year of inaction the Greek
Testament was his constant companion. Change
of scene became necessary, and he spent some time

at his mother's home, Broughton, Hants, and later, with his sister, visited the Normandy coast.

"The summer after his illness," writes his brother, Judge Bompas, "we went on a walking tour to Scotland, and one evening it got dark before we had reached our destination, and we had to sleep out in the mountains with no shelter, and amidst frequent showers of rain. William, though in weak health, was perfectly fearless, and in great spirits, repeating part of Macaulay's 'Lays' and other poems for much of the night."

As his strength returned, his mind reverted more and more to his early desire of entering the ministry. Leaving the communion of his early associations, he decided to seek ordination in the Church of England, and in 1858 was confirmed by the Bishop of London at St. Mary's, Bryanston Square. His remarkable linguistic ability enabled him soon to add by private study a good knowledge of Hebrew to that of Latin and Greek, which he already possessed.

In 1859 he was accepted by Dr. Jackson, the Bishop of Lincoln, as a literate candidate for Holy Orders, and was ordained deacon by him at the Advent ordination the same year, and appointed curate to the Rev. H. Owen, rector of Trusthorpe and Sutton-in-the-Marsh.

This first charge was a trying experience. The parish of Sutton was a wild district, with a rough and primitive population, and most of the men had been smugglers in former times. No school was

established, and there had been no resident clergyman since the time of the Reformation. Mr.
Bompas at once began a great work among the
children, gathering them into his own house, and
teaching them, at first by himself, and later with
the help of his sister and a girl from a neighbouring village. By his care for the children, and by
the unfailing sympathy shown in his visits to his
parishioners, he succeeded in winning their gratitude
and confidence. His plan for the erection of a
school was at first strongly opposed by some of the
farmers, who were unwilling to give land for the
purpose. But Mr. Bompas, with that tact and
gentleness which marked all his dealings, at length
overcame the opposition, and when he left at the
end of two years the building was completed and
opened.

"I can well remember," writes one, in reference
to the young curate's work at Sutton, "as quite a
little child, how he won my heart by carrying my
poor pet cat, that had been hurt by a heavy piece
of wood falling on it, into a place of safety, and
doing all he could to ease its pain. Also, about
the same time, in a heavy gale of wind, he was
going out to dinner at Mablethorpe, and, passing
through Trusthorpe, found a little girl blown into
the thick black mud at the side of a big drain,
and unable to free herself. He not only went to
the rescue, but carried her to her home at the far
end of Sutton, regardless of dinner! The *once*,"
continues the same writer, "that he revisited

WILLIAM CARPENTER BOMPAS
From a photograph taken in Göttingen

Sutton and preached there the people lined the
path from church to gate, and stood waiting for
him to leave the church, that they might get a
word as he passed—a very unusual demonstration
from our true but undemonstrative Lincolnshire
folk of those days."

While at Sutton, in the second year of his clerical
life, a great sorrow came to Mr. Bompas in the
death of his mother, to whose bedside he was summoned in January, 1861.   He was devotedly
attached to her, and was able to take part, with the
rest of the family, in ministering comfort to her
during her last days.

In the midst of early discouragements, Mr.
Bompas found a valuable friend and helper in
Mrs. Loft, of Trusthorpe Hall.   He was always
sure of a hearty welcome at her house, and in
after-years she followed his course with the
warmest interest, and corresponded with him to
the end of her life.

In 1862 he accepted the curacy of New Radford,
Nottingham, a poor and crowded parish, populated
largely by lace-workers.   The number of souls,
about 10,000, within the small triangle of New
Radford was about the same as the population
of the vast diocese of 900,000 square miles of
which he was later to have episcopal supervision.
To this circumstance he referred when preaching
in the parish on his return to England for consecration in 1874.

From Nottingham Mr. Bompas went for a short

time as curate to Holy Trinity, South Lincolnshire,
returning in 1864 to his former neighbourhood as
curate to the Rev. H. Oldrid at Alford, Lincolnshire.
As the earnest curate passed from house to house in
his daily work, his parishioners little thought what a
bright fire of enthusiasm was burning in his heart. He
had been much stirred by the stories told by missionaries of heathen dying without the knowledge of
Christ in far-away lands, and he longed to go abroad
and bear the message of salvation. His mind turned
to China and India, with their seething millions ; but
as he was a little over thirty years of age at that
time, the Church Missionary Society thought him
rather old to grapple with the difficulties of the
Eastern languages. But when one door closes
another opens, and at the right moment Bishop
Anderson arrived from Rupert's Land, and made the
great appeal for a volunteer to relieve the Rev.
Robert McDonald at Fort Yukon. So stirred was
Mr. Bompas by the address that he offered himself
for the work. He was at once accepted by the
Church Missionary Society, and ordained to the
priesthood by Bishop, afterwards Archbishop,
Machray, who had just been consecrated successor
to Bishop Anderson.

How little did those who attended that ordination
service realize the important part those two men
would take in Christ's great work, or that among
the heroes of the Church in Canada in years to
come no names would be held in greater reverence
than those of Machray and Bompas !

THE VOLUNTEER

Only three weeks did Mr. Bompas have in which to prepare for his long journey. But they were sufficient, as he was anxious to be on his way. So complete was his consecration to the work before him that "he decided," so his brother tells us, "to take nothing with him that might lead back his thoughts to home, and he gave away all his books and other tokens of remembrance, even the paragraph Bible which he had always used."

CHAPTER II

FORWARD TO THE FRONT

(1865)

"One who never turned his back, but marched breast forward."—ROBERT BROWNING.

SHORTLY after Mr. Bompas was accepted by the Church Missionary Society, he went to Salisbury Square and inquired how far it was to his mission-field, and the length of time required for the journey. When told it was about 8,000 miles, and that he was hardly likely to reach it that year, a smile passed over his face as he replied, "I see I must start with a small bag."

After he learned more about the country, a longing entered into his heart to start as soon as possible, and reach Fort Simpson, on the Mackenzie River, by Christmas Day. Was such a thing possible? No one before had ever done it in winter, and was it likely that the young, ardent missionary would be the first to accomplish the task? With this determination in view, Mr. Bompas was not long in making preparations for his journey, and on June 30, 1865, he left London for Liverpool,

32

where he boarded the steamer *Persia*, bound for New York.

He travelled in company with the Rev. J. P. and Mrs. Gardiner and family and Miss M. M. Smith, who were going to the Red River. There were many passengers, mostly Americans, and for these an effort was made to hold service the first Sunday, but the captain refused to give his permission. On the following Sunday, however, they were more successful, and service was held in the saloon, attended by crew and passengers. Tracts were also distributed among the sailors, " accompanied by religious conversation."

Reaching New York on July 12, two days were spent at the Astor House Hotel, where they had the exciting experience of viewing a disastrous fire right across the street, when a large block of buildings, including Barnum's Museum, was destroyed. From New York they proceeded to Niagara by the Hudson River and New York Central Railway. On the way Mr. Bompas spent one night at Rochester, to see Captain Palmer, of the American Telegraph Company.

" He informed me," wrote Mr. Bompas, " that a party of explorers were already on their way to Fort Yukon from Sidkar,* on the Pacific coast, with the view of carrying out the company's contract entered into with the Russian Government for laying a telegraph line through Siberia and across Behring's Strait, to join existing lines in America. Should

* Sitka, until recently the capital of Alaska.

the Atlantic cable prove successful, the Yukon line would, I suppose, complete the circuit of the globe."

Mr. Bompas considered the American railways rather noisy and jostling, and the large saloon carriages, holding about sixty people, less pleasant than the English style. At the same time, he thought the general arrangements were " good and expeditious," and admired the system of communication throughout the train and the " booking through luggage by duplicate ' cheques ' or metal badges."

Leaving Niagara, Chicago was reached by way of Detroit. Here were seen " many soldiers returning from the war, some of them wounded, and most looking pale and sickly, reminding one too plainly of the many who never returned." From Chicago they went by rail to La Crosse, and thence by steamer to St. Paul. Here Dr. Schultz, a Red River merchant, and afterwards Sir John Schultz, Lieutenant-Governor of Manitoba, was met, who conveyed their heavy luggage across the plains in his ox-train, and proved in many ways of great assistance.

At St. Cloud the first difficulty presented itself. Since the fearful Sioux massacre of 1862 people were in great dread all over the country, and they found it impossible to get anyone to convey them on towards Red River. After much trouble and delay, they were forced to procure a conveyance for themselves. Before leaving St. Cloud they were told time and time again to beware of the Indians, who were always prowling around. " But," said one informant, " they will respect the English flag, and I advise you to take one along." Such a thing the party did not possess. But Mr. Bompas was equal to the occasion, so, procuring some red and white cotton, he soon formed quite a respectable banner, which was fastened to a small flagstaff erected on the cart. Some distance out on the prairie* mounted Indians appeared in sight, and, like the wind, one warrior swept down to view the small cavalcade. Beholding the flag of the clustered crosses, he gazed for a time upon the little band, and, moving away, left them unmolested.

"On the whole, however," said Mr. Bompas, "we travelled without special discomfort, Dr. Schultz acting as guide. The charge of the horses, making fires, cooking, encamping, driving, etc., of course, threw much work upon us, being without a servant."

Reaching the Red River in safety, Mr. Bompas was much pleased with the whole general appearance.

"The houses," he wrote, "are cleanly and cheerful, and new ones are being built. The settlement extends altogether about twenty-five miles down the banks of the river. In this distance there are five churches. The three which I saw are well built and spacious. The schoolrooms, also, and parsonages are of good size. Mr. Cowley was just removing into a new house of a very substantial character."

Here Mr. Bompas did not have long to wait, for the boats of the great Hudson Bay Company were

* Dr. Schultz was overtaken some distance out on the prairie.

ready to start on their long Northern journey, and he was to go with them. There were four boats, called a "brigade," each rowed by seven or eight men, "mostly Salteaux Indians, heathen, and unable to speak English—a tribe much averse to Christianity."

Then northward fled that fleet of boats, across great inland lakes, over hard portages where the freight had to be carried, past the Company's posts, mission-stations, and Indian encampments, where services were held when possible.

But winter was rapidly closing in upon them, and threatening the daring voyagers. Sixty-three days had they been out from the Red River Settlement when Portage la Loche was reached on October 12, and there they found they were too late to meet any boat going farther north. Here was a difficult situation, but Mr. Bompas was not to be defeated. Engaging a canoe and two French half-breeds, he pushed bravely forward. The journey was a hard one. In some places they had to battle with drifting ice, and the water froze to their canoe and paddles. Still they pressed on, all day long contending with running ice, and the bleak cold wind whistling around them, and freezing the water upon their clothes. At night there was the lonely shore, the camp-fire, the scanty meal, and the cold ground covered with brush for a bed. The next day up and on again—the same weary work, the same hard fight. Such was the struggle for eight long days, till Fort Chipewyan, on Lake Athabasca, was reached.

FORWARD TO THE FRONT

Here Mr. Christie, the officer in charge of the post, gave him a hearty welcome ; here the warm stove sent out its cheerful glow; and here, too, were to be found many comforts for months, if he would only stay and rest. But no, it was ever up and on. Never before had such a man stood within the fort. Who could conquer that northern stream at such a season ? But the missionary only smiled, and asked for canoe and men. They were given a large craft and three Indian lads.

And once more that dauntless herald of the Cross sped northward. For several days the trim canoe cut the water, driven by determined arms. Then winter swept down in all its fury. The river became full of floating ice, jamming, tearing, and impeding their canoe. Axes were brought to bear. They would cleave a passage : the missionary must not be stopped. How they did work ! The ice-chips flew. The spray dashed and drenched them, and then encased their bodies with an icy armour. Colder and colder it grew, and the river became a solid mass from bank to bank. The canoe was dragged ashore, and placed *en cache* on the bank with their baggage. All around was the pitiless wild. It was a dreary sight to this intrepid traveller, with winter upon him, the bleak wilderness surrounding him, and very little food. The enthusiasm of a less ardent spirit would have been completely dampened. But Mr. Bompas was made of sterner stuff, and without delay he and his companions pushed forward through the forest.

FORWARD TO THE FRONT

On and on they travelled by a circuitous route,
through brushwood and thickets, with clothes torn,
hands and faces scratched and bleeding, and uncertain where they were. Night shut down and
wrapped them in its gloomy mantle. All the next
day they struggled forward, without food, and
again night overtook them. Still they staggered
on, and just when wearied to the point of exhaustion the lights of Fort Resolution, on Great
Slave Lake, gleamed their welcome through the
darkness.

It was necessary for the traveller to remain here
until the ice in the lake became firm enough to
cross with dogs and snow-shoes. Mr. Lockhart,
the Company's officer, offered his hospitality, and
during the delay Mr. Bompas continued busy " in
the preparation," as he tells us, " of letters for the
winter express, which is dispatched hence to the
south in December, and also in practising walking
with snow-shoes, in preparation for my journey
forward."

After remaining at Fort Resolution about a month,
" Mr. Lockhart kindly dispatched him across the
lake on snow-shoes, with two men and a sledge of
dogs." Ice was found drifting in the open lake,
and they were obliged to lengthen their course by
following the shore very closely. " However, by
God's help," wrote Mr. Bompas, " we arrived safely
at the next post (Big Island) in five days, when I
was again hospitably entertained by the officer in
charge, Mr. Bird."

FORWARD TO THE FRONT

Here, again, he waited anxiously for the men from Fort Simpson with the winter packet of mails. They arrived on December 13, and four days later started for Fort Simpson, and the missionary with them. Could they make the fort by Christmas Day ? That was the question. Only a short time remained in which to do it. Day after day they sped forward. Saturday came, and still they were on the trail, and the next would be Christmas Day. One hundred and seventy-seven days had passed since leaving London ; and was he to lose, after all, and so very near his destination ? But still the dogs raced forward, nearer and nearer, till—oh, joy! on Christmas morning the fort hove into sight. There was the flag floating from its tall staff ; there were the men crowding around to give their welcome, and among them stood that dauntless pioneer, the Rev. W. W. Kirkby, with great surprise upon his face, as Mr. Bompas rushed forward and seized him by the hand.

Great was Mr. Bompas's delight in having accomplished the journey, and reached the fort on that blessed day in time for the morning service, and thankfully he wrote :

"As I had especially wished to arrive by Christmas, I could not but acknowledge a remarkable token that our lives are indeed in God's hand. It is hardly needful to say how warm a welcome I received from Mr. Kirkby. When I heard what a trying time he had passed through last fall in consequence of the epidemic sickness among the Indians,

39

I felt very glad to have persevered in my efforts to reach him this winter."

No less enthusiastically did Mr. Kirkby write to the Church Missionary Society on June 3, 1866:

" You will imagine, better than I can tell, what a delight and surprise the unexpected arrival of Mr. Bompas was to us. He reached us in health and safety on Christmas morning, making the day too doubly happy by his presence and the glad tidings that he brought. He was a Christmas-box indeed, and one for which we thank God with a full heart. The entire unexpectedness of his coming caused us to see in it more of the loving-kindness of our God. Such a thing as an arrival here in winter is never thought of, nor had it ever before occurred. After the boats leave here in the fall, we have no visitors from without the district until now, when the waters are open again. Our dear brother deserves the greatest credit for the way in which he persevered in getting to us, and the accomplishment of his journey speaks much for his energy and determination. A more auspicious day, too, he could not have had for his arrival. He was just in time for morning service, so that we had, at once, the happiness of partaking of the Holy Communion together. Then followed the Indian service, in which he expressed much delight ; and in the evening, like good S. Marsden of old, he began his work by preaching from St. Luke ii. 10. He remained with us until Easter, and then went on with the

40

packet-men to Great Bear Lake, where I trust God is doubly blessing him.

" Fancy! it is not yet a year since he left England, and in that short time he has travelled so far, entered upon his work, and acquired enough of the language to be able to tell to the Indians, in their own tongue, the wonderful works of God. I admire that way of doing things exceedingly, and would accord all honour to him who thus performs his Master's work."

CHAPTER III

THE EXPLORATION OF THE NORTH-WEST

'Forward! . . .
Into the sleet and snow,
Over bleak rivers that flow
Far to the North and Westward.'
WILLIAM WILFRED CAMPBELL.

THE progress of civilization and Christianity in the Canadian North-West, as in many other parts of the world, is due in a large measure to great fur-trading companies. With a wonderful devotion to the cause in hand, they pushed beyond the bounds of civilization and entered regions never before trodden by white man. They built forts, gained the respect of savage tribes, and ruled them with a firm hand. By their boats missionaries travelled over the noble streams into the wilderness, ministered to the natives who gathered around the forts, and received supplies from the companies' stores.

That they had their faults is quite evident, and there are only too many to-day ready to lay grave charges at their door. But we must not forget what an important part they played in preserving Canada as a British colony. Neither must we omit the fact that the first clergyman of the Church of

EXPLORATION OF THE NORTH-WEST

England, the Rev. John West, was brought into the North-West by the Hudson Bay Company in 1820, or that upon the magnificent gift of £12,000 from Mr. Alexander Leith, a chief factor of the same Company, the bishopric of Rupert's Land was established in 1849.

Considering that these great companies, and especially the Hudson Bay Company, pioneered the way, and opened up the vast territory over which Mr. Bompas travelled and laboured so many years, it seems well to give some account of these early explorations.

As friction between bodies produces heat, fire, and light, so by the rivalry of fur-trading companies the northland of Canada was opened up and a new era ushered in. Eager to outstrip one another, they were ever pushing farther and farther into the country, and, as has been well said, " The great explorers of the period (1763-1812) were all connected with the fur trade."

Away to the north stretched a region, a land of wonder and strange stories. Indians told of a " great river " in the far North-West, and showed specimens of copper found along its banks. The Hudson Bay Company, acting upon these reports, decided to make a thorough investigation, with the object of solving the North-West Passage by land, to ascertain what mines were near the mouth of the Great River, " to smoke the calumet of peace with the Indians, and to take accurate astronomical observations."

EXPLORATION OF THE NORTH-WEST

The man chosen for this work, Samuel Hearne, the "Mungo Park of Canada," was a trustworthy servant of the Company, who, on November 6, 1769, started on his voyage of exploration from Prince of Wales Fort, on the shore of Hudson Bay. Owing to the desertion of over half his men, the attempt proved a failure, and he was forced to turn back.

Two months later he started again, and followed a north-westerly course over streams, lakes, and then inland across the "Barren Grounds." Food was very scarce, and they were reduced to great straits. "For a whole week cranberries, scraps of leather, and burnt bones were their only food." To add to their troubles, when 500 miles had been made, their only quadrant was blown over and broken. So again Hearne was forced to retrace his weary steps to the Bay.

Nothing daunted by these failures, this noble-hearted explorer once more started on his northward quest. This time he was more successful. With a strong band of Indians who were waging war against the Eskimos, he floated down stream, and ere long gained the sea, the first white man to reach the Arctic Ocean from the interior.

"The most unpleasant part of Mr. Hearne's story," wrote Bishop Bompas in his "Diocese of Mackenzie River," "is that the party of Indians with whom he travelled, entirely without his sanction, made an unprovoked attack on a number of Esquimaux encamped on the Coppermine River, and in the night barbarously massacred the whole

44

body of men, women, and children, and spoiled their tents. The site of the massacre became known afterwards as the ' Bloody Falls.'

" It is remarkable that there is a bird in those parts which the Indians there call the ' alarm bird,' or ' bird of warning '—a sort of owl, which hovers over the heads of strangers and precedes them in the direction they go. If these birds see other moving objects, they flit alternately from one party to the other with screaming noise, so that the Indians place great confidence in the alarm bird to apprise them of the approach of strangers or to conduct them to herds of deer or musk oxen.

" Mr. Hearne remarks that all the time the Indians lay in ambush, preparatory to the above-mentioned horrid massacre, a large flock of these birds were continually flying about and hovering alternately over the Indian and Esquimaux tents, making a noise to awake any man out of the soundest sleep. The Esquimaux, unhappily, have a great objection to being disturbed from sleep, and will not be awakened—an obstinacy which seems to have cost that band their lives."

Hearne, like Columbus, was not to have the honour of giving his name to the great river he discovered. This was reserved for another intrepid explorer, Alexander Mackenzie, of the North-West Company. In 1789 he started from Fort Chipe-wyan, on Lake Athabasca, in search of the " Western Sea." He, too, was confronted with great diffi-culties. Wild Indians told " of demon-haunted

caves and impassable falls." Terrified by these
tales, his Indians refused to go further. With
infinite patience Mackenzie induced them to continue seven days longer, and if in that time they did
not discover the sea he promised to turn back.
Before the end of the week the mouth of the river
was reached, and the explorer knew it was the
Arctic Ocean he had gained instead of the Western
Sea.

" It is hard," says Bishop Bompas, " to overpraise
the intrepid courage, cool prudence, and inquiring
intelligence of that noble traveller. . . . Sir
Alexander Mackenzie took the greatest pains to
conciliate all Indians whom he met by presents and
promises of peaceful trade, and he energetically
restrained all attempts at murder or rapine made by
the Indians who accompanied him. He did not
meet with Esquimaux, and it is little wonder that
these and the Mackenzie River Indians were shy of
him, as it was then customary for the Athabasca
Indians to make annual war expeditions down the
Mackenzie for purposes of plunder, massacre, and
rapine, as well as for the kidnapping of women and
slaves."

In after-years many eminent explorers, such as
Franklin, Richardson, Simpson, and Rae, entered the
country, the accounts of whose journeys and thrilling adventures may be read elsewhere.

Several years after the discovery of the Mackenzie
River, trading-posts were established at various
places along this stream and its tributaries. To

these the Indians brought their furs, and a thriving business was carried on. For a time there was a keen rivalry between the Hudson Bay Company and the North-West Company, but at length a union was effected under the name of the former.

Not satisfied with the great advance which had thus been made, these "lords of the forest and lakes" turned their attention in another direction. Ever before their vision rose the majestic peaks of the Rocky Mountains. Beyond those barriers were unknown regions. What possibilities lay in that *terra incognita* they could only conjecture. News reached them of a great river flowing to the west, the estuary of which had been explored by the Russians several years before, and named by them the " Quickpak." This stream they knew must drain a large territory, which might prove valuable for fur-trading purposes.

There was a man in the Company's service especially fitted for the task of pathfinder into the new region. This was Robert Campbell, a Scotchman by birth, over 6 feet of upstanding flesh, bone, muscle, and iron nerve, as dauntless a pioneer as ever shot a swirling rapid or faced a howling blizzard. To him, therefore, the task was consigned in the spring of 1840 by Sir George Simpson, Governor of the Company.

At once he began the undertaking, and after a hard and dangerous voyage up the Liard River, over lakes and portages, a stream was reached, which Campbell named the Pelly, in honour of Sir H.

Pelly. A raft was hurriedly made, on which they floated several miles down the river to view the country. Considering they had gone far enough from their base of supplies, the raft was abandoned, but not before Campbell had cast into the stream a sealed tin can with notice of his discovery, the date, and other information.

This discovery of the Pelly River only served to increase the interest of the Company, and it was resolved to push forward the investigation. In 1842 birch bark in sufficient quantity for the building of a canoe was sent up to the Pelly River, and the same year the construction of a fur-trading post was begun, and named Fort Pelly Banks. Early in June, 1843, Mr. Campbell started down the stream in the canoe which had been built, accompanied by two French Canadians and an Indian interpreter. After a long voyage they reached the mouth of the river, where it flows into another of considerable size. This Campbell named the Lewes, after Chief Factor John Lewes. Here a large camp of Wood or Stick Indians was found, who gazed with curiosity, mingled with dread, upon the hardy adventurers from the East. It was Campbell's earnest desire to continue down the river in order to explore the country. This he was unable to do, owing to the many stories told by the Indians of the wild people along the river, which so terrified his companions that they refused to proceed. There was nothing left but to return, which he did most reluctantly, the Indians treacherously pursuing in the hope of slaying them.

CANOE TRAVELLING IN NORTH-WEST CANADA

EXPLORATION OF THE NORTH-WEST

In the spring of 1848 Campbell once more returned, and erected a post for trading purposes at the confluence of the Lewes and Pelly Rivers. This place was called Fort Selkirk, and occupied a dangerous position, owing to the animosity of a tribe of Indians, known as the Chilcats, along the Pacific Coast. From time immemorial they had kept the natives of the interior in abject submission, having defeated them in a great battle. They refused to allow them to cross the mountains to trade with the white men on the coast, as they themselves did a thriving business as "middle men." When they beheld the hated white race establishing a post in what they considered their rightful domain, and drawing away the principal part of the trade, their anger knew no bounds. Crossing the mountains, they floated down the river, and without a word of warning attacked the fort and razed it to the ground. Campbell was not present at the destruction of his trading-post, as two years after its erection he had started down the river to see at any cost what lay beyond.

In the meantime another entry had been made into the Yukon region away to the north. In 1842 Mr. J. Bell, in the employ of the Hudson Bay Company, crossed the Rocky Mountains, and descended the Porcupine River for three days' journey. In 1846 he returned and moved down the river to its mouth till he reached a great stream, which the Indians told him was the Yukon. Believing this to be in British territory, Mr. A. H. Murray established a trading-post at this spot the following year, and called it Fort Yukon. It was here that the first missionary work was carried on by the Church Missionary Society, the scene of Archdeacon McDonald's wonderful labours for the Master.

At this post Mr. Campbell arrived from Fort Selkirk, the first white man to make the journey. He had ascended the Porcupine River, crossed the Rocky Mountains, dropped down the Peel River, and ascended the Mackenzie to Fort Simpson. Great was the surprise of the men at this latter place to see Campbell return in an opposite direction from that in which he had started out.

In this brief outline of the discovery of the Mackenzie and the Yukon Rivers we have seen the brave efforts of these noble pioneers. We shall see later how they were followed by the great King's messengers with the glorious gospel of salvation.

CHAPTER IV

THE FATHER'S BUSINESS

(1865-1870)

" While life is good to give, I give."
E. ARNOLD.

A WRITER tells us he once saw a statue of a knight of the olden time, clad in mail, with his good sword at his side. His pose was one of conscious strength, and his face alight with intensity of purpose, as he lifted before him a scroll which bore for a legend the single word " Credo."

In this picture we see the young knight, William Bompas, with heart aglow, touched by the altar-flame, taking up his great work in that far north land, proving by deed the faith he confessed, and anxious to pass it on to others.

Previous to the year 1858 the North-West America Mission had not advanced into the far northern territory of vast distances, having confined its efforts to the Algonquin nation of Indians. On June 6, in the year 1858, which has been called the " Annus Mirabilis of missionary enterprise," Archdeacon Hunter resigned for a time his charge at Red River, and started north with one of the Hudson

Bay Company's " brigades." The Roman Catholics were already establishing missions at various places, so, not to interfere with these, it was decided to go further and carry the Gospel to the regions beyond.

Archdeacon Hunter was well received at the various forts along the way, and after a journey of 2,000 miles, occupying two months and ten days, reached Fort Simpson, the principal station in the Mackenzie River District. He remained in the north the following winter, and visited Forts Liard, Norman, and Good Hope. Seeing a number of Tukudh Indians from beyond the Rocky Mountains, he longed to carry the good tidings to that densely ignorant people. But this was reserved for another hero of our Church.

It was the privilege of a young man stationed at Red River to continue and extend the work thus begun by Archdeacon Hunter. This was the Rev. William West Kirkby (afterwards Archdeacon), who, in 1852, had been sent out as a schoolmaster by the Church Missionary Society. Upon Archdeacon Hunter's return from the North, Mr. Kirkby was hurried forward to take his place. With Fort Simpson as his head-quarters, he laboured faithfully among the whites and Indians in the vicinity, and succeeded in building, so he tells us, " a little gem of a church." Concerning his work here, Mr. Bompas bore testimony a few years later:

" Few missionaries have endured more privations and hardships from the climate and isolation of his position. . . . In spite of all opposition he has established a fine mission-station, built a beautiful church, learned their (Indian) language, printed in it a useful book of elementary instruction, and now he has translated two Gospels."

During the spring of 1862 Mr. Kirkby resolved to cross the Rocky Mountains, and carry the message of peace to the far-off Yukon region. On May 29, after he had asked the blessing of God " on those who journeyed, and on those who remained behind," Mr. Kirkby began his long journey in a canoe, which he called the *Herald*, accompanied by two Indian lads.

Down the mighty Mackenzie River he wound his tedious way, up the Peel, and then over the Rocky Mountains. Standing there on the summit which separates the rivers flowing into the Arctic Ocean from those rolling down to the Pacific, the noble soldier of the Cross knelt down and prayed that the entrance of the Gospel light into those new regions might be abundantly blessed by God.

Then on he pressed, against many difficulties. The mosquitoes were bad, and caused his temples and the back of his ears to stream continually with blood.

" Our course to-day," he wrote, " was more varied than before : at one time walking up to our knees through dirty swamps, at another, climbing up the craggy sides of the mountain ridge ; now fording a river ; then treading with weary steps over large patches of unthawed snow. The rivers were neither very wide nor deep, but the current in all was very strong. In all, we crossed twenty-five to-day. . . . The current of one was very strong ; but by all three of us holding fast together, we managed to ford it."

A hearty welcome was given him at La Pierre's House, a Hudson Bay Company's post.

" I never thought to see the day," said the officer in charge with tears in his eyes, " when a minister of the Gospel would be at La Pierre's House."

Proceeding on his way down the Porcupine River, Fort Yukon, another Hudson Bay Company's post, was reached on July 6. Notwithstanding the warning Mr. Kirkby had received about the danger he would encounter from the medicine - men, he preached Christ boldly. The result was marvellous. The Indians crowded around him incessantly, and one after another renounced their evil way, and promised to lead better lives.

" Oh, it was a goodly sight," said Mr. Kirkby, " to see that vast number, who had never prayed before, bending their knees, and trying to syllable the name of Jesus."

After a stay of seven days, the missionary, on July 13, began his long return journey. This was much more difficult, as the way was nearly all up stream. But by God's grace Fort Simpson was reached on August 29, after an absence of three months.

" I have travelled over 3,000 miles," thankfully

wrote Mr. Kirkby, " and have been honoured by God to carry the glad tidings of salvation far within the Arctic Circle to a people who had never heard it before."

The news of Mr. Kirkby's successful journey to the Yukon so stirred a missionary meeting at St. Andrew's, Red River, that a young catechist offered to go to the Indians in that far-off region, and the congregation proposed to raise the funds to send him. This was Robert McDonald, afterwards Archdeacon of the Yukon, a name destined to occupy the very foremost place among the heroes of the Canadian Church. He reached Fort Yukon that same fall (1862) and was bravely holding the post when the young and ardent recruit, William Bompas, entered the field.

Upon reaching Fort Simpson, Mr. Bompas learned that Mr. McDonald had recovered from his sickness, and was able to continue his work. Though this news filled him with thankfulness, yet he was disappointed for himself, as his heart had been set upon the Yukon region as his special sphere of labour. Nevertheless, he began with enthusiasm to master the Indian language at Fort Simpson, assisted by Mr. Kirkby, with whom he remained till Easter, 1866. Then he pushed forward to Fort Norman, on the Mackenzie River, north of Great Bear Lake, where he remained till August. The Hudson Bay Company built him a house, and engaged a schoolmaster, Mr. Murdo McLeod, to assist in teaching the Indians, which encouraged him very much.* He tells us that he did " not find the Indian children deficient in intelligence, but only in application. Their restlessness and want of thought appear to be the chief difficulties to be overcome.

" With respect to the adults, I have not been dissatisfied with the reception given to the Word, though I cannot speak of results at present. God's book is treated with respect, and if I visit their tents Bible in hand, it is seldom that I cannot find some one ready to listen to it. My chief impediment is the imperfect knowledge of the language, but I am thankful to speak even a few words in the name of Jesus."

In August Mr. McDonald arrived from the Yukon, and, accompanying him, Mr. Bompas returned to Fort Simpson, where those three heroes of the Cross assembled to consider the Master's vineyard and arrange plans for the future. The question was, where to place Mr. Bompas. After a long and earnest discussion, it was considered best to give him a roving commission rather than a settled station. With this plan Mr. Bompas was well pleased, as it accorded best with his " judgment and wishes."

" I am quite willing," he tells us, " to push on to the extreme north, to try and carry the Gospel among the Esquimaux ; but meanwhile it seems

* This school was established principally for orphans left by the epidemic of scarlet fever during 1865. The school was broken up in 1868.

An Indian Summer Camp at Peel River. From a photograph by the Rev. C. E. Whittaker

best for me to try and learn first one language thoroughly, and that the Slave, that I may be fit for itinerating throughout the different posts of the district."

It mattered little to him where he was sent, as his feelings were those expressed by an English poet:

> " Should fate command me to the farthest verge
> Of the green earth, to distant barbarous climes,
> Rivers unknown to song . . . 'tis naught to me,
> Since God is ever present, ever felt,
> In the void waste as in the city full."

After the conference, Mr. Bompas returned to Fort Norman, taking with him two Indian boys to be trained at the school, and then plunged into earnest work among the natives, visiting their camps, making journeys some distance away, and patiently studying the language.

" My time," he tells us, " was occupied in visiting the separate tents, and trying to convey the simple truths of the Gospel to the natives. Some few of the Indians, especially one of the chiefs and the Indian who hunted with me, took great interest in my instructions. Living in the Indian tents was not hard to me. The habits of the Indians are quiet and inoffensive. Their hours of eating, sleeping, etc., are regular, and they are mostly occupied in some useful way—fishing, snaring rabbits, net-making, turning snow-shoes and sledges, and other manual labour, while the women are chiefly engaged in dressing deer-skins.

" The month of December was occupied by me

at the fort, chiefly in conversing with Indians, who
arrived almost daily in large or small bands, and
nearly all of them visited me at the schoolhouse
for instruction.

" One of the Indians, of whom I thought better
than any, died during this month, after a few days'
illness. He had built a house near the fort for the
express purpose of being near the mission. He
hunted for us until his illness, and showed every
desire to receive what instruction I could give. I
baptized him before his death ; his name was
Antoine. Another Indian also, whom I baptized
in the spring by the name of Christian Kaia, has
behaved very well. He took me in his canoe to
the Indian camps, hunted for me, housed me, and
waited on me with every care and attention."

Strongly did these Great Bear Lake Indians
appeal to Mr. Bompas's noble nature. He sym-
pathized deeply with them in their many troubles,
and of them he wrote most pathetically :

" Do the noble ladies of our land, when they wrap
around them their highly prized fur, consider that
they cannot choose but be indebted for this luxurious
boon to the half-naked savage roaming the woods,
houseless and homeless, in a temperature nearly
100° below the freezing-point, wrapped in his
single blanket, and kindling in the deep snow his
solitary fire, owing his preservation and food—not
daily food, perhaps—to the one great Father, who
regardeth not the rich more than the poor, for they
are all one in His hands ? Oh, pray for the souls

62

of these poor Indians, that they may become our brethren in Christ, that so their pitiable state on earth may be forgotten in the joys of one common heaven above !"

Leaving Fort Norman on January 10, 1867, he started on a long journey to Fort Rae, on Great Slave Lake, in company with Mr. King, the officer in charge of the Hudson Bay Company's post at that place. They were twenty days in making the trip, passing on the way one large brigade of Dog Rib Indians, whom Mr. Bompas visited for a few hours.

" The name of Jesus," he says, " was that which I sought feebly to proclaim, and with this they did not seem familiar. Two I saw nearly in a dying state."

He found the Indians at Fort Rae greatly diminishing in numbers, owing to European diseases, which they contract " through intercourse with the whites. This is a call to us," he adds, " to be earnest and active in ministering to them the Gospel, that a ' remnant may be saved.'

" My feeling in regard to this country is much the same as that expressed by the Moravian missionaries in a similar sphere in Greenland—namely, that for any other object than that of walking patiently and humbly with our God this country offers but a poor position ; while if we ever keep in mind our Saviour's words, 'Whosoever shall humble himself as this little child, the same is greatest in the kingdom of heaven,' then we shall, I think, view our sphere of labour here as affording a good school for heaven."

THE FATHER'S BUSINESS

He earnestly longed to acquire the Indian language, that he might the better impart the truth, and yet he found many difficulties in the way.

"The little I already know," he writes, "the Indians often ascribe to magic, or 'medicine,' as they call it, but I trust I know how to ascribe it entirely to the help of God's Spirit. Beyond this, a familiarity with the Indians' habits and feelings and modes of thought, the hardening of one's own constitution to bear the exposure of associating with them in their tents, the discovery of the best means of approaching them with the truth, etc., are all matters of time, and in this country progress is slow."

It appeared to him to be of little use to teach the Indians to read their own language until books were printed in it, and he longed for "a small quantity of large printing type, with ink and paper," that he might teach "the Indian lads to read in Slave. Had I these things," he continues, "which I have mentioned, I think I could cheerfully resign myself to a lifetime spent in the wilderness, devoting such of my time as is not occupied among the Indians to the study of God's word in the original languages— a favourite study, which the bustle of home-life sadly interrupted, and which the infidel assaults of our day and generation urgently demand."

Mr. Bompas remained at Fort Rae until the latter end of June, and then went to Fort Resolution, on the opposite shore of the same lake. He travelled in company with a Roman Catholic priest, Père

THE FATHER'S BUSINESS

Gascoigne, who had spent the winter at Fort Rae. During this trip Mr. Bompas endeavoured to bring about a dispassionate consideration of the differences between Protestantism and Romanism, but in vain.

From Fort Resolution Mr. Bompas went to Fort Chipewyan, on Lake Athabasca, where he remained during the summer. Here good work was carried on among the Cree and Chipewyan Indians, when they assembled around the fort to receive their supplies. Though for fifteen years the Roman Catholics had held sway at this post, Mr. Bompas was very anxious to start a Church of England mission here, and the Hudson Bay Company's officers gave him every encouragement.

" A mission here," he says, " would form a sort of connecting-link with that at Fort Simpson, which hitherto has been so far isolated, and we might then, I think, consider that the whole country is brought to some extent within the sound of the Gospel, with the exception of the Esquimaux, for service among whom I would gladly volunteer at any time if this and nearer stations can be otherwise filled."

Mr. Bompas shows how good work done in one section of the country affects another many miles away. He mentions that at the post were Indians who had been brought up in the mission-schools at Red River and the neighbourhood " who are now married and with families, and who, in their education, habits of life, and deportment, do great credit to their instructors. The seed sown at Red River is thus bearing fruit at a distance of more than 1,000 miles."

He pleaded earnestly for a man to take up work at Fort Chipewyan, and urged that "the small Protestant community here needs the rites of baptism, marriage, and burial performed for them. It is a Cree-speaking student from St. John's College, Red River, that I should rejoice to see labouring here."

Early in January, 1868, Mr. Bompas left Fort Chipewyan and travelled up the Peace River to Fort Vermilion, and found himself in the country of the Beaver Indians, whose physical condition he described as " very pitiable. They are very careless and neglectful in their dress, and, though quick and intelligent, appear idle and dissipated. There are but few among them sound in health, and they seem fast dying off. I do not think there is any hope of saving their lives in this world, as well as their souls for the next, except through the ameliorating influence of Christianity, brought to bear on them by means of a mission established in their midst."

" The most necessary adjunct to winter travelling in the North is a dog-sledge, for dogs alone are there used for hauling provisions and fuel over the winter snows. The strength and endurance of a train of three or four dogs is wonderful. Each dog is expected to haul a weight of 100 to 150 pounds. . . . Hard blows and unfeeling usage are too often the experience of the dogs in the

DOG SLEDGE IN NORTH-WESTERN CANADA

A couple married at Whitehorse by Bishop Stringer started in November with this team of dogs, and, after a journey of 1200 miles, arrived at Fairbanks in the spring.

North, and hence their temper is snappish and their intelligence and affection but small.

"Much pride or zeal is shown in the North in decking the sledge dogs in gay trappings with ribbons, beads, coloured cloth, and with numerous jingling bells. A number of dog-trains together form an animated scene."

A good dog-team in the North costs from 100 to 200 dollars, averaging about twenty - five dollars a dog. Some of the best in the country are bred by the natives, nearly every grown-up Indian having his own dog-team and sledge or toboggan. The Indians make their own sledges and harness, the former being made of birch wood, and the latter of moose-skin.

The affection of the dogs towards their master is of the kind that has been called "cupboard love." They attach themselves quite readily to the one who feeds them. They resemble mankind to a certain extent in this respect, and also in the matter of work, some being very willing, while others are lazy.

Their life, as a rule, is a hard one. At times they suffer much, not only from the cruel lash, but their feet become bruised and sore, owing to the sharp crust and ice, and blood often marks the trail. The snow, too, gathers in lumps between their toes, and often the driver is forced to stop and clear this away. Sometimes the dogs themselves will pick out the snow and ice with their teeth. To obviate this, little moccasins are made for the feet, which give the animals much comfort. When a dog is disabled he is turned loose to follow in the best way he can.

They can travel from twenty-five to thirty miles a day, under ordinary conditions, for two or three weeks, and longer if given an occasional day's rest. " They show a marked difference of character," says the Rev. John Hawksley, who has lived for over twenty years in the North, " some being mild and gentle, with a certain amount of affection, while others are most ferocious, and very quarrelsome with the other dogs in the team. Others, again, are very uncertain, at one time licking your hand while harnessing them, at another snapping fiercely at you." They do not mind being shifted about in the team. The leader, who has been carefully trained for his position, is seldom changed.

The dogs are fed only once a day, after camp has been pitched for the night. If fed in the morning or while on the trail, they become so lazy and indifferent that no progress can be made. Their food consists of either dried fish or rice, cornmeal, rolled oats or flour, boiled either with bacon or dried fish well cut into small pieces.

Seldom does the traveller ride during a long northern journey. He is thankful if the dogs draw the load, and at times he is forced to assist. Day after day he must follow the sledge, running by the side of the dogs, urging them on, or plodding ahead breaking a trail through the deep snow. This is all done on the light and springing snow-shoes, which have been well named "northern slippers."

"Anyone who has tried walking in the rough country of the Arctic region in summer-time will readily admit the increased facility of movement in winter over smooth snow on snow-shoes. The ground is mostly marsh, clothed with a coarse grass, which eats out the soil into high tufts or lumps, on or between which the ankles of the pedestrian twist and writhe. These tufts are locally known as "women's heads," being, from the long grass pendent from them, like dishevelled hair. Certainly, to walk over them may be compared to what it would be to walk over the heads and shoulders of a crowd.

"Snow - shoe walking requires care to avoid troubles. If the snow-shoe lashing or any other bands are too tight on the limbs, or if the feet are held too stiffly, a very painful affection of the muscles supervenes, known as the snow-shoe sickness. This sickness sometimes causes the legs to swell like those of an elephant, and renders them so powerless that the feet may have to be lifted with the hand by lines attached to the front of the snow-shoe. Such an accident, when the end of the journey may be 100 miles off, and no provision nearer, and hence no chance of resting, is not pleasant."

In addition to the labour of travelling, Mr. Bompas had the severity of the climate to contend with. Though at times the weather is mild and pleasant, yet only too often the thermometer plunges down to 60° and even 70° below zero. This extreme cold is bearable owing to the dryness and perfect stillness of the atmosphere.

" For outside travelling," continues Mr. Bompas, " it is possible to keep warm on the coldest day without heavy clothing by walking very fast, which pace is often alternated with running by a good voyager. . . . It is the hands and feet which require the most careful covering of blankets and leather, the covering of the hands being locally termed mittens, and of the feet moccasins."

Though each day's journey was made with difficulty, yet at night there was the bright camp fire in some sheltered spot. The process of this camping is interesting, and has been well described by Mr. Bompas.

" As sundown approaches, a spot is selected in the woods, where some dead trees are seen standing. The snow is scraped away, by using a snowshoe for a shovel, from a circular space sufficient to seat the party. This space is next thickly strewn with pine-branches lopped down for the purpose, and which are locally termed brush. The axes are then in requisition to fell a sufficient number of dead trees for the consumption of firewood for the night.

" With a few splinters of dry wood and shavings cut from them, or with a piece of birch bark which burns like a torch, a fire is started and piled to a sufficient height with logs. Water is procured by

FEEDING THE DOGS

melting some of the surrounding snow, and kettles are brought for preparing the evening meal. Dogs are fed with fish, and when supper is consumed, shoes and socks are dried for the next day's travel, and the travellers seek repose wrapped in their blankets on the pine-brush before the fire embers, till shortly after midnight, when preparations begin for another day's march.

" To sleep in the woods is much easier than to sleep without woods. In the Saskatchewan plains, which are mostly bare, a traveller's life may be lost by his being overtaken with a storm in the open plain, far from water, shelter, or fuel. The fact that the cold is not so extreme there as in the far North may make the danger only greater, for if the snow melts about a sleeper, it will soon freeze him to death. For this reason one falling asleep in the snows of Europe will rarely wake again, whereas in the far North a lost traveller overtaken in a storm without fire or shelter, by burying himself in the snow, may probably sleep well and awake in the morning none the worse.

" Want of fuel in a winter camp is a great trouble, but a benign Providence arranges that dry wood may be found almost anywhere. The most difficulty in finding fuel occurs in the approach to the Arctic coast. Where dry pines are lacking, a fire can be made of green pines, by felling a number together and igniting them in the heads with the brush or branches upon them.

" If there are no pines, fire can be made with dry

willows. If these are lacking, even green willows are supposed to burn when once ignited, though the theory is rather a difficult one to reduce to practice. Should there be none of these, there may probably be no fire, unless as a last resort a sledge can be chopped up for the purpose.

" There may be inconvenience also in the lack of materials for starting a fire. In the absence of lucifers or sulphur matches, fire is commonly made with flint and steel and a piece of country touchwood, which consists of a fungoid growth or excrescence on the bark of the birch or poplar. A small particle of this touchwood is kindled to a spark with flint and steel ; the touchwood is then placed in a handful of shavings cut from dry wood, and the whole is waved together in the air till it bursts into a flame. When a steel is missing, a knife may be at hand, or fire may be obtained by snapping a gun. An Indian chief has told of his life being saved at a last emergency by obtaining fire from a piece of green stone, carried for a whetstone, and an iron buckle from his dog harness.

" If a traveller in the woods happens to meet with an accident by cutting his foot with his axe while chopping firewood, his position is not an enviable one, and on this account it is not customary in the North, except with natives, for the voyager to travel alone. In case of such a mishap, the lamed one will be carried by his companions on the dog-sledge, if they have one, to the nearest house, which may be a hundred miles distant.

THE FATHER'S BUSINESS

" As to finding the proper direction to travel through the woods, a native Indian is seldom at a loss, though a stranger may soon lose himself. For one lost in the woods, ' when neither sun nor stars appear,' the best hope of knowing his position or the direction in which to travel is by observing the bark and branches of trees. These in an exposed position may be somewhat blasted towards the north compared with their southern aspect, and hence the points of the compass may be surmised."

Mr. Bompas believed that Fort Vermilion offered remarkable advantages for a mission-station, and was the only place he had seen in the north where an ultimate Indian settlement appeared hopeful. He thought there were facilities for farming, rearing cattle, horses, etc., that would render missionary work more cheerful and promising as far as the present world is concerned than farther north.

Writing to his sister in England from this place, he said :

" In your letter I am amused at your regret that you cannot promise me no snow and ice in heaven. All I can say is, let us be thankful for it here while we have it, and say, ' Praise Him, snow and vapours.' Depend on it there would be a gap in the display in the wonders of God in Nature if this country were left out. Nowhere in Nature is God's power more forcibly shown, as you will find explained in Job xxxvii. and Psalm cxlvii. Besides this, you must know that I have already returned to Southern climes, being now in the latitude of Scotland, and

with a length of day in winter nearly like yours.
We can no longer say with Habakkuk, 'There is
no herd in the stall, and the fields yield no meat,'
for there are plenty of horses and cattle here, and
the fields would grow any quantity of corn and
vegetables.

"Food is abundant here. The Indians live on
moose and beaver; we on moose alone. It is well
that there is the beaver for the Indians to fall back
on, for moose-hunting is rather precarious. It is
only in a wind that the hunter can elude the
animal's quick scent, and only when the snow is
quite soft that he can escape its keen sense of hearing. Last fall, when there was calm weather, and
the surface of the snow became hard, through rain
falling on it, some of the Athabasca Indians were
nearly starved to death, there being no beaver
there—by so precarious a thread does the life of
these poor wandering Indians hang. The beaver
are numerous here. About 4,000 beaver skins
have been traded at the fort this winter, and there
are but about fifty Indian hunters.

"I have paid the Indians a couple of visits in the
woods since I have been here, but not to stay long
with them. Lately they have been, most of them,
at the fort. I have tried to learn something of
their language, which is a new dialect for me.
Sometimes I think they were the first people that
were made, because they call a finger-ring 'O' and
a star 'Sun.' What can I teach, except to look to
Jesus and ask Him to give them good hearts?

THE FATHER'S BUSINESS

" You can have little idea of the way in which we count here by years what you count by days. You would say, ' I will get it to-morrow.' We say, ' It has not come this year, perhaps it will come next' ; or, ' I must order such a book from home ; if no mishap occur, in three or four years I may hope to see it.' A bit of white chalk would, I think, have been more use to me the last twelve-month than fifty sovereigns, and I have often thought I would barter everything I brought out with me, except the Bible, for one or two Sunday-school primers. . . . But I hope I can say I am learning in whatever state I am therewith to be content, and to rely on the promise that ' My God shall supply all your needs according to His riches in glory by Jesus Christ.' "

While Mr. Bompas was at Fort Vermilion carrying on his Master's work, a change had taken place at Fort Simpson. After sixteen years' absence from England, nine of which had been spent on the Mackenzie River, Mr. Kirkby returned home for a well-deserved rest, and also with a view to the printing of the Gospels of St. Mark and St. John, which he had translated into the Chipewyan language. It was his earnest wish that his work at the post should be carried on by Mr. Bompas, who returned from Fort Vermilion for that purpose, about August 20, 1868, took charge of the mission premises, and continued the services. The latter's time on week-days was occupied chiefly in " schooling about a dozen children, all of them natives of

79

this country, about half of them children of white men, and the other half pure Indians."

That fall a medical man, Dr. Mackay, arrived at the fort, "who had been sent by the Fur Company chiefly for the purpose of investigating the diseases of the Indians, with a view of recommending remedial measures." He was given a room in the mission-house for the winter, and the missionary supplied him with much assistance in the way of interpretation, and felt very "grateful that the Fur Company had taken interest enough in the Indians' welfare to send a medical officer to so great a distance on their behalf." Mr. Bompas believed that "in this country one is sometimes tempted to think too much of the physical aid, and yet the misery here, as elsewhere, is the fruit and punishment of sin, and the Physician of souls is He to whom recourse must be had for a medical cure. Still, I should be delighted for the Gospel and medical science to go hand in hand."

During the winter and spring he remained at Fort Simpson; but a change was soon to take place which would remove him to the far north among hardships and dangers of the most thrilling nature, the account of which must be reserved for another chapter. In this has been given the outline of a work carried on over a vast extent of country, where thousands of miles had to be travelled, and obstacles and dangers overcome, that the Father's business might be performed and precious souls brought home.

CHAPTER V

THE COUNTRY AND ITS INHABITANTS

"What charming solitudes! and what life was there!
Yes, life was there! inexplicable life."

CHARLES MAIR.

OF the country in which Mr. Bompas was to play
such a grand part for so many long years, we are
able to give an account, chiefly in his own words.*
It is a region of about 1,000,000 square miles—
the fourth of all Canada. Two mighty rivers, the
Mackenzie and the Yukon, pour their icy waters
into the Arctic Ocean and the Behring Sea.
Between these the Rocky Mountains lift their
hoary peaks as a huge barrier.

"The great Mackenzie River is the longest in the
British dominions, being, from its source to its
mouth, upwards of 3,000 miles long. It bears the
name of Mackenzie only after passing through
Great Slave Lake, whence its course to the sea

---

* The substance of this chapter is taken from the Bishop's
two volumes, "The Diocese of Mackenzie River" and
"Northern Lights on the Bible," by kind permission of the
Society for Promoting Christian Knowledge and Messrs.
J. Nisbet and Co.

81

is about 1,200 miles. It averages about a mile in breadth, with a swift current running about three to four miles an hour. From about 150 miles above Great Slave Lake to the sea there is no great obstruction to the navigation, the few rapids being inconsiderable. In the upper part of the stream it is called by the names of the Athabasca and Slave River.

" The banks of the Mackenzie River are mostly high and clothed with pines. The shores are stony, except in reaches where soil is being cut from muddy banks by the encroaching water. Islands occur at intervals in the course of the stream. The chief features of interest along the river occur where the mountains or jutting crags border the channel. There are first the Nahany Mountains, to avoid which the river takes a sudden bend to the north. Next is noticed the bold precipice known as the ' Hill by the River-side,' a sheer cliff which drops into the water on the right bank of the stream. About 150 miles below this is Bear Rock, an imposing headland immediately below Fort Norman. In the same vicinity are seen constant natural fires burning on the river-banks, and fed by underground coal or mineral pitch. These have been on fire for at least a century—in fact, ever since the discovery of the river.

" Just above the Arctic Circle, the Mackenzie River narrows into a gorge or cañon, between high perpendicular cliffs, known as the Ramparts. These cliffs are fantastically scarped by Nature into a

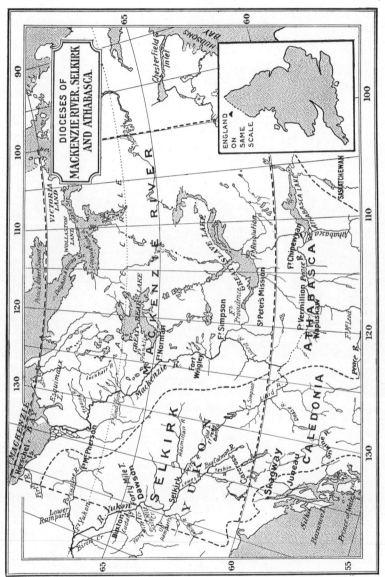

MAP OF THE DIOCESES OF MACKENZIE RIVER, YUKON, AND ATHABASCA

The name of the Diocese of Selkirk was changed to "Yukon" in 1907

semblance of towers and turrets, and present a pleasing aspect. The gorge is about ten miles long, and seems to form a stupendous portal into the Arctic world. Immediately beyond these cliffs is situated Fort Good Hope. Below this point the river sometimes expands into the appearance of a lake, and at other times narrows, when hemmed in by rocks, till the single stream reaches Point Separation, about lat. 68°. From thence the river divides into numerous channels, which widely expand as they approach the sea, till at the coast the delta of the river measures probably about fifty miles across."

The principal lakes in the far North are three— namely, Athabasca, Great Slave and Great Bear Lakes. Athabasca Lake may be about 150 miles long; Great Slave Lake is counted about 300 miles long ; Great Bear Lake is only about 200 miles in length, but as it will measure about the same in width, it probably contains more water than Great Slave Lake.

" In attempting a succinct view of the natural features of the diocese at large, it may be stated generally that its northern border, consisting of the country within about 100 miles of the Arctic coast, is known as the ' Barren Lands,' from its being quite denuded of trees by the blasts of the frozen ocean. To the south of this belt the whole country is generally clothed with pines, except so far as it is intersected by lakes and small marshes. The lakes are of every dimension, and so numerous that in

scanning the country from a height you will sometimes deem the surface to be more water than land.
The soil among the pine-trees is generally covered
with a yellowish moss, which forms the natural
food of the reindeer, and a more succulent moss
generally occupies the marshes, though these and
the small lakes are often fringed with grass, which,
near the trading-posts, is mown for the cattle.

" One noticeable feature of the country is the
burnt wood. From various causes fires are apt to run
through the forests in the drought of summer, and
these reduce the pine-trees to bare and blackened
poles. In a few years after such a fire an under-
growth springs up, and soon young saplings begin
to replace the timber trees that have been destroyed.
The charred poles, however, of the consumed forest
remain standing for many years. Such a burning
of the forests will often change the course of the
migratory reindeer, and perhaps leave a country
hungry that has been rich in provisions. The
spectacle of a blazing forest, when one pine-tree
after another flares up in sparkling splendour, is a
sight of startling magnificence."

Crossing the Rocky Mountains westward, we
come upon the Yukon River. It is a noble stream
of over 2,000 miles in length, flowing into the
Behring Sea about lat. 62° 30′ N. Only a portion
of it flows through British territory, about 639
miles, the remainder being in the United States
territory of Alaska. It flows through the entire
length of the Diocese of Yukon, and has many fine

MILES CAÑON ON THE YUKON RIVER

feeders, the most important of which are the Stewart, the Pelly, with its branch the Macmillan, and the Teslin. Though generally known as the Yukon for its entire length, this river for some distance from its source is called by various names, such as the Lewes, the Sixty Mile, and many others. The principal lakes through which this stream flows are Lake Bennett, twenty-five miles long, Marsh Lake, nineteen miles long, and Lake Laberge, thirty-one miles in length. Besides these there are splendid lakes and rivers over the entire country, filled with many fine fish.

The climate in the Yukon is unequalled anywhere. The winters are clear, cold, and crisp. The thermometer falls very low at times, but so dry and still is the air that the cold is felt far less than in many places of a higher temperature where the air is moisture-laden. The summers are warm and pleasant. The snowfall is not heavy, except on the mountains, while the rainfall in summer is light.

In considering the inhabitants of the far North, we can only touch the hem of the question, on which so much has been written. For those who wish to make an exhaustive study of the natives of this land the admirable article, "The Canadian Denes," by the Rev. A. G. Morice, in the Annual Archæological Report of 1905, will be most helpful. Though Mr. Morice differs from Bishop Bompas in certain points, we will in this short account follow the Bishop's views as set forth in his writings.

THE COUNTRY—ITS INHABITANTS

The natives of the far North may be divided into three classes : the Tenni, Tukudh, and Eskimos.

The Tenni, who live towards the south, are known by different names, such as the Chipewyans, Yellow Knives, Dog Ribs, Big River Indians, Slave Indians, Nahany or Mountain Indians, and others. They are of a sallow complexion, of the Mongolian type. They have coarse features, thick lips, and prominent cheek-bones. They live in conical tents or lodges, with a frame of poles, and covered with dressed deer or moose skin. " In spring they make canoes of birch bark for water travel and chase. In the fall of the year they make birchwood snow-shoes for winter voyaging. Their tents are floored with a litter of pine-branches, and warmed with a pine log fire in the centre. Their dress is of moose or deer skin trimmed more or less with beads or dyed porcupine quills, except so far as they may be able to purchase clothing of European manufacture.

" Many of the Indians have erected wooden log-houses, after the fashion of the whites, which they are quite competent to do, but they seldom inhabit these long. Their fondness for roving, or an increasing scarcity of wild animals round their fixed abode, soon drives them again to their tent. Moreover, if a death occurs in their house the Indians have a superstitious dread of remaining there.

" The whole of the Tenni race seem to be of a sickly habit, and are rather dwindling in numbers.

PRINCIPAL STREET OF MOOSEHIDE, AN INDIAN VILLAGE, THREE MILES BELOW DAWSON

They do not seem to be much addicted to ardent spirits, nor are these now supplied to them; but they have an inveterate propensity to gamble. Though almost wholly free from crimes of violence, and not much inclined to thieve, yet heathen habits of impurity cling, alas! still too closely to them, and they exhibit the usual Indian deficiency in a want of stability and firmness of character. This Indian race seems to have been free from idolatry before the arrival of Europeans among them, and they had some knowledge of a good and evil spirit, and of rewards and punishments after death."

The Tukudh Indians live farther to the north, and extend westward beyond the Rocky Mountains. They, too, are known by various names, such as the River, Lake, Valley, and Mountain Indians. They have sharper features, are " more lively and intelligent, as well as more cordial and affectionate, than the Tenni. Their eyes are inclined to be small and pointed, rather as the Chinese. From this circumstance, probably, they obtained from the French the sobriquet of the Loucheux, or squint-eyed, for they are not really affected with squint.

" The Tukudh make their tents in the shape of a beehive, with bent poles for the frame, and the tent covering is formed of deer-skins with the hair on, and turned on the inside, the skins being softened by scraping. Their camps thus become nearly as warm as a log-house."

Many customs of these northern Indians are very

interesting. " The women's dress mostly consists of a long leather coat trimmed with cloth or beads, and sometimes a cloth hood for the head. The women's faces until recently were often slightly tattooed with dark lines on the chin, formed by drawing a thread loaded with gunpowder or colouring matter under the skin. The men were formerly addicted to painting their faces with vermilion, but this has fallen into disuse among the tribes in contact with Europeans.

"The Indians are fond of rings, earrings, bracelets, and necklaces, and they formerly pierced the cartilage of the nose for the insertion of a shell ornament. Belts are tastefully manufactured by the Indian women of porcupine quill-work. This or bead-work, and the making of shoes, form their chief employment. The old women employ themselves in twisting grass, or roots, or sinew into twine for sewing or fishing-nets. The men and boys are often busied in shaping bows, arrows, snow-shoes, sledges, or other articles.

" The Indians were formerly accustomed, instead of burying their dead, to place them on high scaffolds above the ground; but this habit was probably owing to the ground being for many months in the year frozen too hard to dig it. The raising on scaffolds was also a greater preservative than burying underground, from the ravages of animals of prey. Since mingling with the whites, however, the Indians conform to European habits of burial. . . .

An Old Indian Deserted by his People

THE COUNTRY—ITS INHABITANTS

" None of the Indians of Mackenzie River seem to have been acquainted with the use of plants or herbs for medicines. In their medicine-making they used only the charms of drumming and singing. The Esquimaux, with the drumming and singing, combine an address to an invisible spirit supposed to have power over the disease.

" In sickness the Indians are very pitiful. They soon lose heart, and seem to die more from despondency than disease. Their need is often not so much medicine as good nourishment and nursing ; but this is hard to obtain. Food is often scarce for those in health to seek it, and for a sick Indian it may be hard to find a friend in need. The constant removals are trying to the weak and infirm, and in times of distress those who cannot follow the band are left behind to perish. Indians have been known to devour their own children in cases of absolute starvation ; but such cases are rare, and may, perhaps, be attributed to a temporary mania. Those who are believed to have perpetrated such an act are feared and shunned.

" Chocolate is a favourite beverage with the sick, where it can be obtained, and is looked upon as a medicine. The Indians universally give it the name of ' ox-blood,' because it was mistaken by them for the blood of the musk-ox when first they saw it used by the whites. Rice, which is called ' white barley,' is another luxury coveted by the sick. Flour is known by the Tukudh Indians as ' ashes from the end of heaven.' Tobacco

97

is ' warmth and comfort,' and the pipe the ' comforting stone.'

" All articles in use by the whites are named by the Indians without hesitation, according to their employment. A table is ' what you eat on '; a chair, ' what you sit on '; a pen, ' what you write with.' A watch is called ' the sun's heart.' A minister is with them ' the speaker,' and the church ' the speaking-house.' So a lion is called ' the hairy beast,' and the camel ' the one with the big back.' A bat is called ' the leather-wing,' because such is its appearance. Thus an Indian is never lost for a name. A steam-boat, before it was seen by the Indians, used to be called ' the boat that flies by fire '; but since they have seen it, ' the fire-boat ' seems to be name enough.

" The Esquimaux differ much in appearance and habits from the Indians. In complexion they are as fair and fresh-coloured as ourselves, and do not differ much in feature from northern Europeans, but their eyes are rather smaller, and their faces and hands somewhat chubby. . . .

" In stature the Esquimaux of the mouth of the Mackenzie River are, many of them, large and tall, and of muscular frame ; but the women are mostly below the average height of Europeans. The dress of men and women is nearly alike, but the coats differently shaped. The material is white deer-skin, tastefully decorated with beads and trimmed with fur. The men wear a circular tonsure on the head. They have also the inconvenient custom of

A Heathen Indian Chief, with the wooden Masks worn on different occasions, festive, solemn, or judicial

His cap is made of eagle's down, his robe of beaver and ermine, and his leggings are woven from wild goat's hair.

piercing each cheek with a hole, to admit the insertion of a large bead, often surrounded by a white disc or tablet of ivory nearly 2 inches in diameter. . . .

" The Esquimaux, both men and women, are immoderately fond of tobacco, which they smoke differently from other people. The bowl of their pipe is less than half the size of a thimble, and two or three whiffs are all they use on each occasion. This smoke, however, they swallow, which produces a transient intoxication or even unconsciousness, under the influence of which they occasionally fall from their seat. . . .

" The skill of the Esquimaux workmanship is considerable, especially in carving needle-cases and other small ornaments out of the ivory of the walrus tusks. Their spears, bows and arrows, and other implements, are all neatly contrived. Their canoes are well framed and covered with seal-skin. These have no natural tendency to keep upright, but the reverse ; yet the owner will ride them over the ocean waves as on a prancing steed. When his waterproof coat is secured over the mouth of the canoe, he will turn a somersault, canoe and all, from side to side in the water. They have a singular way of throwing a spear from a hand-rest at the musk-rat, so as not to overbalance the canoe, the management of which probably resembles somewhat that of a bicycle.

"Their provisions consist mostly of the flesh and oil of whales, walrus, and seal. These they hunt, not in their canoes, but embarked ten or a dozen together in a larger boat covered with walrus hide. In their common travels this large boat is managed by the women, who convey the tents, bedding, and utensils therein, while the men paddle about and hunt in their light canoes. The Esquimaux wives thus become superior oarswomen.

"The dwellings of the Esquimaux vary at different seasons of the year. In the fall and early winter they dwell in houses partly excavated and lined with logs covered with poles, and over these with earth or snow. They are thus much warmer than they would be quite above ground, and it is not their habit to use fire in their dwellings. If fire is required for cooking they make one outside. If fuel is at hand they prefer to cook their food; but if fuel is wanting or cooking inconvenient, they eat their meat or fish raw without trouble. In fact, meat or fish frozen can be eaten raw without so much distaste, the freezing having an effect on the tissues somewhat similar to the cooking. The taste of whale blubber is not unlike raw bacon, and it cannot easily be cooked, as it would liquefy too soon. Seal-oil is the favourite luxury of the Esquimaux, and it is indeed sweet, but somewhat mawkish and sickly.

"When the winter is advanced, the Esquimaux leave their excavated dwellings, and build houses or even villages of frozen snow. These are constructed with such ease and speed that, as Milton's imagined palace, they seem to rise like an exhalation from the

A Snow House made on the March

earth. The blocks of frozen snow are cut out of the mass with large knives, and built into solid masonry, which freezes together as the work proceeds, without the aid of mortar. Being arched over, a dome-shaped house is formed, with a piece of clear ice for a window, and a hole, through which you creep on all fours, for a door or entrance. One-half of the interior is raised about 2 feet, and strewn with deerskins as beds and sofas, in which the long nights are passed in sleep, for which an Esquimaux seems to have an insatiable capability and relish.

" In summer the Esquimaux camp in deer-skin tents. They then visit the trading establishment of the Hudson Bay Company at Peel River, about 100 miles from the sea-coast, and there they barter their furs for tobacco, kettles, and axes. They do not purchase European clothing. In the autumn they often hunt for reindeer or fish for herring, which they store for winter use ; and they seem to prefer these when somewhat rotten.

" The character of the Esquimaux is, unhappily, still rather treacherous and murderous. They are great thieves and soon angry. They are, however, capable of attachment and gratitude, and are some of them quite free from ill-will. They are willing to accept instruction in the Christian religion, though they have not yet learned to obey its dictates. Though in some respects disgusting in their domestic habits, yet in their manners to a stranger they are courteous and even ceremonious."

THE COUNTRY—ITS INHABITANTS

Concerning the Indian languages the Rev. John Hawksley says :

" They are radically different. In the Diocese of Mackenzie River the natives of the northern part, in the Peel River district, speak a totally different language to those of the southern, and the same condition exists in the Diocese of Yukon.

" The Bishop had sufficient knowledge of these various languages spoken by the different tribes in his vast field of work to enable him to communicate with them in their own tongue.

" The Indians do not give up the use of their language when they become Christianized ; on the contrary, they cling tenaciously to it. Quite a number speak a broken kind of English, but only when compelled to do so."

Speaking further of them, he says :

" They nearly all wear European dress, and like it. None of the Christian Indians retain their old dress, though they sometimes wear a modification of it when out in the woods hunting, because of its suitability for that purpose.

" Their capacity for civilization is very limited ; none become business men. Some do take up voluntary lay-readers' work, and four of the Tukudh tribe have been ordained deacons.

" The Indians of the North do not seem to be dying off. There are the average number of births, and in some cases large families. The children do not seem healthy, and many die in infancy."

CHAPTER VI

AMONG THE CHILDREN OF THE COLD

(1870)

" Love took up the harp of life, and smote on all the chords
    with might—
Smote the chord of self, that, trembling, passed in music
    out of sight."

TENNYSON.

WE left Mr. Bompas conducting the Indian school at
Fort Simpson, according to Mr. Kirkby's desire. But
the committee at Red River had other plans, and
the Rev. W. D. Reeve, afterwards Bishop of Mackenzie River Diocese, was placed at Fort Simpson,
while Mr. Bompas was sent to the far North. It
suited his roving disposition well to take that long
trip down the Mackenzie River, up the Peel River,
over the Rocky Mountains to the Porcupine
River, and then 600 miles to Fort Yukon. It
was a thrilling moment when he reached the scene
of Mr. McDonald's great labours, in July, 1869.
It was for that place he had started four years
before, when the appeal for help reached England.*

* On August 9, 1869, the United States Government, as
represented by Captain Charles Raymond, took formal posses-
sion of Fort Yukon by hoisting the Stars and Stripes. Mr.
Bompas was present on that important occasion.

AMONG THE CHILDREN OF THE COLD

But though much interested in Mr. McDonald's work, still, a call was ever sounding in his ears which he could not silence. On his way to the Yukon he had met a number of Eskimos at Fort McPherson, who requested him to go with them down to the coast. It was this cry from Macedonia which was continually before him, so, leaving the Yukon, he ascended the Porcupine River, spent the winter at the lonely Rampart House, and in the spring went back over the mountains to visit the Eskimos.

These poor natives, with their strange, uncouth manners, strongly appealed to his noble nature, and he expressed his feeling for such as these in the following beautiful words :

"At the funeral of the great Duke of Wellington it was considered to be a mark of solemn respect that the obsequies should be attended by one soldier from every part of the regiments of the British Army, and it is a part of the Saviour's glory that one jewel be gathered to His crown from every tribe of the lost human race. It is an honour to seek to secure for our Lord one such jewel from even the remotest tribe."

Leaving Fort McPherson on April 18, Mr. Bompas started down the river in company with two Eskimos, a man and a boy, hauling a small sledge with blankets and provisions. On the way he received a message from the chief of the Eskimos to defer his visit, as the "Esquimaux were starving and quarrelling, and one had just been stabbed and killed in a dispute about some tobacco." But this message had no effect upon the missionary ; he was doing his Master's service, and he knew that same Master would take care of His servant, and, undaunted, he pressed bravely forward.

For three days they continued to travel without any difficulty, camping at night on the river-bank, and making a small fire of broken boughs. But the glare of the spring sun was very severe, and Mr. Bompas was stricken with snow-blindness.

This snow-blindness is very common in the North, and has been described by Mr. Bompas in the following words :

" As the sun rises higher and has more power in the months of March and April, to walk long over the snow in the sunlight becomes distressing to the eyes from the dazzling brightness. This is especially the case in traversing a wide lake or in descending a broad river, where there are no near forests of dark pines to relieve the gaze, but an unbroken expanse of snow.

" The effect of this is to produce after a time acute inflammation of the eyes. These in the end may be so entirely closed as to involve a temporary blindness, accompanied by much smarting pain. . . . The inflammation generally lasts for at least three days, after which it gradually subsides. In the meantime it may be ameliorated by dropping one drop of laudanum into the eye, though the sensation of this is like an application of liquid fire. The voyager feels very helpless during the acute stage

of snow-blindness, and, like Elymas the sorcerer or
St. Paul himself, he ' seeks some to lead him by the
hand.' "

For three days, in awful darkness, he was led by
the hand of the native boy, making about twenty-
five miles a day, till the first Eskimo camp was
reached. It was only a snow-house, and to enter it
with closed eyes, stumbling at every step, was a
most disagreeable introduction. And yet such
sufferings were little considered by Mr. Bompas.

" They are delights," he once said. " The first
footprint on earth made by our risen Saviour was
the nail-mark of suffering, and for the spread of the
Gospel I, too, am prepared to suffer."

After one day of rest in the snow-house, Mr.
Bompas recovered his sight, and then, moving
forward, reached another camp. His appearance at
each place, so he tells us, " excited a great deal of
observation and curiosity, as they had never had a
European among them in the same way before."

In this camp he was disturbed " by yelling and
dancing" on the very spot where he was lying.
This was caused by an old woman "making
medicine—that is, conjuring in order to cure a man
who was, or was thought to be, sick." Mr. Bompas,
unable to stand the terrible confusion, tried to stop
them by saying that medicine-making was all a
wicked lie, whereupon the old woman threw herself
upon the missionary, and in no gentle manner
vented upon him her wrath. After this he left the
place and betook himself to another camp, where he

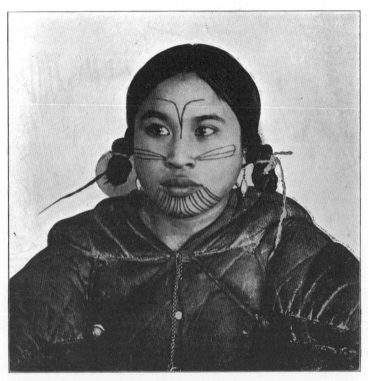

AN ESKIMO BRIDE ON HER WEDDING DAY

From a copyright photograph by permission of Halftones, Limited.

lay down and " enjoyed a good night's rest." Next morning, seeing the man who was the cause of all the trouble, Mr. Bompas found he was suffering from a sore head, for which he gave him a " small piece of soap and a few grains of alum to rub it with." When he saw the man some time later, he was told that his conjuring was very strong.

What a forlorn hope lay before this missionary in trying to uplift and save such wild, uncouth creatures, who were ever around him ! Yet there were many things which appealed to him. He looked deeper than the mere surface, and, studying them very carefully, saw there was much cause for encouragement. He noticed how ingenious the Eskimo was in the forming of implements " out of any old iron which he is able to obtain, such as files, saws, etc., from which he will forge variously shaped knives, gimlets, and other tools, with which he constructs his boats and canoes, as well as arrows, bows, spears, fishing - hooks, nets and tackle, sledges, and all other implements for the chase, as well as furniture for his tent."

Then he watched his skill in building the snow-house, which he could " compare to nothing but the skill of the bee in making its honeycomb. . . . The snowy material is so beautiful that the work proceeds as if by magic." People who were so clever and artistic he well knew must have a love for the beautiful, and were capable of higher things.

He studied their religious instincts, and found

they were very low. They were addicted to lying, stealing, and even stabbing. " They practised heathen dances, songs, and conjuring, and placed much dependence upon spells and charms." And yet, sifting through all this, he found they believed in two spirits : one " an evil, named Atti, which seems to symbolize cold and death, and which they seek to exorcise or appease by their charms and spells ; the other a dim idea of a good spirit connected with the sun, as the source of warmth and life." Their faint idea of heaven was that of a " perpetual spring, and the name they give to ministers who bring them tidings of the world above is ' Children of the Sun.' " He also learned that they possessed a tradition of the creation, and of the descent of mankind from a single pair.

Though he found them at times very treacherous, yet there was a spirit of true hospitality still existing, which he felt could be fanned into a flame, and which would work a great change. His own difficulty was the language, and he maintained that the best hope would be to bring a Christian Eskimo from Labrador, as the Moravian missionaries there and in Greenland had mastered the language in the course of many years' labour.

"A native of Labrador would probably be able to converse fluently with the natives in the course of a few months, and might be able in that time to give them a better knowledge of Christianity than a European missionary could in as many years."

AMONG THE CHILDREN OF THE COLD

Though the language was a great drawback, still Mr. Bompas determined to do the best he could. He collected many Eskimo words, and with his remarkable linguistic ability made fair progress in a short time. He found they expressed great willingness to be taught, and says :

" They have received the little instruction I have been able to give them with great thankfulness. At the same time, their ignorance and carelessness are so great that they seem quite unable at present to apprehend the solemnities of religion. The chief idea they have in seeing my books is to wish that they could be metamorphosed into tobacco, and indeed, at present, smoking seems to be the sole object of their lives."

He accompanied them on their various hunting and fishing journeys, and lost no opportunity of studying them and winning their affection. He stood by their side as they fished for hours through holes in the ice, and, observing their great patience, he himself became strengthened in the greater task of fishing for souls, and expresses the thought in the following words :

" We may admire the patience of an Esquimau fishing for hours over the blow-hole for a seal ; and such should be the perseverance of a watcher for souls. ' Lord, we have toiled all night, and have taken nothing : nevertheless, at Thy word I will let down the net.' "

During the cold weather Mr. Bompas slept with the Eskimos in their small, crowded houses, and the inconvenience he suffered must have been great, as the following words will show :

" The Esquimaux sleep in their tents between their deer-skins, all together in a row extending the whole breadth of the tent, and if there are more than enough for one row, they commence a second at the foot of the bed, with the head turned the other way. For myself, I always took care to commence the second row, keeping to the extremity of the tent, and thus generally rested without inconvenience, except, perhaps, a foot thrust occasionally into my side. At the same time, it must be confessed that the Esquimaux are rather noisy, often talking and singing a great part of the night, especially the boys ; and if any extra visitors arrive, so that the tent is overfull, it is not exactly agreeable."

When the warmer weather arrived, Mr. Bompas began to camp by himself outside, and found it much better. The days became so long that he found it difficult to tell what time of day or night it was, as he "thought it most prudent" not to carry his watch with him. Seldom did the missionary speak of his hardships, but, reading between the lines of the few words he utters, one can see they were of no ordinary nature.

In a letter to Mrs. Loft in England, Mr. Bompas gave a vivid description of these Eskimos :

" It would be easy for you to realize," he wrote, " and even experience the whole thing if so minded. First go and sleep a night in the first gipsy camp you can find along some roadside, and that is precisely like life with the Indians. From thence go to the nearest well-to-do farmer, and spend a night in his pigsty (with the pigs, of course), and this is exactly life with the Esquimaux. As this comprises the whole thing in a nutshell, I think I need give you no further description. The difficulty you would have in crawling or wriggling into the sty through a hole only large enough for a pig was exactly my case with the Esquimaux houses. As to the habits of your companions, the advantage would be probably on the side of the pigs, and the safety of the position decidedly so. As you will not believe in the truth of this little simile, how much less would you believe if I gave you all particulars ? So I prefer silence to exposing myself to your incredulity, but if I had to visit them again I should liken it rather to taking lodgings in the den of a Polar bear. The first time, in God's good providence, he did not show his claws.

" Harness yourself to a wheelbarrow or a garden roller, and then, having blindfolded yourself, you will be able to fancy me arriving, snow-blind and hauling my sledge, at the Esquimaux camp, which is a white beehive about 6 feet across, with the way a little larger than that for the bees. . . . As to one's costume, you cannot manage that, except that a blanket is always a good cloak for us ; but take a large butcher's knife in your hand, and that of itself will make you an Esquimaux without further additions.

" If you will swallow a chimney-ful of smoke,

117

or take a few whiffs of the fumes of charcoal, you will know something of the Esquimaux mode of intoxicating themselves with tobacco, and a tanyard will give you some idea of the sweetness of their camps. Fat raw bacon, you will find, tastes much like whale blubber, and lamp oil, sweetened somewhat, might pass for seal fat. Rats you will doubtless find equally good to eat at home as here, though without the musk flavour ; but you must get some raw fish, a little rotten, to enjoy a good Esquimaux dinner.

"Fold a large black horse's tail on the top of your head, and another on each side of your face, and you will adopt exactly the Arctic lady's headgear. Then thrust a knife through the centre of each cheek, and leave the end of the knife-handle permanently in the hole, and you will experience the agreeable comfort of the Arctic cheek ornament. After this, get a dozen railway trucks, tackled together, and load them with large and small tow-boats, scaffold-poles, a marquee, three or four dead oxen, the contents of a fishmonger's stall and of a small rag-shop, and then harness all your family, and draw the trucks on the rails from Alford to Boston, with a few dogs to help, and thus you will have a very close resemblance to an Esquimaux family travelling in winter with their effects over the frozen ice. As I have formed one of the haulers on such an expedition, I speak from personal experience."

Writing to his brother George, he says : " Do you

know that the Esquimaux took me for a son of
Cain, probably Mahujael, for they said on my visit
that in the first family in the world two brothers
quarrelled, and the one killed the other, and the
murderer had to wander away, and they concluded
that the white men who now came to meet them
were probably sons of the murderer. . . . I should
think it probable that the Esquimaux circled round
the pole from Northern Siberia, which they would
first reach on the dispersion of Noah's sons from
Babel. They may be descendants of Javan, to
whose name their word for tribe, 'kavani,' has
some resemblance. All the races in this part of
the world show evidence of having crossed from
Asia by Behring's Straits, and the Tukudh have a
tradition to that effect. These, as the nearest, must
have been the last to cross, but their language is
allied to that of the Chipewyan race, who must have
preceded them, and who extend the whole breadth
of the continent from Hudson Bay to the Pacific
coast in British Columbia. The Crees must have
preceded these, as they are beyond them to the south,
and retain so many Eastern customs that they have
been mistaken, like most other nations, for the
so-called lost ten tribes of Israel."

Several years later, referring to these Eskimos,
he wrote :

" Both the Rev. Mr. Canham and myself often
showed the Esquimaux the *Illustrated London
News*, when, on meeting with an elephant, they
would recognize it, apparently by its trunk, ex-

claiming ' Kaleh !' as an exclamation of surprise.
The interpreter, an Esquimaux who speaks English
well, told me that they knew the animal, because,
though not now alive in their country, they thought
it was not long since it was so, from finding its
body or skeleton. As elephant bodies are known
to have been found on the Siberian coasts, it is
still less strange that they should be found near
the Mackenzie, for the current sets eastward from
Behring's Straits. The bodies might, however, lie
embedded in the ice for thousands of years without
decomposition, and may have been floated hither
at the time of the flood."

His great friend among the Eskimos was the old
chief, Shipataitook by name, who had at the first
invited him to visit them, and had offered the missionary the use of his camp, and entertained and fed
him with the greatest kindness and cordiality. To
this old chief Mr. Bompas was indebted for his life
not long after, and ever remembered him with the
greatest affection.

When the ice had gone out of the Mackenzie
River, the Eskimos began to move up stream to
trade with the Hudson Bay Company at Fort
McPherson, taking the missionary with them. It
was a voyage of 250 miles, and much ice was
encountered. For days they made slow progress
and laboured hard. Then they became angry with
one another, and also cast threatening glances upon
the white man in their midst. They imagined that
in some way he was the cause of all their trouble,

BIG CHIEF AND HIS WIVES. FROM A PHOTOGRAPH TAKEN AT UNGAVA

and the angry glances were followed by threatening gestures, and Mr. Bompas saw that the situation was most critical. One night, after a day of unusually hard work, when little progress had been made, the natives became so hostile that Mr. Bompas feared they would take his life ere morning. But, notwithstanding the impending danger, the faithful servant committed himself to the Father's keeping, and, wearied out, soon fell asleep.

Old Shipataitook was to be reckoned with. He had taken a fancy to the brave young white man, and could not see him murdered without making an effort to save him. He had heard the threatening words, and when the plotters were about to fall upon their victim, he told them to wait, as he had something to tell them before they proceeded farther. Then he began a strange story, which, falling upon the ears of the naturally superstitious natives, had a great effect. He told them he had a remarkable dream the night before. They had moved up the river, and were almost at Fort McPherson, and as they approached they saw the banks lined with the Hudson Bay Company's men and Indians, all armed ready to shoot them down in the boats if they did not have the white man with them.

When this story was told, all plotting ceased, and in the morning, when Mr. Bompas awoke, he found no longer angry glances cast upon him, but the natives were attentive in their care.

On June 14 the ice left them and the river

became clear, and without more detention they continued on their way, "and arrived safely, by God's help," says Mr. Bompas, "at Peel's River Fort on June 18, about midnight."

Here a most hearty welcome was given him by Mr. Andrew Flett, the officer in charge of the Fur Company's post, and of him Mr. Bompas wrote in the following words :

"His influence over the Esquimaux, as well as the Indians, has been very beneficial, for the whole time of his residence among them—now nearly ten years—and by consistent and honourable conduct, as well as by his attention to the duties of religion, he has done much to assist the work of the missionary. Of his personal kindness to myself I have had much experience during the past twelve months."

In this beautiful heartfelt testimony to the work and kindness of one man we see how the missionary was cheered in his great labour by earnest words of sympathy and an ever-open door of hospitality, where he could rest from his great journeys. To Mrs. Flett also Mr. Bompas was greatly indebted ; for in his study of the Loucheux language she gave him much material aid. Upon the lay members of the Church of Christ devolves a noble work in cheering the hearts and upholding the hands of their leaders in their strenuous battle against the powers of darkness.

Never again was Mr. Bompas able to visit that band of Eskimos along the Mackenzie River, but he ever held them in mind, and often his heart went out to them, and he declared that " there was nothing warmer than the grasp of a Husky's hand."

But his visit had not been in vain. He had lived among them, and shared their humble camps, and, though they could not understand him, nor fully comprehend his message, yet they could understand his love for them, and long years after they spoke of him in the highest terms.

Bishop Stringer, who more than twenty years later travelled a good deal with Takachikima, son of Chief Shipataitook, says :

" Takachikima was a young boy at that time. Several times he asked me about the white man who lived with his father long ago, and he bemoaned the fact that they treated him so shamefully. ' Why would they not listen to him ?' he used to say. ' We were like dogs. We know now what our fathers missed.' "

CHAPTER VII

SOWING BESIDE MANY WATERS

(1870-1873)

" When Thy word goeth forth, it giveth light and understanding to the simple."—Ps. cxix. 130.

NOT long could Mr. Bompas rest at Fort McPherson;
there was great work before him, and, like his Divine
Master, he had to be ever going about doing good,
sowing the seed of the Gospel beside all waters in
that great northern region. Two thousand miles
away was the Peace River Valley, which needed
his attention, and towards this he once again set
his face. The Mackenzie and Slave Rivers had to
be ascended, and this took him ten weeks to accomplish. Then six weeks more passed before he
reached Fort Vermilion on the Peace River, having
travelled since May, 1869, 4,700 miles, all in a
canoe.

Travelling in the North during the summer is by
boats, and of this Mr. Bompas has given a vivid
description.

The boats for long journeys are generally built
by the French half-breeds in the employ of the
Hudson Bay Company, assisted by the Indians.

They are not decked. Some of the Indians can build well-modelled, substantial boats, though they prefer canoes.

" The average distance accomplished in a day's journey, whether in summer or winter, is from twenty-five to thirty miles, with many delays in summer, either by rain or contrary winds, sometimes involving detention in one spot for days together.

" The travel is tedious and monotonous. In summer the day's voyage begins about 3 a.m. and is continued to 7 or 8 p.m., with a halt of about an hour twice a day for breakfast and dinner. The progress in boat voyaging is either by tow-line, hauled by four men on the river-bank, or by eight or ten heavy oars, unless a fair wind permits of hoisting a sail. The canoes are propelled by the Indian paddles. Any impediment to the navigation in the way of rocks, causing an impassable rapid, occasions delay, and the boats have to be hauled over the land till the obstruction is passed. In other places, the cargoes only have to be carried by land.

" An accidental breakage of the boat on the stones obliges the steersman to insert a piece of wood by way of a patch, which causes a detention of some hours. The breakage of a canoe by a stick or stone is more frequent, as the canoes are constructed of tender birch bark. This, if torn, is patched with a piece of fresh bark, sewed with roots, and cemented with gum or pitch.

" As the trading posts are mostly from 200 to

300 miles apart, houses are generally seen on a summer's voyage about once a week. Between these a few Indian tents may be passed, but on most days no human being is encountered ; yet so incessant is travelling that it is hardly possible to land in any spot along the river-bank, without traces appearing of some person having been there previously, who is betrayed by a chopped stick or by his long-extinguished fire.

" What is termed in the North a rapid, or by Americans a ripple, is an interruption to navigation occasioned by a shallow or rocky point in the river, where the water is hurried turbulently among the stones or in eddies, sometimes with small cascades, till it gains a less confined channel.

" The test of skill in the Canadian boatmen is the passing of these rapids, especially in the descent, when the boat (mostly lightened of its cargo) is often urged with headlong speed down the swift waters, the traveller trusting to the coolness and skill of the helmsman and bowsman to avoid the stones. It is needful to urge the boats more rapidly than the hurrying current, in order to have headway enough for steering, and a quick eye and ready hand are quite essential.

" The boat's cargo is generally carried past the obstruction by a land track, technically termed a portage. There are sometimes as many as fifty to one hundred of these interruptions in a single voyage, so rocky are the channels of these northern rivers, and so impeded their navigation.

" Such, however, is not the case with all the rivers. The great Mackenzie has no obstruction for about 1,100 miles from the sea. Then, after one long rapid of about fifteen miles, the navigation is again undisturbed for about 300 miles more."

On the Peace River Mr. Bompas tells us that " large masses of driftwood descend the river from the mountains with the ice in spring, and some of these, lodging along the banks, form drift-piles, not without danger for a passing voyager. His canoe may be wrecked and sunk among the snags, and himself whirled by the eddying current into mid-stream, or sucked under the boiling rapid."

In addition to the difficulty of travelling by water, the flies are a continual pest. " An African traveller, who passed down the Mackenzie, stated his experience to be that the flies of the North were more virulent than the insects of Africa.

" And these are of ' divers sorts.' Early in spring appear the large blue horse-flies, which bite a piece out of the skin. These are succeeded by the mosquitoes, the summer infliction, which are at times so numerous as to cover the clothes and fill the mouth and plate at meal-time.

" In some travellers lately arrived, with a soft skin, the mosquito bites produce a kind of fever, and greatly disfigure the face and neck."

This magnificent river " received its name from Peace Point, one of the angles in its course, where about a century since the Indians were persuaded by the traders to terminate their former wars and feuds, to bury their weapons, and to devote themselves to peace and commerce."

Arriving at Fort Vermilion in October, this messenger of peace remained there during the winter, teaching the natives for miles around. But in the spring of 1871 he again went down Peace River, and, after visiting Fort Chipewyan and Fond du Lac, on Lake Athabasca, once more ascended Peace River as far as Rocky Mountain Portage.

" It is now, I believe," wrote Mr. Bompas, " nearly thirty years since a Protestant minister visited the upper part of Peace River, and I am thankful to have been brought by God's providence thus far. . . . These head waters of the Peace River in the Rocky Mountains, about ten days' travel hence, have been the scene of a great excitement during the last twelve months, in consequence of the discovery of new gold-mines there. About 2,000 miners are said to have been working there during the past summer, and of these some hundreds will probably remain to pass the winter among the snow. Some of them, of course, have not been very successful, but a considerable quantity of fine gold-dust has, I believe, been procured. This discovery will doubtless tend to the opening up of the country. Wagon roads are being made at Government expense from the coast to supply the miners with provisions and necessaries, and already the traffic is considerable. In the end it may turn out that one of the readiest ways of access to this part of the country will be from the Columbian side. The rivers here actually seem to cross through the mountains, and are doubtless intended, in God's providence, to be a channel of communication from east to west."

Mr. Bompas formed hopes of visiting these miners, but was unable to do so. He was much encouraged by what he heard, that "nearly all abstain from work on the Sabbath, notwithstanding the excitement of their occupation, and that the mining operations are restricted by the frost to about four months in the year."

"We hear," he wrote further, "of several parties from the Columbian side of the mountains being sent out to explore a route for the proposed railway from Canada to the Pacific, and in this way I trust the progress of civilization, and Christianity also, in this wild country may be facilitated. God's providence is plainly working in the changes that are going forward, and I trust they will redound to His glory."

In a letter to his sister in England, Mr. Bompas describes another phase of his work in this region, and lets in a little light which is most interesting.

"This spring my chief character has been that of public vaccinator, I should think I must have vaccinated about 500, and as 2,000 Indians are said to have died last summer of smallpox at one post only, in the plains, vaccination is not uncalled for. The smallpox also broke out last fall at Peel's River, only about two months after

I left there. Five died, and many others, including Mr. Flett's family, were attacked. . . . Knowing the danger of the smallpox to the Indians, it has been a pleasure to me to vaccinate them, though rather troublesome sometimes to persuade them to submit to the operation."

In the same letter he describes the death of Mrs. Donald Ross, the wife of one of the Hudson Bay Company's clerks :

" I had not seen her," he goes on to say, " since I was here three years ago, and this spring she fell into consumption. . . . She expressed a wish to see me before her death, and they were bringing her down to me in the boat, when she died, and her body only came to me to be buried. I have this morning buried her little girl, born about three months before the death of her mother. Mrs. Ross was a very quiet, kind woman, and seems to have been fully prepared for her death. She expressed herself quite happy to the last, and during the last night was often asking for the candles to be put out, for she said, ' It is all broad daylight with me now.' Her delight was in hearing the Bible read, especially the fourteenth chapter of St. John. I feel this death rebukes me for having expressed in a letter this spring a fear that our Saviour gathers no lilies from this desert land, for here are two."

Having ministered to the Indians around Rocky Mountain Portage, Mr. Bompas in the fall moved down the river, sowing the Gospel seed as he went. Reaching Fort St. John, he gathered the Indians around him, who gladly received his instruction. It was here that a fearful massacre of several of the Hudson Bay Company's men, by the Tsekanies Indians, took place years before, and on that spot where the awful deed of violence was committed, the noble ambassador delivered his great King's message. Only a few days did he remain here, and as he continued on his way he received letters from the committee at Red River, instructing him " to proceed next spring (D.V.) to the Youcon district, to replace Mr. McDonald, who has obtained leave of absence. This quite accords with my own views," continues Mr. Bompas, " of what is fitting and necessary, and, with God's permission, I shall hope, if life is spared me, once again to visit the far North, being the district to which I was appointed on leaving England."

From Vermilion he crossed overland till he struck the Hay River, and, following its course, reached Great Slave Lake in safety in the spring of 1872.

" Hay River," he tells us, " takes its rise near the Rocky Mountains, not far from the source of the Peace River. In descending the river, I witnessed its stupendous cataract, which is, I think, one of the wonders of the world. It is a perpendicular fall of about 150 feet high by 500 feet wide, and of surpassing beauty. The amber colour of the falling water gives the appearance of golden tresses twined with pearls, while in the spray was a rainbow reaching from the foot of the fall to the rocks far

133

above its brink. We viewed the fall only from the brink, as the access from below is precipitous. I named the cataract the Alexandra Falls. The waterfall which I have described impressed me much more with its beauty than did Niagara, which I saw on entering the country about seven years ago. Both at Niagara and Alexandra Falls I spent a Sunday. The beauty of the scene was much enhanced by the rainbows in the spray."

Though Mr. Bompas longed to take up work at Fort Yukon, still it caused him much anxiety to leave the Athabasca district vacant.

"If I have to leave this district a second time unoccupied," he writes, "the Indians will lose all confidence in the permanence and reliability of our instruction, and will be thrown more completely than ever into the arms of Rome."

Then the earnest traveller was feeling the effects of his long journeys. For seven years he had been ever moving from place to place, and, like the great Apostle of old, he had endured much "in journeyings often, in perils of water, in perils by the heathen, in perils in the wilderness, in weariness and painfulness, in watchings often, in hunger and thirst, in cold and nakedness."

"As I am now once more directed to return to the far North," he writes, "I do not think reliance should be placed on my being able to return hither again ; for even if life should be prolonged, which is doubtful, I cannot reckon on being able to accomplish repeatedly so long a journey from north to

INDIAN DANCERS

Stereo copyright, Underwood and Underwood, London and New York

south. I hope God's good providence will order the arrangements made according to the Divine will."

A question might naturally arise here concerning the advisability of Mr. Bompas's extensive travelling. Could he not have done much better work by remaining in one locality, and cultivating it thoroughly, instead of spreading over so much country ? No doubt there is much truth is this ; but there is another side which needs careful consideration.

The Indians in the North at the time of Mr. Bompas's arrival were mostly in heathen darkness, and the work of evangelization had only been begun in a few places. To the Indians the Gospel message was new, and in their unenlightened minds the progress could only be slow, like leaven in the meal. Having sown a little seed among one band of Indians, it would be necessary for the missionary to pass on to others. This was what Mr. Bompas did. He was, to use a naval metaphor, a " detached cruiser," speeding from place to place, that he might bring in the Gospel dawn to widely scattered bands.

And, further than this, we find the Indians were ever on the move themselves. They were forced to travel in order to obtain a living. They were to be met with in so many places : a little group by some river bank, or a few encamped near a lake. These he would meet as he passed to and fro. The seed would be cast, and then more sown when he met them again.

SOWING BESIDE MANY WATERS

In reality this has ever been the principal method of work among the Indians in the North. The missionary establishes himself in some place where the natives congregate. For months they will be away hunting, but at certain seasons they return to the mission. They may remain only a few weeks, and in that time the work of instruction must be carried on. The lessons learned in this short time are not forgotten. A missionary along the Yukon River unexpectedly came upon a camp of Indians miles away from the mission. It was night, and he found them sitting around the fire repeating what he had taught them, and singing a hymn learned but a few weeks before.

Pushing on his way down the Mackenzie River, Mr. Bompas spent the fall and winter and spring in the regions to the north and west of Fort McPherson. During the fall he " visited a tribe of Esquimaux encamped on the sea-coast about 200 or 300 miles west of the Mackenzie River, and found their camps full of American goods, which they trade from the whaling vessels in the Arctic Sea, inside Behring Straits, somewhere about Point Barrow."

He also visited La Pierre House, west of the Rocky Mountains, and the reception he met with from the Loucheux Indians there filled him with thankfulness, and encouraged him much in his work. Writing of these Indians, he says :

" I have been much cheered in my work among them by finding them all eager for instruction and warm-hearted in their reception of the missionary.

SOWING BESIDE MANY WATERS

Each day I spent in the Loucheux camps was like a Sunday, as the Indians were clustered around me from early morning till late at night, learning prayers, hymns, and Scripture lessons as I was able to teach them. I never met with so earnest desires after God's word, nor have I passed so happy a time since I left England; indeed, I think I may say that, had I ever found at home such a warm attachment of the people to their minister, and so zealous a desire for instruction, I should not have been a missionary. These mountain Loucheux seem the 'fewest of all people,' but I cannot help hoping they are 'a chosen race.' "

On April 28, 1873, he wrote the following letter to his sister in England from Peel River:

" As I have again an opportunity of writing home, I will send a line to tell you that, by God's providence, I have been safely preserved during the past winter with the Indians in their camps, and walking with them over the snow, and that in the coldest part of the country and in the coldest season, yet I have not suffered from cold, hunger, or fatigue. God's good providence has most visibly watched over and protected my ways, in answer, I suppose, to the prayers of friends at home, and I have been much happier the past winter than any time previously since I left England.

" News reaches us this spring that men are to be sent here shortly to cut an ox-road across the Rocky Mountains, with a view to steamboats being placed as soon as possible on the Yukon and Mackenzie

Rivers, and a communication opened between Rupert's Land and the Pacific. It is therefore probable that in a few years civilization will reach this remotest spot on the earth's surface, and the two ends of the earth here meet. I have this winter again visited Fort Yukon, where the American steamer came again last summer, and thence, via San Francisco, you could reach Europe in two months.

" The Indians here have treated me like Christian brothers all winter, and I quite look on them in that light. They are all eager for instruction, and warm-hearted, so that it is a pleasure to be among them. I must have walked more than 1,000 miles among the Indians this winter, but that is nothing—not so much as I used to walk in a winter in the streets of London. On the last day of my winter's marching I composed about 200 lines of poetry on the Loucheux, which I shall enclose to you. I was walking about eighty days, and in camp with the Indians about as many. I am now trying to learn a little more Eskimo from the interpreter here, though I do not know that I shall be able to instruct the Esqui-maux at once, as I hope (D.V.) next winter to visit Fort Yukon again."

Later we find Mr. Bompas far west, beyond the Rocky Mountains, carrying on his work along the Yukon River. Of this he says:

" There is much that I might tell you of my labours. The summer has been spent in visiting all the Indians on the Upper Yukon. I am thankful to relate that the Word of Life was received with

penitence and tears. Some of these Indians have
now been under instruction for nearly ten years, and
I thought it right to baptize the more advanced of
them, to the number of thirty-five adults and eighty
children. Already, I regret to say, has an epidemic
reached these tribes, and of the newly baptized
infants, one at least, and perhaps more, has ere this
been summoned to glory as the first-fruit of this flock
of lambs freshly gathered into the Saviour's fold.
Directly my time of instruction with them (the
fishing for men) was over began the literal fishing
for salmon, the Indians' harvest here, and they let
down their nets for what is likely, I think, to be a
plentiful draught, reminding us of New Testament
scenes."

Travelling up the river, he was much pleased
with the beauty he observed on every hand.

" It is a splendid river with high wooded hills on
each bank, occasionally broken into bold and cragged
rocks. The margin of the river is rather flowery
with lupins, vetches, bluebells, and other wild-
flowers ; and I was surprised to see a few ferns in
the clefts of the rocks, so close to the Arctic circle.
Gold has not yet been found in the Yukon, but I
brought down with me good specimens of iron ore,
of which there seems to be a great quantity close
to the river's bank. This may some day be
utilized."

These words were penned in the summer of
1873, and what changes this missionary was to see
before the closing of the century ! Instead of the

iron which he thought "some day would be utilized," the gleaming gold would be luring thousands into the country.

Mr. Bompas ascended the Yukon for 300 miles, and everywhere he was gladly received by the Indians, who gathered around him to hear the message he had to deliver. But a change was soon to take place in the life of this noble man, and while quietly and humbly pursuing his work, a letter reached him, summoning him back to England to be consecrated Bishop of the huge diocese. To the hardships and dangers of travel there was to be henceforth added "the care of all the Churches."

CHAPTER VIII

HOME AND HONOURS

(1873-1874)

" Called to the work and ministry of a Bishop."
Prayer Book.

WHILE Mr. Bompas was performing his wonderful journeys in the far North, and enduring so many hardships for the Master's sake, men no less earnest were following his movements and planning and praying for the success of the Church in North-West Canada.

Owing to the statesmanlike plans of Bishop Machray, of Rupert's Land, it was decided to divide the vast district, comprising more than one-half of all Canada, into separate dioceses. The Bishop realized that more effective supervision was needed in the large field, as the distances were too great for one man to think of undertaking. The distance from the Red River to the farthest posts on the Mackenzie River was as great as " from London to Mecca," and it would have taken him two years to visit the northern posts with profit. Crossing to England, the Bishop set forth the proposal for the division of his diocese into four parts, which was accepted by all concerned.

"The reduced Diocese of Rupert's Land would comprise the new province of Manitoba and some adjacent districts; the coasts and environs of Hudson's Bay would form the Diocese of Moosonee; the vast plains of the Saskatchewan, stretching westward to the Rocky Mountains, the Diocese of Saskatchewan; and the whole of the enormous territories watered by the Athabasca and Mackenzie Rivers, and such part of the Yukon basin as was within British territory, the Diocese of Athabasca."

For Moosonee, the veteran missionary, John Horden, had been consecrated Bishop in 1872; and in the following year John McLean, Archdeacon of Manitoba, and William Carpenter Bompas were summoned home to be consecrated Bishops of the new Dioceses of Saskatchewan and Athabasca.

Mr. Bompas shrank much from the thought of becoming a Bishop, and in July, 1873, he set his face homewards with the express purpose of turning the Church Missionary Society from the idea. It was a long journey that lay ahead of him, fraught with many dangers and difficulties. The clerk at Fort Yukon in charge of the American Fur Company's post kindly supplied him with provisions and with two Indian lads who had volunteered for the trip. Soon all was ready, and then the start was made up the Porcupine River, and after two weeks of hard and persevering labour he reached the Rocky Mountains. Here the Indians left him to return to Fort Yukon, and alone and on foot the missionary began his journey across the mountains. Three days was he in accomplishing the task, and in a furious snow-storm, "which rendered the mountains almost as white as in winter," reached Fort McPherson, Peel River, on August 6.

" The force of the Arctic storm in the mountains," says Mr. Bompas, " is greater and less endurable than elsewhere—not because the winter temperature is more severe on the mountain than below, for it is milder on a height, but because the wind is more violent, and the snow is whirled with blinding fury and freezing bitterness in the face of the traveller.

" Happily, in the mountains there is generally some angle or jutting crag where shelter can be had from the blast till the storm is past, and if fuel is found at the same point wherewith to kindle a fire, the voyager is comfortable.

" The effect of the sharp frozen snowdrift, blown from the mountain-top in the traveller's face, is first to make his eyes water, and then effectually to seal these up, through the freezing of the exuding moisture. Frost-bites on the cheeks soon follow, and, if travel is continued, these will be running with blood. It is in such a case that the expression of the Almighty is recognized, ' Who can stand before His cold ?' (Ps. cxlvii. 17).

" When a storm is blowing on the mountains, the appearance of these from the distance is as if they were fringed with hair, the snowdrift blown in heavy clouds from the ridge having such an aspect. . . .

"Though, while earth remains, winter storms will never cease, yet we may well believe that, in heaven above, when there shall be no more night and no more sea, the surging tempest will sink for ever into an unruffled calm; and the storms of our earthly lives are intended to prepare us to enjoy more fully that haven of repose."

Starting again by canoe, with two other Indian lads, Fort Simpson, a distance of 800 miles, was made on September 2, "after three weeks of fatiguing towing." Pushing on his way, after a difficult journey, contending with the cold and swift stream, he reached Portage la Loche on October 8, having travelled 2,600 miles since July, "and all, except about 300 to 400 miles, against a strong current."

Owing to the cold weather he was forced to remain at the Portage for ten days, and when the swamps were sufficiently frozen he "started on foot through the woods to Buffalo Lake in company with two servants of the Hudson Bay Company." Reaching the lake, he travelled with some difficulty on the fresh ice around the margin, and at the farther end found a camp of Indians, who guided him to Isle à la Crosse. Here a stay of ten days was made, and then he left with dogs and sledge for Green Lake, with three employés of the Hudson Bay Company. The weather becoming milder, they were forced "to cross one of the intervening rivers on a raft."

146

From Green Lake they entered " on the plain country of the Saskatchewan," and after a walk of five days reached Fort Carlton. While here Mr. Bompas visited the Prince Albert Settlement on the banks of the North Saskatchewan, and says : " This settlement is the first that has been formed by the immigrants in that neighbourhood, and it bears every sign of increasing prosperity and success."

From Carlton House, Touchwood Hills was reached with a horse and sledge. Here, through the kindness of the postmaster, he was furnished with a carriole and dogs, and, after a journey of 400 or 500 miles, reached the Red River Settlement.

" I enjoyed the kind hospitality of the Bishop of Rupert's Land and Archdeacon Cowley," wrote Mr. Bompas, " and was much interested in seeing the progress of the mission work in the colony. I reached, by God's good providence, the first houses of the settlement on the last evening of the old year, and after nearly six months' travel in the wilds, I awoke on New Year's morning to a new life of civilization and society."

It is said that when Mr. Bompas reached the episcopal residence and inquired for Bishop Machray, the servant mistook him for a tramp (in his rough travelling clothes), and told him his master was very busy and could not be disturbed. So insistent was the stranger that the servant went to the Bishop's study and told him a tramp was at the door determined to see him.

" He is hungry, no doubt," replied the Bishop ;

147

"take him into the kitchen and give him something to eat."

Accordingly, Mr. Bompas was ushered in, and was soon calmly enjoying a plateful of soup, at the same time urging that he might see the master of the house. Hearing the talking, and wondering who the insistent stranger could be, the Bishop appeared in the doorway, and great was his astonishment to see before him the travel-stained missionary.

"Bompas!" he cried, as he rushed forward, "is it you ?"

We can well realize how Mr. Bompas must have enjoyed this little scene, and the surprise of the good and noble Bishop of Rupert's Land.

We will let Mr. Bompas describe the rest of the journey :

"From Manitoba the dog-train was exchanged for the stage-coach for Moorhead, the terminus of the American railway towards the North-West. In this the cold was piercing and freezing, even though the travellers were wrapped in buffalo-skins. The poor horses were utterly exhausted in drawing the vehicle about fifteen miles through the snow, and though changed thus often, yet at last the journey had to be suspended during a storm, and in the end the horses, though changed every stage, occupied a week in performing the same distance as that travelled by the dogs in four days, more easily and pleasantly—that is, 160 miles.

"The journey was next continued by railway, but from the fires not being lighted in the cars the cold was intense, and the train was shortly brought to a standstill in a snow-drift. Though two locomotives were tugging at it, no progress could be made till the guards with shovels disengaged the carriage-wheels from the snow which entangled them.

"In Canada the journey by stage-coach was resumed. This was shortly after overturned into a ditch by the wayside while scaling a snow-drift. The outside passengers were deposited in an adjoining field, where, to be sure, the snow provided them with a sufficiently soft bed to fall on. The inside passengers had a more uncomfortable shaking.

"The journey was next proceeded with by train to Montreal, before approaching which the cars left the rails, causing some apprehension and delay, which might have been increased had not the guard been provided with a powerful winch for the purpose of replacing the carriages on the track.

"In passing through Canada, I was much pleased with the cities of Toronto, Ottawa, and Montreal. The first I should consider the pleasantest place of residence, but the Parliament buildings and Government offices at Ottawa are very handsome, and Montreal shows the greatest activity in business. I had the honour of waiting upon the Governor-General of Canada, the Metropolitan of Canada, the Bishop and the Dean of Toronto, the Deputy Minister of the Interior, and others, all of whom received me most affably.

HOME AND HONOURS

" From Montreal, following the Grand Trunk
Railway to Portland, I embarked in the steamship
Scandinavian, of the Allan line. At starting, the
masts, yards, and deck of the steamer presented
a woeful appearance, from being thickly coated and
hung with ice, yet 200 miles were made the first
day. By the constantly increasing head-wind, however, the daily speed was decreased down to 100
miles per day, at which rate the Captain thought it
prudent to shut off half the steam, and diminish the
speed to a minimum, for fear that something should
give way in the plunging vessel. After thirteen
days, under the careful seamanship of Captain
Smith, Liverpool was reached on February 13, in
the safe keeping of a protecting Providence."

This account is given to show some of the difficulties the traveller experienced in the early days
in his trips to and from England. Mr. Bompas,
after this journey, decided in favour of the dog-
team.

" On the whole," he said, " the dogs may be
counted to hold their own in competing with horse-
flesh or steam, whether on land or water."

At last the soldier was home from the front, the
hero among his friends, and after the years of
hardships he might have enjoyed a well-earned
rest. But his thoughts were far away across the
ocean in his vast field of labour, and the voice of
the children of the wild was ever urging him to
make haste. The restraints, conventionalities, and
luxuries of civilized life worried him ; the narrow-

ness of the streets was unbearable, and he longed
for the smell of the camp-fire, the free, fresh air of
the North, the great untamed streams, the snow-
capped mountains, and his dusky flock.

During his stay in England Mr. Bompas had
many commissions to fulfil, which occupied much
of his time. There were purchases to make for
people in North-West Canada, including six gold
watches for as many female residents, and a pair
of corsets for another. Obtaining the latter caused
much worry to the missionary. But he was never
known to back down, and finally the purchase was
made. Is it any wonder that he preferred the life
among the Indians, who worried so little concerning
the wherewithal they should be clothed ?

Mr. Bompas was unsuccessful in dissuading the
Church Missionary Society from carrying out
their plan, and on May 3 he and John McLean were
elevated to the Episcopate. The consecration took
place in the parish church of St. Mary's, Lambeth,
Dr. Tait, Archbishop of Canterbury, being assisted
by Bishop Jackson of London, Bishop Hughes of
St. Asaph, and Bishop Anderson, late of Rupert's
Land. The sermon was preached by the last-
named prelate, who thus referred to the two new
Dioceses of Saskatchewan and Athabasca :

" To-day the noble plan will be consummated by
the consecration of two more Bishops. One will
preside over the Church in the western portion of
the land, labouring among the Indians of the plains,
and along the valley of that river whose source is

in the Rocky Mountains, the River Saskatchewan.
The other will have the northern diocese as
his own, along yet mightier lakes, and with rivers
which roll down an immense volume and discharge
themselves into the Arctic Ocean."

After some words addressed to Bishop McLean,
the following charge was given to Bishop Bompas :

" In leaving for the more distant sphere of
Athabasca, brother, it is to no untried work that
you proceed. It is matter of very deep interest to
notice the links in the chain of God's providence
which has guided you to this hour. Nine years
ago to-morrow it was my privilege to preach the
anniversary sermon of that noble Society which
mainly sends you forth. I had then heard that he
who was bearing the standard of the Cross in the
most advanced position of Fort Yukon was sinking
in rapid decline. I read a touching extract from a
letter which I had just received from his nearest
fellow-labourer, in which were these words :

" ' Oh, plead for us, my lord—plead with God for
men and with men for God, that they may come
to gather in the harvest here ! The time is short,
the enemy is active, the Master will soon be here,
and then blessed will those servants be who are
found working and watching.'

" On this I grounded my appeal, and said :
' Shall the minister fall in the forefront of the
battle, in the remotest outpost, and shall no one
come forward to take up the standard of the Lord
as it drops from his hands, and occupy the ground ?'

HOME AND HONOURS

These were the words which commended themselves to your heart. You offered yourself to the
Society, and within three weeks of your offer you
were on your way to the far North-West. He
who was thought to be sick unto death was raised
up, restored, to find you by his side, ready to aid
and sustain him in his work.

" You have been there for more than eight years,
in labours abundant, and your love has not lessened
nor your zeal slackened. You have brought home,
as the fruit of your labour, portions of Scripture,
prayers, and hymns, in seven different dialects or
tongues. You are ready to take the precious
treasure out with you—the translations printed and
prepared by the Society for Promoting Christian
Knowledge. You have also one complete Gospel,
that of St. Mark, which the British and Foreign
Bible Society has enabled you to carry through
the press.

"But you left good treasure behind, in souls
warmed with the love of Christ and softened by
the spirit of Grace. You have the hearts of the
Indians and the Esquimaux."

But Bishop Bompas was not to return alone to
his great work, for a few days after his consecration, May 7, he was united in marriage to Miss
Charlotte Selina Cox, by Bishop Anderson, assisted
by the Rev. John Robbins, Vicar of St. Peter's,
Notting Hill, and the Rev. Henry Gordon, Rector
of Harting.

Mrs. Bompas was a woman of much refinement

and devotion to the mission cause. Her father,
Joseph Cox Cox, M.D., of Montague Square,
London, was ordered to Naples for his health.
During this trip, in which he was accompanied by
his family, his daughter, afterwards Mrs. Bompas,
acquired that love for the Italian language which
ever after continued to be a great source of
pleasure to her. No matter where she went in the
northern wilds of Canada she carried her Dante
with her, which she studied, with much delight, in
the original.

During her stay at Naples she attended her first
ball given by the British Ambassador, and met the
King of Naples (the notorious King "Bomba"),
and often afterwards recalled his remark in Italian,
"What have you done to amuse yourself at the
carnival ?"

When quite young, Mrs. Bompas had little
interest in missions, and says : " My brother, who
was Vicar of Bishop's Tawton, Devonshire, used to
hold missionary meetings at the Vicarage, and I
remember thinking them the dullest affairs, and
the clergymen who addressed us, and whom my
brother, perhaps, would introduce as the distinguished missionary from Japan or Honolulu, I
looked upon as the most dismal old slow coaches
it was anyone's unhappy fate to attend to."

Her interest at length became aroused, and later,
when the martyrdom of Bishop Patteson startled
the Christian world, she became much excited, and
reached, as she tells us, " the enthusiastic stage

when we resolve to become missionaries ourselves, and are all impatient to be off anywhere—to China, Japan, or to the Indians of the Mackenzie River."

Shortly after this she cast in her lot with the Bishop of Athabasca, and became " consecrated to mission work."

CHAPTER IX

THE LONG OUTWARD VOYAGE

(1874)

" All we have we offer,
All we hope to be:
Body, soul, and spirit,
All we yield to Thee."
THRING.

THESE words were never better illustrated than in
the lives of the Bishop and Mrs. Bompas, who on
May 12, 1874, set their faces towards their great
field of labour. Friends and loved ones came to
bid them farewell, among whom was Bishop
Anderson, late of Rupert's Land, who presented the
Bishop with a beautiful paten for his cathedral in
the new Diocese of Athabasca. The good steamship *China*, of the Cunard Line, received them, and
soon she was cutting her way through the water
bound for New York. Consecrated, married, and
sailed all in one week! Such was the record of the
Bishop, who declared it was the hardest week he
ever experienced. Never again was he to look upon
the shores of his native land, or visit the scenes of
childhood ; the northern wilds of Canada needed
him, and there he remained till the last.

156

THE LONG OUTWARD VOYAGE

Accompanying the Bishop and Mrs. Bompas were several missionaries, forming in all a most interesting company : the Rev. Robert Phair (afterwards Archdeacon) and Mrs. Phair, Mr. and Mrs. Shaw, Mr. and Mrs. Reader, Miss Moore, Mr. Hines, and Miss Bompas, eldest sister of the Bishop, who was returning to Lennoxville, in the province of Quebec.

The Bishop was kept busy during the voyage, not only in looking after the welfare of his party, but also in cheering up the steerage passengers, thus making the tedious trip more bearable by his words of comfort.

" A strange motley set were these poor emigrants," says Mrs. Bompas, " about 150 in number, some whole families—father, mother, and children—dragging their thinly filled mattresses along with them, and all carrying a few tin implements for cooking. A number of young girls there were, all neatly dressed, with jet-black hair, and a pretty scarlet ' snood' around their heads."

On Sunday a hearty service was held in the saloon, at which most of the passengers and some of the seamen were present. The Bishop gave an address, and Mrs. Bompas led in the singing of the two hymns, " Thou art gone up on high," and " Lord, as to Thy dear Cross we flee," in which all joined most earnestly.

Off Newfoundland they encountered icebergs and much rough weather, but reached New York safely on Whit-Sunday, and attended the morning service at St. Mark's Church, where, for the first time, the Bishop and Mrs. Bompas knelt together and received the Holy Communion. In the evening the Bishop preached at the request of the Vicar. Here a shadow was cast over the party by the death of the Phairs' little child, who caught cold on the steamer.

"I have been in to see it," wrote Mrs. Bompas, "lying like a little wax doll, so blessed to see it at rest after its sufferings."

From New York they took the train for Niagara, and, having visited the famous waterfall, travelled on to Chicago and thence to St. Paul's. After a tedious trip they arrived at the Red River, and took the heavy, flat-bottomed boat bound for Winnipeg, as the village around Fort Garry was already called. Slow progress was made up the river, and on one occasion the boat stopped to take a raft in tow, making the journey very tiresome. But the time was whiled away in the study of the Indian languages and in reading.

At length Winnipeg was reached one Sunday morning, and the great-hearted leader, Bishop Machray, gave them a most cordial welcome. Bishop Bompas preached that evening in St. John's Cathedral, and public thanks were offered to God for their "merciful guidance hitherto."

During the week Messrs. Shaw and Reader underwent their examinations for Deacons' Orders, and the next Sunday were ordained in the cathedral. Mrs. Bompas describes this service.

"We started early for St. John's Church, the

cathedral of Manitoba. A pretty walk across the prairie took us into a neat little square-towered church standing near the river. There was a good congregation, fairly good choir (the boys of St. John's College, which is close to the Bishop's). Service nice and quiet. William preached. Bishop ordained candidates. After service the Bishop invited us into his house to luncheon, so we all went, and there were a number of other guests. After a short time he came and took me and sat me in the seat of honour."

That evening Bishop Bompas preached in the cathedral, and after service Bishop Machray walked part of the way home with him and Mrs. Bompas. Not until thirty years later did this missionary stand in that building again, and then in touching words referred to that Sunday and his departed friend.

Ahead of them lay the long journey of two months by open boat to Fort Simpson. They had missed the boats of the Hudson Bay Company, and after some difficulty another was obtained, in the hope of overtaking the former. It was a " brilliant cloudless " June morning when they crossed the prairie towards St. John's Cathedral, and sighted the " river looking still and silvery in the morning light," and found the boat, their home for weeks to come, " moored just below St. John's College." Farewells were said, the boat pushed off, and they moved on their way, leaving the Bishop of Rupert's Land waving his hand from the bank of the stream.

THE LONG OUTWARD VOYAGE

It was a tedious journey, as day after day they glided forward. Not only was the heat intense, but the swarms of mosquitoes proved a great annoyance.

"I had come prepared for intense cold," wrote Mrs. Bompas, "and we were destined to endure tropical heat. All up the Saskatchewan, Stanley, and English Rivers the banks slope down like a funnel, and the July and August sun scorches with vertical rays the heads of the travellers. We were seated in open boats, each with a crew of ten or twelve men, who spread our sails when the wind was fair, and took them in when the wind failed us. Eighty-six was on some of those days our average temperature, and I had come provided with the thickest of serge dresses, as none of my friends had realized the possibility of anything but frost and cold in these northern regions. Besides this, we had to encounter swarms of mosquitoes, crowding thick around us, penetrating our boots and stockings, and invading our robabou soup and pemmican, etc. I remember the bliss it was in those days in camping-time to escape from the rest of the party, and, getting rid of boots and stockings, to sit with my feet and legs in the cool water of the river, to soothe the intolerable irritation of the mosquito bites."

But in the midst of all this there were times of refreshing, and at various places hearty were the greetings that awaited them. One morning they reached St. Andrews, on Red River, and there before them appeared a pretty stone church, with wide square tower and a comfortable-looking parsonage-house, with a nice veranda, and a few scattered cottages around. It was a pleasant home scene, and there they found the Vicar, the Rev. John Grisdale (afterwards Bishop of Qu'Appelle), and about sixty others, who had been waiting all the morning to receive them. After luncheon had been served a little service was held on the veranda, and, as they left, the bell of the church rang out a peal of farewell, and all on shore gave a hearty cheer.

Welcome also awaited them at St. Peter's Mission, where Archdeacon and Mrs. Cowley gladly received them, and at The Pas, where the native clergyman, Mr. Budd, was stationed. At this latter place service was held in the yard for Indians, and the Bishop gave an exposition of the Creed in the Cree language.

All along the way Indians were encountered camped on the bank, and at times a halt was made while the Bishop spoke a few words to them. One night they stopped near a number of natives, and service was held. Among the party was a poor woman totally blind. The Bishop knelt by her side and told her of the blind man in the Gospel story, and repeated to her several passages of Scripture, to which the woman listened with much eagerness, and seemed greatly pleased.

The many long, hard portages formed a great impediment to their progress, and through the scorching heat, fighting myriads of mosquitoes, the party had to carry the provisions overland and drag the boat up the rapids. The Bishop willingly took his share of the labour, and though of great strength, overtaxed himself in lifting a heavy box and sprained his back, or, rather, re-sprained it, as he had been injured some weeks before in hauling at the boat. He suffered much agony from the sprain, which troubled him somewhat during the rest of his life.

An incident happened on this trip which serves to show the Bishop's forgetfulness of self when others were to be considered. A young Indian lost his hat overboard, and, being unable to obtain it, suffered much from the heat as he toiled at the oar. The Bishop, seeing his discomfort, at once placed his own hat upon the Indian's head, and insisted that he should wear it. The sight of the native with the flat, broad-brimmed episcopal headgear caused great amusement to the entire company.

At Fort Providence they found the Rev. W. D. Reeve (afterwards Bishop) and Mrs. Reeve, and took them on board. "It was pleasant," wrote Mrs. Bompas, "to see the greeting between the Bishop and his old colleague."

On September 24 they came in sight of Fort Simpson, and much excitement took place. The red flag of welcome was soon hoisted, and Mr. Hardisty, the chief officer, and the whole settlement came to the shore to meet them. So hearty was the reception that they did not perceive the

TROUT-SPEARERS BRINGING SUPPLIES FROM A MISSION STATION
FROM A PHOTOGRAPH TAKEN DURING A HEAVY FALL OF SNOW

shadow, the grim shadow of starvation, that was hanging over the fort and land. There was only one week's provisions in the Company's store, and game was very scarce. At this point the new party arrived, bringing six extra mouths to be fed, besides the boat's crew, and yet the Company's officers received them with the utmost courtesy and good temper, and did their best to look and speak cheerfully. Most of the men around the fort had to be sent away, and there was difficulty in collecting dried scraps of meat for the wives and children. At length there came a time when there was not another meal left. The poor dogs hung around the houses, "day by day growing thinner and thinner, their poor bones almost through their skins, their sad wistful look when anyone appeared. Even a dry biscuit could not be thrown to them." But just when matters reached the worst two Indians arrived, bringing fresh meat, and the great tension slackened.

"From that moment," says Mrs. Bompas, "the supplies have never failed. As surely as the provisions got low, so surely, too, would two or three sledges appear unexpectedly, bringing fresh supplies."

Little wonder that the Bishop acquired that great trust in Providence that caused him to say that "a restful trust in Heaven's bounty will lead to a cheerful content even in the far North, and make a man exult in the consciousness that his God is still present with him there."

CHAPTER X

BISHOP OF ATHABASCA

(1874-1876)

" He bowed himself
With all obedience to the King, and wrought
All kind of service with a noble ease,
That graced the lowliest act in doing of it."

TENNYSON.

FORT SIMPSON was chosen by the Bishop as his abode at first. It is situated at the confluence of the Mackenzie and Liard Rivers, and formed the most central and convenient point for managing the vast diocese. This position had been occupied years before by the Hudson Bay Company, and here, in 1859, Mr. Kirkby built the church and mission-house. *

All around stretched the huge diocese of 1,000,000 square miles—and such a diocese! It has been well described by the Bishop himself in the words which follow :

* In 1874 the mission-house, which had been some distance away, was removed to the fort, and another building, given by Mr. Hardisty, of the Hudson Bay Company, was placed alongside for a schoolhouse. In 1881 these were removed from the fort and re-erected near the church.

166

"No shepherd there his flock to fold,
No harvest waves its tresses gold;
No city with its thronging crowd,
No market with its clamour loud;
No magistrates dispense the laws,
No advocate to plead the cause;
No sounding bugle calls to arms,
No bandits rouse to dread alarms;
No courser scours the grassy plain,
No lion shakes his tawny mane;
No carriages for weary feet,
No wagons jostle in the street;
No well-tilled farms, no fencèd field,
No orchard with its welcome yield,
No luscious fruit to engage the taste,
No dainties to prolong the feast;
No steaming car its weighty load
Drags with swift wheel o'er iron road;
No distant messages of fire
Flash, lightning-like, through endless wire;
No church with tower or tapering spire,
No organ note, no chanting choir."

Writing of the extent of his diocese, he says:

"To represent the length and tediousness of travel in this diocese, it may be compared to a voyage in a row-boat from the Gulf of St. Lawrence to Fort William, on Lake Superior, or a European may compare it to a voyage in a canal barge from England to Turkey. Both the length and breadth of this diocese equal the distance from London to Constantinople.

"If all the populations between London and Constantinople were to disappear, except a few bands of Indians or gipsies, and all the cities and towns were obliterated, except a few log huts on the sites of the capital cities—such is the solitary desolation of this land. Again, if all the diversity of landscape and variety of harvest-field and meadow were exchanged for an unbroken line of willow and pine trees—such is this country."

In this region the Bishop and his devoted wife began their great work together. At once an Indian school was started, carried on at first principally by the Bishop himself. Mrs. Bompas says:

"My ears often grew weary of the perpetual 'ba, be, bo, bu; cha, che, cho, chu.' These, with a few hymns translated into their own language, and a little counting, were the first studies mastered by our Simpson scholars."

November 22 was a day long to be remembered at the fort, when the first confirmation took place in the little church, and four candidates received the Apostolic rite. The service was very simple, quiet, and impressive, and the church well filled. The Bishop gave an earnest address to the candidates from Eccles. xii. 1, "Remember now thy Creator in the days of thy youth." Outside, the world was cold and dismal, but within that little sanctuary in the far North there was much warmth and peace.

The following Sunday another service of great interest was held, when the Rev. W. D. Reeve was admitted to the priesthood. Such a service was never before performed in the diocese, and all who attended were much impressed.

Only a short time could the Bishop spend at Fort Simpson; other places needed his attention, and he had to be much on the move, visiting trading-posts and Indian encampments on the various rivers and lakes. About 300 miles away was Fort Rae, on Great Slave Lake, and the heart of the missionary yearned for the natives and whites gathered there.

On December 8, with Allen Hardisty, a young native who was being trained as a catechist, and several men from Fort Rae, the Bishop set out on his journey.

Concerning the preparation for this trip Mrs. Bompas gives us the following very interesting description :

" It was a clear, beautiful morning, November 27, 1874. The great frozen river glittered in the sunshine—not a smooth glassy surface, as you might fancy, but all covered with huge boulders of ice, and these, again, all thickly strewn with snow. Some of these boulders assume grotesque forms—you might imagine them great monsters which had come up from the river depths—while others look like birds, and some, again, have the appearance of a beautiful foaming wave, caught by the ice just in the act of curling.

" Here are our ' trippers,' as they are called, and all ready to start, and my Bishop in his fur cap and warm wraps, which I have made for him. His large mittens, formed of deer-skin and fur, are suspended from the neck, as is the custom here. William takes with him Allen Hardisty, an Indian who is being trained as a catechist. He packed the sledges last evening with their bags of clothing and provisions for the way—blankets, cooking implements, etc. There are the three sledges, and the dogs ready harnessed. I am rather proud of my 'tapis,' which, amid sundry difficulties, I contrived to get finished, with some help, in time. Now comes the word, ' Off ; all ready !' our farewells are said, the drivers smack their whips, the dogs cry out and start in full scamper, the trippers running by the side of the sledges at such a pace that all are soon out of sight."

The trip was a hard one, and, failing to obtain any deer on the way, they struggled on for days without provisions, gaining the fort in an almost exhausted condition. But what did such sufferings matter to the Bishop ? The Indians were reached, and, sitting by their camp-fires telling them of the great message he had come to bring, he forgot the days of want and the weariness of the way.*

Meanwhile, at the fort, Mrs. Bompas was anxiously awaiting the Bishop's return. Mr. Reeve took charge of the settlement, while Mr. Hodgson conducted the Indian school. It was a weary time—a time of darkness, for grease had given out, and there were few candles, as the deer were very thin. Never before had there been such a scarcity. Every particle was saved with jealous care, and doled out with the greatest caution.

* In 1876 the Rev. W. D. Reeve and family removed to Fort Rae, to establish a mission there. (From notes found among Bishop Bompas's papers.)

But, notwithstanding the darkness, a cheerful time was spent at Christmas, when Mrs. Bompas brought in twelve old Indian wives and gave them a Christmas dinner. They tried their best to use the knives and forks, but at last gave up in despair, and had to " take to Nature's implements."

Then a Christmas-tree—a grand affair—was given for the Indian and the white children of the officers of the fort. The presents were made by hand, and Mrs. Bompas wrote :

" Years ago, in my childhood, when my busy fingers accomplished things of this kind, my dear mother used to tell me I should one day be the head of a toyshop. How little did she then dream in what way her words would be fulfilled! I actually made a lamb—' Mackenzie River breed '—all horned and woolly, with sparkling black eyes."

Many were the wonderful things made for that tree, and great was the delight of those little dark-skinned Indians as they looked upon their first Christmas-tree.

After the excitement had subsided dreary days of waiting followed, when one Sunday morning bells were heard, and a dog-team swung into the fort, and there, to the astonishment of all, appeared the Bishop, " with white snowy beard fringed with icicles, in a deer-skin coat and beaver hat and mittens—a present from Fort Rae." What rejoicing there was ! and more rejoicing still when he poured into Mrs. Bompas's lap the long-looked-for home letters, which had been eight months reaching her.

" Dear, precious letters," says the faithful recorder of these early days, " for which I had so longed and prayed and wept for eight months past. The long silence was broken, the electric chain laid down between England, Darmstadt, and Fort Simpson!"

The Bishop lamented that it was impossible in such a huge field to carry on systematic work. He draws attention to the fact that St. Paul in his great journeys " found it possible to found small communities of Christians in only hasty visits to the various cities encountered in his travels. But," he adds, " St. Paul's labours were among civilized races," and he believed that to work well among the Indians a teacher must be " willing to surrender his life to a permanent residence in the heathen country as an adopted home "—to teach by example as well as by precept. But the Bishop became by no means discouraged in his efforts, and made wonderful journeys in the face of hardships and dangers, many of which remain unknown.

Shortly after his return from Fort Rae an incident happened which almost deprived the Church of this heroic missionary. He wished to visit Fort Norman, some 200 miles farther north of Fort Simpson, and made ready to travel in the dead of winter with several of the Hudson Bay Company's men who were going that way. On the morning of the departure Mrs. Bompas went to the Indian camp and asked the natives who were to accompany the travellers to look after the Bishop. One of the boys—Natsatt by name—spoke up and said :

BISHOP OF ATHABASCA

" Are we not men ? Is he not our Bishop ? *Koka* " (*i.e.,* " that's enough ").

And so they started. As a rule, the Bishop was a great traveller, always keeping in front of the dogs, and running like a deer, with great powers of endurance ; but on this occasion he lagged behind the sledge, travelling slower and slower all the time. Natsatt kept looking back, and when at length the Bishop disappeared from sight, he became uneasy, and presently said :

" Me no feel easy. Me not comfortable.

Leaving the rest of the party, who swung on their way, he went back to look for the Bishop ; and there he found him helpless in the middle of the trail, bent double, with hands on his knees, trying to walk, having been seized with fearful cramps. At once Natsatt rubbed him thoroughly, made a fire as quickly as possible, and, after the sufferer was well warmed, with a great effort succeeded in getting him back to the fort. The day was extremely cold, 40° below zero. A few minutes more, and the Bishop would have perished on the trail.

Poor Natsatt, this noble young Indian, several years later, while hunting beaver, was drowned. He was the only support of his old mother, and was also one of the faithful choir members at Fort Simpson.

This story serves to show the affection felt by the Indians for their Bishop, and good reason was there for this love. He had given up much for them, and in their troubles and sorrows was always ready to help. Though his great object was the saving of the souls of the natives, yet he believed this work could often be helped by caring for their bodies. He had never studied at a medical college, but his keen powers of observation and the study of some of the standard medical books that he had always at hand stood him in good stead on many an occasion. He had witnessed so often the sufferings endured by his flock owing to snow-blindness in the spring that when he returned home for consecration he took advantage of the visit to attend several lectures at an eye hospital, and was henceforth able to treat the patients who came to him with splendid success. Great was the faith the Indians had in the Bishop's healing powers. Only a few years ago an Indian along the Yukon River who had been treated by the police doctor for some time was heard to say, " P'lice doctor no good "; and then with animation continued, " Ah ! Beeshop heem moche good !"

Wherever he went the Indians came to be cured, bringing their sick and afflicted, and truly many an Apostolic scene was enacted in the great northern wilds. Shortly after he was made Bishop he amputated a man's leg above the knee, and the operation proved most successful.

The story of poor old Martha is a touching one. Her daughter's child, little Tommy—a miserable misshapen creature—was very sick. They sent for the Bishop, who did all in his power, but in vain: the child soon passed away. Through his tender care he won their hearts, and not long after the child's death Martha came to him one cold, dark night and begged the Bishop " to give her medicine to do her heart good ; she had pain there ever since Tommy died." And there, in the quietness of the mission-house, the noble teacher talked with her, telling of the great Physician of souls, and sending her away comforted.

Great was the love the Bishop had towards the children of his flock, and this love often blinded his eyes to many of their imperfections, and at times caused him to take part with the children against the mission teachers. On one occasion, hearing the sobs of a child who was being chastised, he marched to the schoolroom door and sought admittance. This not being complied with at once, with a mighty push he drove open the door, seized the child from the teacher's grasp, and, placing it upon his knee, began to soothe it with parental affection.

A beautiful scene is that which shows us the Bishop seeking for one of his flock, a little girl who had wandered into the wilderness. Jeannie de Nord was a child of ten years, with a complexion scarcely darker than an ordinary English gipsy. A rogue she looked, and a little rogue she was, up to all sorts of f.n and mischief. Her father, old De Nord, had left her with an aunt while he went away some distance to hunt. The aunt was neglectful of her little charge, and Jeannie, unable to bear this, started in search of her father. So little did the aunt care that two days elapsed before the word spread that Jeannie was lost.

No sooner did the Bishop hear of it than, like the true shepherd he was, he started with others in search of the little wanderer. They pushed on over the snow, following the girl's tracks, for she had taken her snow-shoes with her. She had no food or blanket, and the nights were cold, and starving wolves roamed the forests. And where was Jeannie ? She had reached her father's abandoned camp one night, cold and tired. Groping about, she found his gun, which had been left there, and with the cunning of the wild she discharged the weapon, and from the spark thus obtained started a fire, which kept her warm through the night. All the next day she wandered in vain, searching for her father, and, tired and hungry, crept back to the abandoned camp and fell asleep. It was in the night that the rescue-party drew near, and some distance away discharged a gun to attract the girl's attention. Jeannie heard the report, and, thinking it was her father coming back, with a sigh of relief fell asleep again on her cold bed. When she next opened her eyes, it was to see standing before her the tall figure of the anxious Bishop, and to feel his strong loving arms around her as he lifted her from the ground, while the only word she uttered was " Ti tin die " (*i.e.*, " I am hungry ").

The shepherd had found the lost lamb, but oh, at what a cost! The Bishop's clothes were soaking from the overflowing streams they had crossed as

they wandered about, and he could hardly reach
Fort Simpson, so great were the cramps which
seized him, and for dáys he endured great suffering.
But what did it matter? Little Jeannie de Nord
was safe, and none the worse for her experience.

Four years later the Bishop was called upon to
lay poor Jeannie to rest. Her father made her
work harder than she was able. One day she
started with the dogs and sledge for the woods, to
bring in a deer her father had killed. The journey
was a long one, and when she returned to the camp
tired out she complained of not feeling well, and,
lying down on her bed of brushwood, died the next day.

Such a scene as this wrung the Bishop's heart,
and he did all in his power to bring the little ones
into the mission-schools, where they could receive
proper care. An interesting sight it was to see
this shepherd returning from some long trip,
bringing with him several wild, dirty little natives
for his school.

Not only did the Bishop bring the Indian children
into the mission-school, but time and time again he
and Mrs. Bompas received some poor little waif as
their own. A few years after his consecration little
Jenny, a mere babe, was thus taken to their hearts.
She came to them, so Mrs. Bompas tells us,

> " At holy Christmas-tide,
> When winter o'er our northern home
> Its lusty arms spread wide;
> When snow-drifts gathered thick and deep,
> Winds moaned in sad unrest,
> My little Indian baby sought
> A shelter at my breast."

Upon this child they bestowed their affection; but, alas! notwithstanding the greatest care, it gradually wasted away. Long and patiently they watched by its side, and did everything possible to alleviate its sufferings. It was a sad day to them both when the little one passed away.

Some time later another was received into their home and hearts. This was Owindia ("The Weeping One"), who was baptized Lucy May. A terrible tragedy had been enacted at one of the Indian camps, from which the babe had been marvellously rescued. Her mother had been cruelly murdered by an angry husband, and as there was no one to care for her, the Bishop and Mrs. Bompas took the motherless child. Great was the joy they received from the little one, and, with much pride, several years later she was taken to England, where she died some time after. Mrs. Bompas beautifully tells the story of this waif in her little book, "Owindia."

CHAPTER XI

A SYNOD IN THE WILD

(1876)

" Do Thou in ever-quickening streams
　　Upon Thy saints descend,
　And warm them with reviving beams,
　　And guide them to the end."

As soon as possible after his consecration Bishop
Bompas began to organize the forces at his command, and made preparations for the holding of a
Synod. But his men were few and far removed,
and months passed before word reached them at
their distant posts. At last the difficulty was overcome, and on September 4, 1876, the first Synod
of the vast diocese was held at Fort Simpson.

The general idea of a Synod is a large city,
splendid church or cathedral, enthusiastic gatherings of earnest people, hearty services, imposing
processions, and learned discussions, where

" Grey champions bowed and thoughtful,
　　Young knights of mettle fine,
　Meet as of old in councils vast,
　　Grave questions to define."

179

A SYNOD IN THE WILD

But reverse all this, and behold a Hudson Bay post in the northern wilds along the great Mackenzie River, a few houses clustered together, a small church, a congregation composed mostly of Indians, and a Bishop with only three clergy, besides a few schoolmasters and catechists.

Though small, it was still an interesting assemblage which met on that early September day, unlike any Synod ever before held. Foremost of the three clergy was the Ven. Archdeacon Robert McDonald,* who had come from Fort McPherson, on Peel River. Noble champion of the faith, he had endured more than all the rest in sickness and hardships for the Master's sake. Next came the Rev. W. D. Reeve, who at that time was steadily making his mark in the great work, and upon whom in after-years devolved the care of the Churches in the diocese of Mackenzie River. The third was the Rev. Alfred Garrioch, recently ordained. Besides these there were Messrs. Allen Hardisty and William Norn, catechists, and George Sandison, a servant of the Hudson Bay Company.

There were many things to consider at this meeting. In August, 1875, the first provincial Synod of the ecclesiastical province of Rupert's Land had been held at Winnipeg, and the Bishop wished to confirm the resolutions then made. There were also questions to discuss concerning each post, and many details to be considered. But the most

* Appointed Archdeacon in 1875. (From notes among the Bishop's papers.)

important work of this Synod was the division of the diocese into four parts. The Bishop found it impossible to be always at hand to settle any question that might arise in the remote portions of his field. The year previous to this meeting he had traversed, so he tells us, " the extreme breadth of the diocese from north-west to south-east, a distance of about 2,000 miles, covering, in going and returning, about double that distance, and visiting all the mission-stations and other posts on the route.

" These extended travels," he said, " prove inconsistent with domestic life, and Mrs. Bompas, being left alone in the rigorous climate, and among the sometimes chill hearts of our northern clime, has lost her health from exposure to cold and insufficient food. There is no doubt that the domestic hearth, when it can be had, will convey Christian lessons to the Indians."*

The arrangement of the force under the Bishop's command at this time was as follows :

1. *Tukudh Mission.*—Rampart House, Mr. K. McDonald, catechist ; La Pierre's House, Henry Venn, native catechist ; Fort McPherson, Peel River, Archdeacon Robert McDonald, missionary.

2. *Mackenzie River Mission.* — Fort Norman (Trinity Mission), Mr. J. Hodgson, schoolmaster ; Fort Simpson (St. David's), the Bishop, missionary ; Mr. Alfred Garrioch, catechist.

3. *Great Slave Lake Mission.*—Fort Rae, Rev.

* Archdeacon McDonald in a letter to the writer.

181

W. D. Reeve, missionary ; Hay River Fort, Mr. William Norn, catechist.

4. *Athabasca Mission.*—Fort Chipewyan, Rev. A. Shaw, missionary ; Mr. Allen Hardisty, catechist ; Fort Vermilion, Mr. G. Garrioch, catechist.

These were the workers scattered over the vast diocese, and after careful consideration the following plan was agreed upon :

To the Rev. R. McDonald was entrusted the Tukudh Mission, in the extreme north-west, on the Yukon and its tributaries ; to the Rev. W. D. Reeve, the Mackenzie River Mission ; the Great Slave Lake Mission to the schoolmasters ; while the Bishop kept the Athabasca Mission, comprising the southern district and the Peace River, to himself.

At this time the estimated population of the diocese was 10,000, of whom half were Roman Catholics, 3,000 with the Church of England, and the remainder heathen. The Bishop had 100 children in the various schools, and the same number of communicants.

But it was not all business that was carried on at this first diocesan Synod ; there was something of a very different nature, and that was the charge given by the Bishop to his little band of men. Portions of it must be set down here, not only for its interesting and instructive nature, but because it is the only address delivered by the Bishop to his clergy of which we have any record.

" 1. At this, our first meeting in diocesan Synod,"

he began, "it is right that I should congratulate you on the band of union which this Synod forms, to link us not only to one another, but also (through our connexion with the newly formed province of Rupert's Land) first with Manitoba and the whole of the North-West Territories, and more remotely with the Churches of Canada and England.

"2. The Right Rev. Bishop Machray, as our Metropolitan, forms the connecting-link between the four dioceses of Manitoba and the North-West Territories, while the Archbishop of Canterbury, being our Primate, assures us that our connexion remains unbroken with the ancient Mother Church of England. Again, the Church of the Dominion of Canada, containing now two ecclesiastical provinces (a northern and a southern), should not be considered as disunited but connected by the arrangement, just as the two provinces of the English Church (a northern and a southern), at York and Canterbury, offer no obstacle to, but only complete the union of, the Church of England as an undivided whole.

"3. It is also a matter for congratulation, in these dangerous times, that, by the provisions of our provincial Synod, our Church is secured in safe attachment to the faith and formularies of the Church of England, which all must admit to be Scriptural and moderate. At the same time we are happy in being removed by distance from the controversies at home."

After speaking at length about the contention between the Church of England and the Roman

Catholic Church in his diocese, the Bishop continued : " The day of trial, we are assured, shall declare who amongst the builders of Christ's Church has wrought with God's own materials, the gold, silver, and precious stones of His holy word ; and who, on the other hand, have used the wood, hay, and stubble of man's invention. ' If any man's work abide, he shall receive a reward. . . .' It is important for us to see that our own work be deep and thorough. Let us not accept any as Christian converts in connexion with our mission but such as we believe to have been the subjects of a real change of heart by the grace of Christ and His Holy Spirit. Others must, of course, be admitted to instruction, and from such an endeavour should be made to select those whose hearts are touched to form a band of inquirers for more careful and constant training with prayer and pains.

" 4. The most common and the most open vices of the Indians, and those which seem to keep them most from the reception of the Gospel, are the practices of gambling, conjuring, and impurity. To their abandoning of these habits, therefore, our efforts should be specially directed, and no Indian should be considered as a Christian convert until he has entirely abandoned them. Dishonesty also, although not originally habitual to the Indians, has now become very general with those about the forts, and efforts should be made to check it.

" 5. The practice, which it would be wrong to discontinue, of baptizing all the Indian children who are brought to us for the purpose throws upon us a great obligation to provide for them, as they grow up, instruction in the Christian faith. It seems impossible, at present, to keep the Indian children regularly at school in any numbers, and the only alternative seems to be to arrange a short form of elementary instruction, which shall be systematically taught to the children by rote at their camps, or whereve⁻ opportunity may offer.

" 6. It is a melancholy fact that there is still but one completed church in our diocese, and this, though more than two years have now elapsed since a grant of £500 was offered us by the Society for Promoting Christian Knowledge for erecting additional churches. The school-church at Fort Norman is, however, now approaching completion. Let us all make an effort to have some plain buildings erected at our different mission-stations for Christian worship. The House of God is the chief visible sign which we are still allowed to retain of God's presence amongst us, and I take it to be of great importance that the heathen should be reminded, by this constant memorial before their eyes, that the introduction of Christianity into their country by the missionaries is a reality, and more than a mere tale ; and I do not know of any way in which we may better seek to call down a Divine blessing on the land in which we live than by exerting ourselves for the erection of places of worship in the name of the Saviour whom we serve. All might do something in this matter by providing

185

us with labour, materials, or furniture for the new churches.

" 7. Our plans for education, in which I have been interested ever since my arrival in the country eleven years ago, have also proved hitherto partly abortive, and I take this to be a lesson that, in missionary work, efforts for education must follow and not precede the work of evangelization. Meantime the missionaries themselves have to undertake educational duties. I am still, however, earnestly desirous that at least one school be formed in the diocese, where the elements of a sound English education for children should at all times be procurable. It is very desirable that this subject be further considered by us in Synod and private conference, with the hope, by God's help, of arriving at last, by perseverance, at some successful scheme of education.

" 8. Economy of funds and scarcity of provisions oblige us at present to confine our mission agents and stations to as few in number as possible. The stations proposed to be occupied at present are the Forts Vermilion, Chipewyan, Rae, Simpson, Norman, McPherson, and Rampart House, at each of which it is earnestly desired that a church may be erected.

" 9. I am glad to be able to testify, in returning from my recent journey, that the Indians of the Tukudh Mission are making fair progress in Christian instruction. I had the pleasure of administering the rite of Confirmation to more than one hundred of them. At Fort Norman, also, I was pleased to find among the Protestant Indians a readiness to learn. At Fort Simpson I was very pleased to find, during the first winter after my return from England, a marked increase of attention and attachment to our mission among all resident at the fort. I cannot feel, however, that this has been sustained as I could have hoped during the past winter; but I would trust the Christian spirit among you may now be revived and increased again. At Fort Chipewyan I am glad to hear of a regular attendance at Divine service, and at Fort Rae of a spirit of inquiry among the Indians. I would fain hope that the efforts now making to extend and strengthen our mission in the southern portion of the diocese may be permanently successful."

When the Synod ended the little band of workers had to hurry away to their distant posts, as winter was fast approaching. And away, too, went the Bishop. There were stations to visit which needed his attention, and he was delayed for some time. On his return in November he found Mrs. Bompas quite ill. Concerning the Bishop's return Mrs. Bompas speaks in her journal of that time :

"On the 11th I was in bed, feeling very poorly and distressed, a bad headache in addition to my other pains, when suddenly, about 4 o'clock p.m., my French girl (whom I had got over from the French Mission to help me in my extremity) went to the window, hearing the sound of sledge bells.

In another moment she turned quickly to me and said, ' C'est votre mari, madame.' Never shall I forget that moment of joy and thankfulness. He was at my bedside the next instant, looking so well and handsome, his beard all hoary with frost, in fur cap, mittens, and deer-skin coat, etc., etc. Almost from the moment he arrived he set to work to make me more comfortable. My room hitherto, I confess, had been very cold and comfortless, and I seemed to have no strength to make it less so. But now every day seemed to take something off my burden and anxieties. Oh, it seemed impossible to be thankful enough ! I could only lie in my weakness and pray to be more thankful."

That sickness, which was so hard to bear, was in reality a blessing in disguise, as after-events proved conclusively.

With the opening of navigation Mrs. Bompas started on her long journey of over 1,000 miles to Winnipeg. Of this trip she wrote :

" I am thankful to have come to the end of my long journey from Athabasca, which, by God's mercy, I accomplished with less fatigue than I anticipated. I met with much kindness on my way at the various mission-stations, and also at the Company's forts, and I visited many Indian camps, where one seldom fails to meet with a hearty welcome. Sometimes I had prayers with some of the women and children in my tent. They seem to like to come, and enjoy singing hymns. . . . My boat's crew from Isle à la Crosse to Cumber-

land was composed of Stanley men, and a more
orderly, well-conducted set I never saw. They had
a nice little service every morning and evening
among themselves, which I always attended; it
consisted of a hymn (beautifully sung in parts), a
few words of Scripture, and a few of the Church
prayers. Some days the poor men were quite worn
out with hard work at the portages, and for two
days their provisions ran short and they were
nearly starving, but they sang their hymn and had
their prayers without fail, and when relief came in
the shape of two canoes bringing bags of flour and
pemmican, their shout of delight, I think, must
almost have reached Salisbury Square. . . .

"I came with the Governor-General from the
Grand Rapids. His Excellency and Lady Dufferin
were kind enough to invite me to join their party,
as they heard that I was anxious to get on.

"I am thankful to find all my powers gradually
returning, and the state of woeful emaciation to
which I was reduced giving way under the influences of milk and other luxuries, of which I was
deprived at Athabasca. I deplore my having to
leave my work so soon, but I earnestly trust in
God's mercy to bring me back to it again in the
early spring." *

* *Church Missionary Society Gleaner*, January, 1878.

CHAPTER XII

A RACE WITH WINTER

(1877-1878)

" The watery deep we pass,
With Jesus in our view ;
And through the howling wilderness
Our way pursue."

THRING.

WHILE Bishop Bompas was carrying on his steady
work along the great inland streams, a storm was
brewing in an active mission centre on the Pacific
coast. Mr. Duncan, who had been sent out by the
Church Missionary Society, was working among the
Indians at Metlakahtla with good results. Bishop
Hills, of Columbia Diocese, several times visited the
settlement, and baptized a large number of converts.
But Mr. Duncan objected to the Indian Christians
being prepared for Confirmation, thinking they
would make a fetish of it. Time and time again
the Church Missionary Society sent out ordained
men to Metlakahtla, but Mr. Duncan would not
listen to them, and remained most headstrong in his
views. Matters thus reached a climax. Bishop
Hills well knew if he visited Metlakahtla it would

only add fuel to the flames, as Mr. Duncan, for certain reasons, had taken a dislike to him. He therefore acted a wise part, and wrote to Bishop Bompas, asking him to go to Metlakahtla as arbitrator.

It was late in the season when the letter reached the Bishop, but without delay he prepared for the trip. At any season it was a great undertaking, but at that time of the year the difficulty was very much increased. In a direct line the journey was a long one, but to reach the coast the distance had to be lengthened by a circuitous route over rivers, lakes, portages, and mountain summits.

Then, winter was upon them.

"All the latter part of September," wrote the Bishop, "the frost and snow had been more severe than I had ever known it before at the same season, so the winter had decidedly the first start in our race."

It was a cold, frosty day, that 8th of October, 1877, when the Bishop left Dunvegan in a stout canoe with several Indians on his long race to the coast against stern Winter. For five days they moved up the river, contending with drifting ice which met them coming out of "tributary streams," and on the 13th Fort St. John was reached, where they "were kindly entertained for the Sunday by the officer in charge" of the Hudson Bay post. From this point they left winter "behind for a fortnight, and were fairly ahead in the race." But every day they expected to be overtaken by their competitor, and arose from their " couches anxiously every morning, foreboding signs of ice or snow."

Rocky Mountain House was reached on the 17th, where a large band of Indians was found assembled. The Bishop lost no opportunity of speaking a word to the natives wherever he met them, and the seed thus sown bore much fruit in after-years. For the first time he found no sickness in the camps, which fact he attributed " to their unusually liberal use of soap and water, as compared with the tribes farther north."

Ahead of them was the Peace River Canyon, and, after making a land portage of twelve miles to avoid this dangerous spot, they again proceeded by canoe. But the work was becoming harder all the time. The current was very swift, and the canoe had to be poled all the way. In trying to ascend the Parle Pas Rapids, the current was so " strong that their canoe turned on them, and was swept down the stream, but, being a large one, descended safely."

" On the very morning that we left Parsnip River," wrote the Bishop, " the ice began again to drift thickly to meet us, and had we been only a few hours later, we might have been inconvenienced by it, showing us that stern Winter was still on our track.

" Most of the time that we were passing through the gorge of the Rocky Mountains the weather was foggy, but when the mist cleared we saw the bold crags and hilly heights closely overhanging the river in snowy grandeur. The mountain terraces

and picturesque scenery on this route have been
described by Canadian explorers."

For eleven days the Bishop and his men poled
their craft against the stream, and, with many
dangers passed, reached McLeod's Lake Fort on
October 29. Here they were hospitably received
by Mr. McKenzie, the officer in charge, and an
opportunity was given to see the Indians who were
at the fort. A rest of two days was made here, and
then they started across the lake. This was a
difficult task, as the ice was beginning to stretch
from shore to shore, and they had to force their
way as best they could around the corner of the
solid mass.

From Lake McLeod a long portage of eighty
miles was made over frozen ground to the beautiful
sheet of water known as Stuart Lake, on the shore
of which the officer at Fort St. James gave them a
hearty welcome. Here the Bishop was on historic
ground. Seventy-one years before those famous
explorers, Simon Fraser and John Stuart,* discovered the lake which took the name of the
latter. Fort St. James, which was erected on its
banks " long before Victoria and New Westminster
had been called into existence," was the regular
capital of British Columbia, "where a representative of our own race ruled over reds and whites." †

* " History of the Interior of British Columbia," by the
Rev. A. G. Morice.

† John Stuart was Lord Strathcona's uncle, and was largely
instrumental in bringing the young Scotchman to Canada in
1838.

A RACE WITH WINTER

A stay of four days was made at this place, during which time heavy snow-storms raged over the land and ice began to form in the lake, which threatened to bar further progress. This body of water, which is about fifty miles in length, had to be traversed, and the Indians refused to make the long journey at that season and in such weather. During the delay the Bishop was invited to hold Divine service at the fort on Sunday. Never before had the place " been visited by a Protestant missionary, the Roman Catholics only having laboured in the region, and Mr. Hamilton, the Hudson Bay Company's chief officer there, brought up a family of ten children, without having for more than twenty years any opportunity of seeing a Protestant minister."

After much difficulty the Indians were persuaded to go forward, and, leaving Fort St. James on November 7, arrived at Fort Babines, on the lake of the same name, on the 14th, after encountering a furious snow-storm on the way. The Babine Indians in this region, being all Roman Catholics, were naturally suspicious of a Church of England missionary. " However," said the Bishop, " they treated us well."

From Fort Babines they started on the land-trail over the mountains to Skeena Forks. This was a difficult undertaking, and winter overtook them once again. At the beginning of the portage, the snow was several inches deep, and as they ascended the mountain it deepened continually, till they were forced to dig out their camps, " to sleep in a foot and a half of snow, and without snow-shoes the walking was heavy. We were invading Winter's own domain," continued the Bishop, " and it was little wonder if he was severe with us."

On descending the western slope the next morning, the snow diminished rapidly, and they " camped at night in the grass without a vestige of snow remaining, and only saw stern Winter frowning down from the heights behind."

Having reached the Skeena Forks, they were given a hearty welcome by Mr. Hankin, who informed the Bishop that, till the previous year, the Skeena River had never been known to continue open so late, being generally frozen the first week in November, and now it was the 17th. The next day the descent of the Skeena was begun by canoe, in fear and trembling, lest the ice might " drift down from behind." And the race began in earnest, for a heavy snow-storm swept over the land, and Winter once more made a last effort to block them. But through the tempest sped the determined missionary, and to his joy found that, on nearing the coast, the mild breezes of the Pacific were too much for grim Winter, and he steadily retreated, leaving the little party unscathed.

On November 23 Port Essington, at the mouth of the Skeena, was reached, and after spending one night there with Mr. Morrison, the Bishop proceeded " twenty-five miles by canoe along the coast to the north to Metlakahtla, which he reached on the 24th, "this being the tenth canoe," he remarks, "that we had sat in since leaving Dunvegan."

Mr. Duncan cordially welcomed the traveller, and 124 of the Christian Indians were confirmed and communicants' classes formed. Mr. (afterwards Archdeacon) Collison received both Deacon's and Priest's Orders, and was placed in pastoral charge of Metlakahtla. Thus it looked as if the Bishop's visit would bring about a lasting peace ; but, alas! after he left the condition of affairs became as they were before, and the history of the struggle that followed is a sad one.

Bishop Bompas spent four months on the coast, making several trips in canoes to visit the Indians at various places. His visit was very beneficial, and he wrote that he felt " a good deal invigorated both in body and mind by the change, and not at all loath to return to the more northern regions, which seem to me much less isolated and inaccessible now that I have made the connexion between them and the wild western slopes of the Pacific. It had long been my expectation that Athabasca and Mackenzie districts would gradually become more approachable from the west, and this idea is now confirmed."

The Venerable Archdeacon Collison, of the Diocese of Caledonia, writes from Kincolith, Naas Mission, of the visit of Bishop Bompas to the Pacific coast :

" It was Mr. Morrison who met the Bishop on his arrival at Port Essington after what he described as ' A Race with Winter ' down the Skeena. He was so travel-worn that Mr. Morrison mistook him for a

miner as he disembarked from the canoe. ' Well,
said he, ' what success have you had ?' The Bishop
replied that he had been fairly successful, evidently
relishing the joke. Just then Mr. Morrison saw
the remains of his apron, and, recollecting that he
had heard that a Bishop was expected at Metlakahtla
from inland, exclaimed, ' Perhaps you are the Bishop
who I heard was expected ?' ' Yes,' replied the
Bishop, ' I am all that is left of him.' He remained
at Metlakahtla that winter, where he succeeded in
confirming a large number of candidates. By the
first steamer in spring he came over to me on
Queen Charlotte's Island, at Massett. I had a little
bedroom specially prepared for him in the new
mission-house, but he preferred lying down on the
floor, as he said he was not accustomed to sleeping in
rooms. He was about to lie down just across the
doorway when I begged him to take another position,
as he might be disturbed by some one entering late
or early.

"I returned with him to the mainland on the
steamer. We went up together to the Naas River
by canoe, a voyage of some fifty miles to Kincolith.
The owner of the canoe, who was a chief, was
steering, and I was seated near him towards the
stern, whilst the Bishop was seated forward. As
the Bishop raised his arms in paddling, in which
we were all engaged, it revealed a long tear in the
side of his shirt. Suddenly the chief asked me in
a low tone in Tsimshean, ' Why is the chief's shirt
so torn ?' I replied : ' He has been a long time

travelling through the forest.' He was dressed very roughly, and wore a pair of moccasins. When we reached Kincolith, he purchased a coarse pair of brogans in the little Indian store there. He was in the habit of sitting, after the others had finished their meal, eating a small piece of dry yeast-powder bread, baked by Mrs. Tomlinson or one of her Indian girl boarders, and he would exclaim, ' How sweet this bread is to my taste after roughing it so long on the trails !' He informed us of the privations both missionaries and Indians had endured owing to scarcity of food during certain seasons, on more than one occasion having had to boil and eat the skins of the animals that had been caught in the hunt for their furs. I ventured to suggest to him that this might be avoided if they could only grow potatoes and pit them securely. We had taught our Indians to do this. The Bishop feared they would not mature in his diocese, but promised to remember it. Afterwards I was informed he had introduced the potato with success.

" The Rev. R. Tomlinson and I accompanied the Bishop when he started to return to the head of canoe navigation on the Naas River, and some distance on the trail. We had a prayer-meeting at the point where we separated in the forest, in which we joined in prayer for needful blessings—the Bishop for us and God's work in our hands, and we for him in his journey and labours for the Lord. He gave away his great-coat and a pot to the Indians, and started on the second stage of his return journey accompanied by one young Indian."

While on the coast it was but natural that his thoughts should wander to his native land.

"From the Pacific coast," he wrote, "a few weeks would have taken me to England or any part of the civilized world ; but I preferred to return north without even visiting the haunts of civilization (except so far as the Indians are culti-vated at our missions), on the ground that such a visit renders the mind unsettled or disinclined for a life in the wilds."

Brave soldier of the Cross, how willing he was to sacrifice anything for the Master's cause ! Leaving the coast, he started in the spring up the Skeena River, and once again plunged into the wilderness among his dusky flock.

CHAPTER XIII

ONWARD AND UPWARD

(1878-1884)

" The labourers are few, the field is wide,
New stations must be filled, and blanks supplied."
J. BORTHWICK.

THE Bishop reached Fort St. John, on the Peace River, during the latter part of April, and remarked that his trip from the coast was " unmarked by special interest, though not without much assistance by a kind Providence." He was much interested in the lava plain on the Naas River, " about twelve miles square, caused by a volcanic eruption from a neighbouring mountain. The Indian tale is," wrote the Bishop, " that some cruel children, playing at the mouth of a small stream, were catching the salmon, and, cutting open their backs, put stones in them and let them go again. The Good Spirit, being angry, set the river on fire, and burnt up the children, and the lava plain remains as the memento. I could not help thinking it a mercy, when I heard the tale, that some of our London urchins have never yet set the Thames on fire!"

200

ONWARD AND UPWARD

Seldom did the Bishop refer to the legendary lore of the Indians, with which he must have been most familiar, except " to point a moral," and never " to adorn a tale."

Upon reaching his own diocese, sad news met him of a terrible famine which had ravaged his flock the previous winter. Food was scarce, " owing to the extreme mildness of the season interfering with the chase, and the mission supplies having failed to reach there in the fall." Mrs. Bompas was not in the country, for which the Bishop was most thankful ; but his heart was sore over the suffering, not only of the Indians, but of the missionaries at the various posts. He gives a graphic picture of the sufferings endured in the diocese.

" Horses were killed for food, and furs eaten at several of the posts. The Indians had to eat a good many of their beaver-skins. Imagine an English lady taking her supper off her muff. The gentleman now here with me supported his family for a while on bear-skins. These you see at home mostly in the form of Grenadier caps. Can you fancy giving a little girl, a year or two old, a piece of Grenadier's cap, carefully singed, boiled and toasted, to eat ? Mr. McAulay's little girl has not yet recovered from the almost fatal sickness that resulted. The scarcity brings out the strange contrast between this country and others. Elsewhere money 'answereth all things,' and among India's millions half a million sterling will relieve a famine ; but send it here, and though a great sum among our scattered individuals, who can be counted by tens, yet it would do us no good, as for digestion we must find it ' hard cash ' indeed."

This severe " wasting of the famine " induced the Bishop to launch a plan which for some time he had had in mind. He felt how uncertain it was to depend upon the supplies brought in from the outside, and to obviate the scarcity he knew they must endeavour to raise their own produce.

" A mission-farm in connexion with the mission," he wrote, " seems almost a necessity, for as the wild animals of the wood are ceasing to yield even a precarious subsistence, Providence seems to point us plainly to raise food out of the earth."

Peace River was the region chosen for the venture, " the country there being very picturesque, having some resemblance to the English South Down hills. The grass slopes are a great relief to the eye from the monotonous pine-forests, which are often almost our only view. The soil is fertile, and the country well adapted for farming ; and though Peace River is at present a starving country, yet it is strange to see it spoken of in the papers as adapted by Nature to be a great granary for the two Continents of Europe and America."

A new mission was accordingly commenced at Dunvegan, " as this point is likely to prove one of the most important in the country, being a convenient door of ingress and egress to and from the north."

Mr. Thomas Bunn, who had done " patient

and successful school work at Chipewyan," was placed in charge of the mission, while Mr. G. Garrioch had control of the farm which was started. Another farm in connexion with Dunvegan was begun at Smoky River, " so called from the constant smoke occasioned by the spontaneous combustion underground of coal and bitumen."

At Vermilion the mission was enlarged " by the addition of a school, in charge of Mr. Lawrence from Canada," and in 1880 the Bishop reported that " the mission - farm at Vermilion has been also enlarged, and is in a fair way to be productive enough to provide food for that and other mission-stations."

So encouraged was the Bishop by the success of his farming plan on Peace River that he began to think of a similar undertaking on the Liard River, further north, and he considered this section " better adapted for farming than any other part of the Mackenzie River country."

Besides the farming plan, the Bishop had another in his mind about this time, and that was to have a small mission - steamer placed on the Mackenzie River. As the farms would, he hoped, supply the mission with produce, so the steamer would not only carry all the supplies, but facilitate travel and advance the missionary work in the vast diocese.

He believed a steam - launch, with portable engines of about 20 horse-power, a rapidly revolving screw, and a furnace to burn wood or

coal, could be taken in by the way of the Saskatchewan and Peace Rivers, and the hull built in
the country. Such a launch, he estimated, could
ascend the Mackenzie River, the longest river in
British territory, for about 1,300 miles.

The movement thus begun by the Bishop caused
the Hudson Bay Company to make a start in the
same direction. They wished to remain the "lords
of the north," and for a steamer to be placed on
the river and controlled by others would, they
believed, weaken their prestige among the natives.
When the Bishop saw the Company meant business he at once gave up his own plan, for it mattered
little to him who controlled the steamer so long as
the method of travel was improved. This was not
done till some years later, when, in 1882, the little
steamer *Graham* was built by the Company at Fort
Chipewyan, on Lake Athabasca. In 1885 the screw
propeller *Wrigley* was built at Fort Smith, on the
Slave River ; and a few years later the stern-wheeler
Athabasca was launched at Athabasca Landing for
the Upper Athabasca River.*

But during the waiting season the Bishop had to
continue his long journeys in the open canoe over
the great network of waterways with which he was
so familiar. In May, 1881, he began those marvellous trips which only a giant constitution could
have endured. From the Peace River district he
made a voyage far north to visit the Tukudh

* "The Remarkable History of the Hudson's Bay Company," chap. xxxviii., p. 395.

An Indian Camp, with a Woman holding a Child in the peculiar Indian Cradle

missions. Here he was much pleased with the hearty welcome given by the native converts, "whom," he says, "I have come to regard as my brethren in Christ." "It was a delight to me," he further adds, "to hear adults and children at each mission post read before me from the Tukudh books printed for their benefit; and as they have now begun to teach one another to read, our missionary will be somewhat relieved from the necessity of holding school for all."

But the Indians along the Upper Yukon, whom he "left weeping in contrition for their sins ten years ago," weighed much upon his mind, and he made a strong appeal for men to man the field. One of the Yukon Indians who had come to plead for the Bishop to visit his tribe pointed to a smouldering fire and said:

"That is how you have left us. You kindled the fire of the Gospel among us, and left it untended to die out again. Why have you done this?"

Is it any wonder that this missionary, standing by the smouldering camp-fire, with the dusky natives all around, and listening to their cry, "Come over and help us," sent forth his soul-stirring appeal for men to support his great undertaking in the northern wilds?

He also asked the Church Missionary Society "to take up work in the American territory of Alaska," adding "that international boundaries ought to make no bar to evangelistic efforts," and that " the whole of the Indians on the Youcon are thirsty for instruction, and are already partly evangelized by the efforts of Archdeacon Mc-Donald."

The Eskimos, in their dense ignorance, worried him much, and he sent appeal after appeal for assistance. And the cry was not in vain, for the Bishop's brother, George Bompas, gave a substantial sum for the purpose. While the Bishop was in the North still pleading, the Church Missionary Society sent out the Rev. T. H. Canham to start a mission among the Eskimos. Mr. Canham reached Peel River one year later, and was cordially received by the Eskimos, among whom he at once began to work.

For some time Bishop Bompas did not know who the generous donor was, and when he at length found out he wrote to his brother George in 1884 :

" I have only just heard that you were yourself the kind and generous donor. . . . I feel very thankful for your generosity and for the direction it took. Just at the time of Archdeacon McDonald's absence it was this gift only that has enabled us to support in sufficiency the Tukudh Mission, as well as to press on efforts for the Esquimaux.

" You may, then, view the Rev. T. H. Canham, with whom I have been staying at Peel River during much of last winter, as your own particular missionary. He is making good progress with the Tukudh and Esquimaux languages ; but, both being difficult, it is hard to acquire the two at once."

After spending the summer amongst the Tukudh missions, and travelling from May to August 2,500 miles, the Bishop returned south to Great Slave Lake to meet the incoming mission-party from England, and afterwards proceeded up the Liard River from Fort Simpson, and visited two posts there, Liard and Nelson. This region he considered " debatable ground " between the Dioceses of Caledonia and Mackenzie River. " However," he wrote, " as it appears at present quite inaccessible to Bishop Ridley, and has always been associated with our missions, I have worked it meanwhile, with the permission of Bishop Hills, irrespective of the question to whom it may ultimately be assigned."

Before winter the Bishop returned to Fort Norman, and had a terrible journey. The following letter written by Mrs. Bompas the next summer, and published in the little missionary magazine, *The Net*, describes most vividly what the Bishop endured :

" Fort Norman,
" *July*, 1882.

" The Bishop's return to us was greatly delayed. We counted on his arrival for relief in our most pressing necessities, and I was weary of acting on my own responsibility and judgment, for daily there is very much in which the said judgment is called for. But we looked and longed for him in vain, and the river became more firmly locked with ice.

ONWARD AND UPWARD

Towards the middle of November I was roused one night from sleep and startled to the uttermost by the loud knocking at the door of two Indians, who shouted out to me:

"'We bring you tidings of Bishop; he is starving!'

"It did not take me long to spring up and examine the men as to the truth of their report, and perilous indeed was the adventure which I gathered from them. The Bishop had reached Fort Simpson some days later than was expected. Finding that ice was rapidly forming on the river, so that to proceed northwards by canoe was utterly impossible, he started on a small raft (which was hastily and badly constructed) with one Indian. On this they were beating about for days, in great peril amid the gathering ice. They reached at last La Violdtes' house at Little Rapid, and there had to remain for ten days until the river was fast bound. Then the Bishop started anew to walk with four Indians, one of whom went after a bear in the woods and wholly lost sight of the others. Their supply of provisions was most insufficient, and from losing the right track the journey occupied twelve days instead of, as is usual, six. At length, when within a day's reach of this place, the Bishop was so overcome with exhaustion as to be quite unable to proceed, their only meal, sometime previous, having been a fish and small barley cake between four men. The Indians left him in the woods and hurried on to tell me of his con-

MRS. BOMPAS IN WINTER DRESS
From a photograph by Messrs. Notman and Son, Montreal

dition. My heart sank pretty low at such tidings, yet at the same time came the thought and firm conviction, which I trust was not presumptuous, that the Arms which had shielded my dear husband through so many dangers would befriend him still. But I felt there was no time to lose, and my first effort was to induce one of the young Indians to set off immediately to discover the Bishop in the woods, with Indian sagacity, and take him the relief I would send.

" ' Whu-tale, Bishop is starving in the woods. I send him meat—chiddi, chiddi (quick, quick). You take it to him, eh ?'

" Whu-tale, with true Indian passiveness :

" ' Maybe to-morrow.'

" ' No, Whu-tale ; to-morrow Bishop must be here : he cannot stand until he has eaten meat. I want you to take it now, and go to him like the wind. If you go directly and bring Bishop safe, I will give you a fine flannel shirt.'

" Whu-tale, a little more briskly :

" ' Then it would not be hard for me to go, and perhaps like the wind.'

" The next moment saw me emerging from my house, wrapped in my deer-skin robe, up the hill to the fort, where I had to rouse the Hudson Bay Company's officer from a sound sleep to obtain from him a supply of moose meat. The thermometer was nearly 30° below zero, and wolves in a starving condition had been seen lurking near the fort ; but I thought of neither the one nor the

other, and only rejoiced to get Whu-tale off, and
waited with enough anxiety through the succeeding
hours. After darkness had set in on the following
day, the travellers appeared, trudging along on
snow-shoes, weary and footsore, my husband looking hardly able to stand, and with his beard all
fringed with icicles. It is wonderful how he had
been preserved amid such perils, and brought to me
at last in answer to many prayers."

Here the Bishop stayed all winter, and, notwithstanding his last fearful experience, left again in
the spring among the drift-ice, intending to visit
Archdeacon McDonald at Peel River, whose health
was not good.

Of the risk the Bishop ran in this journey downstream with the drift-ice the following description
in his own words will give some idea:

"The breaking up of the ice in spring in the
large rivers, like the Mackenzie, is sometimes a fine
sight. The ice may pile in masses along the banks
to the height of 40 feet, or be carried far into the
woods. When any check occurs to the drifting of
the broken ice, so as to back the stream, the water
may suddenly rise to the height of 50 feet or more,
and flood the country.

" The rivers and lakes freeze in winter to a depth
of from 6 to 10 feet, and the force and impetus of
large masses of ice of this thickness, when hurled
along the rapid current of a mighty river, are
enormous. Few exhibitions of the power of the

Winter Travelling. A Missionary's Indian Helper

Great Creator are more imposing than when ' He causeth His wind to blow, and the waters flow.' "

Reaching Fort Good Hope, he heard better accounts of the Archdeacon, and, turning back, took Mrs. Bompas from Fort Norman to Fort Resolution, on Great Slave Lake, occupied by Messrs. Garton and Norn, " where," wrote the Bishop, " I have left her, I hope, a little more comfortable than last winter."

From Great Slave Lake he proceeded at once to Fort Chipewyan,* where he was engaged some time placing the accounts in the hands of Mr. Reeve, who had been appointed financial secretary, owing to the accessibility of his station from north to south. During the Bishop's stay here Captain Dawson, of the Royal Artillery, arrived from England with three men, in connexion with the International Circumpolar Expedition. At this place he made preparations for the building of a steamer by the Hudson Bay Company, " so that civilization," remarked the Bishop, " appears approaching us by degrees."

From Fort Chipewyan the Bishop went to Vermilion, on Peace River, and was " much encouraged by the sight of the good crops harvested from the mission-farms." After visiting Dunvegan, and other places along the river, he returned and spent three months at Vermilion, assisting Mr.

* A mission-house was erected here in 1876, and the church opened on Easter Day, 1880.—(From notes found among the Bishop's papers.)

Lawrence with the school. At length, becoming anxious about the lower missions, he started on foot for Chipewyan. This was a journey of about 200 miles, and many difficulties he must have endured before reaching his destination, which he did on March 1, in time to meet the spring letters, and confer with Archdeacon McDonald respecting the latter's intended trip to Manitoba and England.

At this place he heard that Mrs. Bompas was ill, which caused him much uneasiness. After spending a fortnight here with Mr. Reeve, he " found an opportunity of proceeding north again to Fort Resolution," which he reached shortly after Easter. He found Mrs. Bompas " in tolerable health, though having suffered rather severe hardships in winter, through the house not having been properly arranged in the fall to exclude the cold."

Though the Bishop had been absent from home for nine months, he only remained at Fort Resolution two weeks, and then pushed north to the Tukudh Mission, visiting the various stations on the way. Here he remained one year, and " was enabled to see nearly all the Indians at each of the three stations twice, both in winter and spring, and the Eskimos twice, both in fall and spring." His time was fully occupied, as the following will show :

" I held two Confirmations—viz., at Peel River and Rampart House—about forty being confirmed each time. I administered the Communion twice, to about forty communicants at each of these stations. I gave a daily address at Evening Prayer in Indian throughout the year, and the same twice on Sundays, always from the Gospels. I again went through the Eskimo primer with the interpreter, and wrote out additional prayers and lessons, and endeavoured to assist the Rev. T. Canham with the language. I made much effort towards the completion of the two mission-churches at Peel River and Rampart House, and left the former in so forward a state that we held prayers in it in spring, when it was quite filled by the Indian converts. Our cheerfulness was rather damped by the sudden death after New Year of their aged chief, good old Red Leggings, who has been from the first a mainstay of our mission there. I count him one that trusted in the Lord."

These are only the unembellished facts, and how we long for more interesting detail of that year's labour in the North ! But only once does he allow us a brief glimpse into his work at Rampart House.

" The old Indian chief specially asked me to administer the Sacrament to the communicants here, which I did, and about ten days after receiving it occurred his sudden death, for which, I trust, he was fully prepared. For the past six weeks I have been fully occupied in teaching a large band of Indians, and in holding school for the children. The sun here is hidden by the mountains all midwinter, and the days are so short that when the sky is cloudy we use candles at noon, and in clear days we can read by daylight only for two hours. I have spectacles, and my eyes are becoming dim by candle-light through the effect of using them in fire and twilight, which must be my apology for a poor letter just now ; but our darkest winter days are now passing by. The glare of the never-setting sun is also injurious to the eyesight in summer ; but, with these drawbacks, I have come to like the country, and should dread the recommencing life in England much more than ending my days here."

But the Bishop was longing for one change. The incessant moving about was telling upon him, and he asked that the diocese might be divided.

" I feel," he wrote, " much gratitude to Almighty God for the needful health and strength granted me for the past year's travel, but I do not feel so much energy for journeying as before, and may be unable to accomplish the same again."

He maintained that the great extent of the country, 3,000 miles long, rendered his own " superintendence of the missions rather superficial ; " but," he continued, " if the zeal and affection of friends at home would provide an additional Bishop for Peace River, then I think the whole diocese, as large as half Europe, might be viewed as an end worth an effort to accomplish. If the diocese remains undivided, my itinerancies will be inconsistent with domestic life, and I have asked Mrs. Bompas to revisit England next year. If relieved of the charge of the mission accounts, and of domestic

AN INDIAN ENCAMPMENT

From a photograph by Mr. J. M. Lowndes, Calgary

duties, I wish to surrender myself without reserve to the visitation of the mission-stations."

The Bishop did not think that he was sacrificing himself in giving up so much for the work's sake, for the compensation, he considered, was very great, as the following will show :

" This land of retirement and rest offers considerable attraction to a contemplative and sedate mind ; and if grace is given to heart and mind to ascend and dwell above, the turmoil of earth is so far removed that the rest of heaven may almost be begun below ; while our constant dependence on our heavenly Father's care and providence makes the life a good school for trust, and the scarcity of food impresses the truth that man shall not live on bread alone, nor his mind be fed alone by the giddiness of worldly gaieties, ' but by every word that proceedeth out of the mouth of the Lord shall man live.' "

The Bishop had now spent almost twenty years of strenuous life in the North, and one naturally asks what was the outcome of those years of uuceasing labour. Looking back to the year 1865, we find there were then three missionaries in the huge field : McDonald at Fort Yukon, Kirkby at Fort Simpson, and Bompas with a roving commission. There was only one church, that at Fort Simpson. The work of translation had but begun, and thousands of Indians were roaming over the land to whom the name of Christ had little or no meaning. At that time, the attempt to enlighten those children of the wild, seemed almost hopeless, and the difficulties well-nigh insuperable.

Look, now, at the work twenty years later, and see if any changes had been made. Eleven men were in the field upholding the standard of the Cross. Ten stations were occupied and six churches erected, several of which were finished and others partly completed. The Bishop himself thus tells of the progress made in translating the Indian language.

" A manual has been printed in seven dialects of the country, containing a summary of Christian instruction, which even the Roman Catholic Indians tell us is better than the priests' books. Gospels have been printed in Slave and Chipewyan. The Tukudh nation long since signalized the power of the Gospel by turning completely from heathenism to Christianity. Full translations have been made into this language."

These are the facts that can be ascertained to satisfy the world's calculation. But who can estimate the blessings which have flowed into so many lives during that score of years—the hearts made glad, the weary comforted, and the dying soothed by the tidings from on high, delivered by those noble messengers of peace ? These are the things which cannot be counted, and yet their price is above rubies and their influence eternal.

Too often people forget the great force of national importance exerted by a few missionaries scattered over a large extent of country. In the lone wilderness they are doing more than at times appears on the surface. In their efforts to save souls they are indirectly advancing the nation's interests. It has been well said : ' They have promoted civilization ; they have furthered geographical discovery ; they have opened doors of commerce ; they have done service to science ; they have corrected national and social evils ; they have sweetened family life."*

Bishop Galloway, in an address before the Student Volunteer Movement for Foreign Missions at Toronto, in 1902, said :

"The statue erected to David Livingstone in Edinburgh represents the great missionary standing on a lofty pedestal with the calm confidence of the conqueror, his eager eyes turned towards Africa, the Bible in one hand, while the other rests on an axe. These are the suggestive influences that all missionaries stand for—the world's redemption and civilization. They have made the echoes of the woodman's axe keep time with the story of the Gospel in opening up the regions beyond. They have opened hospitals and established orphanages, and founded schools and colleges, and introduced the great doctrines of personal and civil liberty. They have taught the tribes of earth all these great rudiments of life ; they have taught them how to use the plough and the plumb-line, and the saw and the hammer, and the compass and the trowel."

* Eugene Stock's " History of the Church Missionary Society."

CHAPTER XIV

BISHOP OF MACKENZIE RIVER DIOCESE

(1884-1891)

" In Truth for mail enfolden,
Virtue for corselet pure,
And Love for breastband golden,
The soldier shall endure."

BISHOP BOMPAS.

THE long-desired change at last took place, for while the Bishop was writing his letters by the camp-fires of the Indians a definite step was taken by the Provincial Synod of the province of Rupert's Land, and a new diocese was carved out of the southern part of the old. This included the Peace River district, and retained the name of Athabasca.

Here, then, were two dioceses—one the Mackenzie River, stretching from the 60th parallel of north latitude to the Arctic circle, and westward beyond the great mountains, bleak and desolate; the other nearer civilization, and only half as large, but with great prospects before it. Which would the veteran take ? The one that promised greater ease ? No ; that was never his plan. Leaving

226

AN INDIAN CAMP IN WINTER

MACKENZIE RIVER DIOCESE

Athabasca in charge of Bishop Young, who had been consecrated on October 18, 1884, for that special field, he set his face steadfastly towards the frozen North, as far as possible from the restraints of civilization. Great was the Bishop's satisfaction at the division thus made, for he would be able to accomplish more definite work, and carry on his beloved translations.

But just as soon as one care was removed, others came of a most distressing nature, from unexpected quarters. His appeals for men to man the vacant stations of the Tukudh Mission had not been in vain, and in 1881 the Rev. V. C. Sim, a man of great earnestness, came forward, and was placed among the Indians at Rampart House. Splendid work was done by this new recruit, who spared not himself in ministering to his dusky flock, for whom he gave his life. He was incessantly on the move on river and land, following the example of his Bishop. On one occasion he visited some Indians along a branch of the Porcupine River, and camped on the bank. The medicine-man pitched his tent near by, and proved most hostile. For three days Mr. Sim was busy baptizing the Indians who came to him. At night, tired out, he tried to sleep, but in vain, as the medicine-man made night hideous with his noise and the beating of a drum. The missionary became exhausted, and, having given away nearly all his food to needy Indians, was on the point of starvation when he returned to Rampart House in the fall. Even then he

229

could not rest, for he was kept busy during the fall and winter nursing sick Indians. When these recovered he was completely worn out, and his health gave way.

A messenger was sent to the Rev. T. H. Canham, on Peel River, 230 miles away, who hurried at once to Mr. Sim's assistance. For a time the latter seemed to rally, and longed for his letters, which were expected by the annual mail. Mr. Canham, with noble self-sacrifice, made the journey to Peel River, and upon his return, bringing the mail, he found a great change had taken place in the sick man's condition. So weak was he that he could not hear his letters read, and the fond messages from loved ones never reached his ears. Day by day he sank lower, and, lying there in that far-away station, dying at his post of duty, he repeated over and over again those beautiful words of Psalm xlvi. : " The Lord of Hosts is with us ; the God of Jacob is our refuge."

" On May 11, 1885," writes Mr. Canham, " his spirit passed to the presence of his Saviour, whom he had so faithfully served. He was laid to rest in the Indian graveyard—a quiet, secluded spot on the top of a high hill. A neat rail and head-board were made, and placed by an Indian around the grave."

And there in the wilderness fell the brave soldier in the great cause among the Indians whom he loved so dearly. Some time before his death he had made a touching appeal to the Church Missionary Society

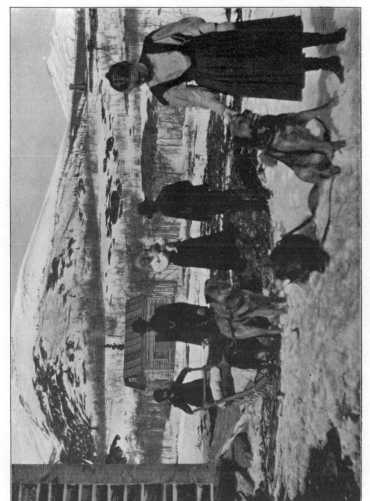

A Dog Team at a Mission Station

for assistance, which resulted in the sending of the Rev. G. C. Wallis to fill the post, who reached Rampart House, after much difficulty, in the fall of 1886.

The death of Mr. Sim was a severe blow to the Bishop, who at that time was doing the work of several men at Slave Lake. Though he wrote little about the sad event, the following extract from a letter sent to Mrs. Bompas shortly afterwards describes somewhat the state of his mind :

" The passing changes of the present shadowy existence are, we know, soon to give place to the noontide blaze of heavenly glory. Your own life and health, like that of myself and all, are precarious and uncertain, but we can do little more than remain in an attitude of penitence and supplication at the Saviour's feet, seeking to be sanctified to His will."

The year of Mr. Sim's death saw the outbreak of the great North-West Rebellion. This was an uprising of the half-breed element along the banks of the Saskatchewan River in 1885. It was brought about through several causes, such as the advance of civilization, the threatened famine due to the rapid disappearance of the buffalo, the " fear that their lands, of which they had received no patents or title-deeds, would be snatched away by speculators," and the dissatisfaction " with the Government's method of surveying the land, which interfered with the old French plan of having all the farms fronting upon the river."

Led by Louis Riel, himself a half-breed (the

leader of the Red River rebellion in 1869), and joined by the Cree Indians of Saskatchewan, they spread terror over the country, committing at the same time a number of unwarrantable murders. The North-West Mounted Police, of whom there were only 500 at hand, bravely held them in check until General Middleton, Commander-in-Chief of the Canadian Militia, arrived from Eastern Canada with a force of 4,400 men. After several sharp encounters at Fish Creek, Batoche, and Cut Knife Creek, the rebels were defeated and the rebellion brought to a close. Riel was found guilty of treason, and sentenced to death.

This rebellion had the effect of drawing the attention of people in Eastern Canada to the richness of the North-West, increasing the number of mounted police for the protection of settlers scattered throughout the country, and of obtaining a stronger Government.*

Though the disaffection did not extend to the Indians of the Mackenzie River Diocese, yet the mission-stations suffered severely, as some of the Hudson Bay Company's posts were in the disturbed districts, and at these places mission supplies had been stored, ready to be forwarded during the summer. These stores were broken into by the rebel Indians, and a large amount of the property stolen. Mrs. Bompas, writing of this, says:

* For a fuller account of this rebellion see " The Story of the Canadian People," by David M. Duncan, p. 368. Published by Morang and Co., Toronto.

A CREE WOMAN
Ah-e-squee-urt (Little Squaw).

MACKENZIE RIVER DIOCESE

" Think what the want of flour, tea, and sugar must be ; of warm clothing ; of fish-nets, and twine to make them ; of soap and candles ; of tobacco ; and, worst of all, of powder and shot, without which it is impossible for the Indian hunters to bring us our supplies of moose, deer, or wild goat's meat ! A number, too, of our charity bales are gone ; and, indeed, knowing as I do the treasures that these bales contain in warm clothing, and other kind and thoughtful gifts for our Indians, and often for the missionaries themselves, it does make one's heart ache to think of what the loss of them will be."

Not only did the rebellion cut off the mission supplies, but it was a sore hindrance to Mrs. Bompas, who was returning from England with recruits for the work in the far North. Several times they essayed to go forward, but in vain, and for a whole year were forced to remain in Winnipeg. This little band consisted of (besides Mrs. Bompas) Miss French, on her way to join her betrothed, the Rev. T. H. Canham, at Peel River ; Mr. and Mrs. Garton, lately married ; and Mr. J. W. Ellington, on his first and only journey to the North. At Winnipeg the sad news reached them of Mr. Sim's death, and of this Mrs. Bompas wrote to *The Net :*

" Mr. Sim, one of our most gallant workers in the far North—the most simple, earnest-minded man— has been honoured by the call to lay down his life in his Master's service. . . . One thinks of the little church he has helped to build, with no one to hold service there ; of the gathering of the

Indians next spring at the different places where he was wont to meet them ; but there is none now to teach and pray with them, to hold solemn service among them, and lead them in the hymns they love so well. There will be infants brought for holy baptism, and sick members to be doctored, but none to minister to them."

In August, 1886, the Bishop summoned his clergy to Fort Simpson to attend the first Synod of the Mackenzie River Diocese. He had more men at his disposal now than when he held his Synod ten years before. Daily services were conducted in three languages in St. David's Church, for Indians and whites. A proposal was made to found a diocesan Indian school, and the Rev. W. Spendlove was appointed to organize it. The latter was also made registrar of the diocese, and elected delegate to attend the Provincial Synod in Winnipeg in 1887. A motion for the division of the Mackenzie River Diocese was also made, and a petition sent to the Church Missionary Society for more men.

Some of the results of this meeting were : the formation of the new diocese of Selkirk (Yukon) in 1891, the Canadian Church brought into closer contact with this northern diocese, and the sending out of Mr. John Hawksley by the Church Missionary Society.

On Sunday, August 29, an ordination service was held by the Bishop, when two candidates, John W. Ellington and David N. Kirkby, were admitted to the diaconate. This ordination was of unusual

INDIANS RELIEVED WITH GIFTS OF CLOTHING AT A
MISSION STATION

A DOG TEAM. FIFTY DEGREES BELOW ZERO

interest, owing to the fact that these two men were sons of missionaries, were of the same age, and had attended school together for about eight years in England. They had separated for another period of eight years, and, without any previous planning, had met in the lonely North, to be ordained to the sacred ministry. Fort Simpson was the birthplace of one of the candidates, David Kirkby, and the church in which the ordination took place had been built twenty years before by his father, the Rev. W. W. Kirkby, that noble pioneer missionary who welcomed Mr. Bompas on Christmas Day, 1865.

The candidates were presented to the Bishop by the Rev. W. Spendlove, who also preached on that occasion. In the afternoon the Bishop gave an address on the duties of the Christian ministry.

At the time of the Synod there was a scarcity of food, the beginning of the great famine, and all were placed on short allowance. One day the dinner consisted of barley and a few potatoes, but it is said that the Bishop was equal to the occasion, justifying the scanty fare by repeating Proverbs xv. 17 : " Better is a dinner of herbs where love is, than a stalled ox and hatred therewith."

The winter that followed the meeting of the clergy was a terrible one. The famine increased. Game was scarce, few moose were to be obtained, the rabbits all died, and the fish nearly all left the river. The Indians asserted that the scarcity of the finny " prey " was caused by the propeller of the new steamer *Wrigley*, which first churned the head waters of the great river the preceding fall, but was unable to reach the northern posts owing to the ice—hence the lack of supplies. But any excuse would serve the Indians, as on a previous occasion when fish was scarce (so Mrs. Bompas tells us) the natives said it was due to the white women bathing in the river. Such a radical change as cleanliness was evidently as much disliked by the fish as by the Indians.

Through the weary days of famine sad reports reached the Bishop of Indians dying for lack of food.

"Forty starving Indians," so he wrote, "are said to have been eating each other on Peace River, and 200 dead there of measles, and a like number at Isle à la Crosse."

"We have been living for some days," says Mrs. Bompas, "on flour and barley soup, and potatoes twice a day. We are four in family, and William gives us all the giant's share, and takes so little himself. One hopes and prays for help. One hears terrible accounts of the Indians all about, all starving, no rabbits or anything for them to fall back upon. Here many of them hunt for rotten potatoes thrown away last. fall. Oh, it is truly heartrending!"

At length so serious became the trouble that the Bishop, to lessen the number at the fort, left for Fort Wrigley. Thus the winter and spring passed, and not until the steamer arrived with supplies did the famine cease. On this steamer

Mrs. Bompas left for England, and never again did she visit the Mackenzie River Diocese. The Indians and all missed her very much, and kept asking continually when she would return.

" I tell the Indians and every one else," wrote the Bishop to Mrs. Bompas, " that I have sent you home against your will. I told them yesterday that Christ died for them long ago, and that was enough. There was no occasion for you to die for them as well, however willing you might be."

In 1887 the Bishop was cheered by the arrival of Mr. John Hawksley from England, sent out by the Church Missionary Society. He was placed at first on the Liard River, where the Bishop had for some time wished to open up regular mission-work. He accompanied Mr. Hawksley to his new field of labour, and spent some time travelling and assisting the young recruit. As an example of the Bishop's love for the Indians, Mr. Hawksley relates that one cold night in September, while sleeping near a camp of Indians, the Bishop was much concerned over one poor old man who was suffering from a severe cough. In the night he arose quietly, and, taking his best and warmest blanket, placed it carefully over the coughing Indian, and then, returning, wrapped himself up in his one thin remaining blanket and slept till morning.

For some time the Bishop thought of going to Manitoba on a short visit, and pathetically he wrote: " My feet now refuse to perform their exercise, and it is perhaps time for me to cease to be a missionary. There is a text for everything, and the one in which I have been driven to find comfort in the past three weeks is, ' Neither delighteth He in any man's legs.' I am rather thinking to change my name and travel incog. when I come outside, to avoid being pestered by reporters and interviewers. Perhaps it would be a good plan to change the Bompas into ' Bon-point ' or ' Bon-rien.' "

Much of his time during his last years on the Mackenzie River was taken up with translation work and the writing of his books, an account of which is given in another chapter. Occasionally we catch glimpses of him on a special day, such as Christmas or his birthday, when presents were given and received. Sometimes the Hudson Bay Company's officers would present him with a " prettily worded paper of good wishes."

The arrival of the mail-packet was always a great event in the quiet life at the fort, when letters months old were received. They generally came twice a year, by boat in summer and by dog-team in winter, when the journey was made from post to post by some trusty courier. As a rule, the letters were much soiled and worn from frequent handling at the various posts, and at times the Bishop complained of the thinness of the envelopes, which was not conducive to secrecy.

An amusing incident happened on one occasion, when the courier was hurrying forward with the mail. In some manner he broke through the ice,

BRINGING THE MAIL IN A HARD WINTER

Provisions failed through the depth of snow, and all the dogs died except one, who was kept alive on a boiled moosehide. The Indians left part of the mail behind, hung up in a tree, and brought on only the larger packets, chiefly advertisements. The letters, which had been anxiously looked for since the summer, did not arrive until a month later. The last 250 miles of the journey took between two and three weeks. One of the Indians had his little boy in the sledge, and kept him in good condition.

and dogs, man, and letters were thoroughly soaked. It was a cold day, so, heading for the shore, the Indian made a good fire, dried his clothes, and then gazed sadly upon the wet letters. At length a thought occurred to him, and, taking the soiled epistles out of the envelopes he stacked them around the fire, near enough to dry, but not to burn. When this was completed to his satisfaction, he began to replace them. But, alas ! though well versed in woodland lore, he had never acquired the gentle art of reading, so that the letters were replaced helter-skelter. Into envelopes addressed to the Bishop went important missives meant only for the Company's officers, or the tender sighings of some fair maiden for a Northern lover, while the Bishop's letters were disposed of in a similar manner. Thinking he had accomplished a very clever feat, the courier pushed on his way, and, reaching the fort, was much astonished at the exclamations and excitement of all. Not until the whole matter was explained by the puzzled courier was its humorous side seen, and then a good laugh ensued.

From beyond the great mountains again came sad news, which gave the Bishop much concern. Before it came from Rampart House, on the Porcupine River; this time from the Yukon, where a new mission had been started. Owing to the touching and stirring appeal of poor Sim, Mr. T. Fowell Buxton, of Easneye, Ware, gave the sum of £100, and the Church Missionary Society sent out a young man, J. W. Ellington. He was stationed by the Bishop at the confluence of the Yukon and Forty Mile Rivers, after his ordination, already mentioned in this chapter; and for some time the place was known as " Buxton," but afterwards it took the name of Forty Mile, which had been familiar to the miners.

Here Mr. Ellington laboured earnestly and to the best of his ability, but his position was a hard one. The miners delighted in playing practical jokes of a most serious nature upon the young missionary, and made life so hard for him that mind and body completely gave way, and in this sad condition he was taken back to England.*

And once again the Indians were without a teacher along the Yukon. Most anxious was the Bishop concerning them, and he longed, as he said, " to steal away quietly to the Youcon," and proposed Archdeacon Reeve to succeed him on the Mackenzie River.

" I fear," he wrote in 1890, " to ask anyone to take my place in Mackenzie River these starving times, and I fear I may have to stay myself. But I write to the Church Missionary Society asking them again to accept my resignation, and send a successor, unless they can relieve me of half the

* Mr. Ellington died at Northampton on May 23, 1902. His father, who died in 1878, served eighteen years as a Church Missionary Society missionary in the Telugu country, South India. His mother, after her husband's death, became a missionary of the Church of England Zenana Missionary Society.

diocese. . . . I feel a presentiment that Archdeacon Reeve will at last come up next year and set me free, that I may go across the mountains or to heaven."

He had no inclination to leave the country, and when it was suggested that he should go to Manitoba he wrote : " I find the needle points west rather than east, and north rather than south."

When urged to return to England, he wrote : " To life in England and to my relations there I feel so long dead and buried that I cannot think a short visit home, as if from the grave, would be of much use. If over fifteen years ago when I was at home I felt like Samuel's ghost, how should I feel now ?"

On January 31, 1890, we find him at Fort Norman, living in the church, with a large stove, and eating more flour, so he tells us, than he had done for twenty-five years. To the loneliness of his position here the Bishop never once referred, but the following words of the Rev. W. Spendlove, ten years later, give a vivid picture of the place :

" We reside in the northern confines of British territory, on the Arctic slopes of this continent, not far from the Arctic circle and Great Bear Lake, amid wild mountainous scenery. Either the wild fury of the storm rages, or dead calm with intense cold prevails, interchanged with bright sun and cheery ice and snow landscape for eight months of the year. Ice-blocked and snow-bound, dense forest covers the banks of the Mackenzie River, and beyond a trackless desert of beautiful perfectly dry snow. Distance, 8,000 miles from England; upwards of 1,500 miles beyond the outer limit of Canadian frontier border of civilization; and our nearest missionary brother fifteen days' journey. Cut off from white people; shut up among Red Indian savages. Oh, what vast solitudes! What extreme loneliness! The effort to procure sufficient food and fuel for these regions is no easy task. Other conditions of life are most disadvantageous. Nothing in Nature to smile upon us for eight months. No sight or sound of civilization. No European Christian to mingle with, or fellow-worker to shake the hand, join in mutual sympathetic intercourse, and say, ' Go on, brother; I believe in you and your work.' "

Such is the grim picture given of that lonely Northern post; and how much more isolated it must have been ten years before! Yet we see the Bishop alone in the log church, deeply engaged in his beloved translations, and poring with delight over the Syriac Testament and Lexicon which Mrs. Bompas had sent out from England. Listen to these words of courage and trust penned in the midst of such dreary surroundings:

" It is only this winter that I find life worth living, and I think God has paid me handsomely for twenty-five years' mission service in Mackenzie River. I have found the winter days very short and dark, and have been cheered by a sense of

God's presence. 'When I sit in darkness, the Lord will be light unto me.'"

"During the past two weeks my mind has been entirely diverted from these inward cogitations to the outward world by a large arrival of letters and newspapers, after I had been utterly in the dark regarding the outer world for six months. It is as though a veil were suddenly drawn over the inward and spiritual world, and the veil as suddenly drawn back from the outward world that had been concealed from me."

Mrs. Bompas tells us that the Bishop was a very self-contained man. "During the years when he was itinerating among the Indians and Eskimos he had lived so much alone in tent or cabin that he had learnt to be wholly independent of external aid. Moreover, he had trained himself to endure hardness as a good soldier of the Cross. His diet was at all times abstemious, almost severely so. To the last he never allowed himself milk or cream in tea or coffee. He was a fairly good cook and bread-maker, and loved to produce a dish good and savoury for his friends, although eschewing all such dainties himself."

Truly his wants were few.

"An iron cup, plate, or knife," writes Mr. Spend-love, "with one or two kettles, form his culinary equipment. A hole in the snow, a corner of a boat, wigwam, or log hut, provided space, 6 feet by 2 feet, for sleeping accommodation. Imagine him seated on a box in a 12-foot room, without furniture, and there cooking, teaching, studying, early and late, always at work, never at ease, never known to take a holiday."

On August 5, 1891, we find him still at Fort Norman, and in a letter to Mrs. Bompas, who was in England, he wrote :

"I am now engaged in packing up, with the view, if God will, of shortly and finally leaving Mackenzie River for the far west. Mr. Hawksley was ordained to deacon's Orders here last Sunday."

And thus the Bishop's work on the Mackenzie River closed. Twenty-six years had he laboured faithfully among the natives of that land, and, instead of seeking rest, he resolutely set his face to new work, the account of which must be reserved for future chapters.

CHAPTER XV

BEYOND THE GREAT MOUNTAINS

(1891-1896)

" These are the tones to brace and cheer
The lonely watcher of the fold,
When nights are dark, and foemen near,
When visions fade and hearts grow cold."

KEBLE.

MEANWHILE changes were taking place beyond the mountains, along the great Yukon River, the Quikpak of the Russians. Gold had been discovered, and the reports of the Government surveyors were attracting miners to that region, and it became necessary that more complete episcopal supervision should be made. The Bishop, writing concerning the matter, said :

" The missionaries now labouring in the district referred to are very isolated, and much need the support of episcopal oversight, which it is hoped may be no longer denied them. From the Mackenzie River it appears impossible to superintend the district. A visit thither from the east side of the Rocky Mountains would involve a journey of 5,000 miles or more, and an absence of two years.

253

BEYOND THE GREAT MOUNTAINS

The Rocky Mountains form a natural barrier between
the Mackenzie River and the large country farther
west."

The result was that in 1890 the Provincial Synod
of the province of Rupert's Land sanctioned the
division of the Diocese of Mackenzie River. Archdeacon W. D. Reeve became Bishop of the eastern
portion, stretching to the Arctic Ocean on the
north and the Hudson Bay on the east, while
Bishop Bompas gave himself up to the work along
the Yukon River. Archdeacon Reeve was consecrated in Holy Trinity Church, Winnipeg, on
November 29. The Very Rev. Dean Grisdale,
in preaching from Acts i. 8, referring to the loneliness and burden of responsibility associated with
the new office, said :

'Of these burdens the noble - hearted Bishop
Bompas has had his full share ; yet now, for the
second time, he has resigned his diocese, that he
might go to the regions beyond."

Even after the division was made Bishop Bompas
had no small sphere of work before him. His new
diocese comprised 200,000 square miles—more
than twice the area of Great Britain, and the third
largest diocese in British America. It stretched
from the Diocese of Caledonia on the south to the
Arctic Ocean on the north, and was separated on
the west by the 141st meridian of west longitude
from the United States territory of Alaska. To
this new diocese the Bishop gave the name of
" Selkirk," and when some called the appropriate-

AN INDIAN VILLAGE IN ALASKA
Stereo copyright, Underwood and Underwood, London and New York

ness of the name into question,* he bravely defended it in the following paragraph :

" Sclkirk, I presume, may be shortened from ' Selig Kirke,' or ' Holy Church,' which does not seem offensive as the name of a diocese. Manitoba means, I suppose, ' Spirit Narrows,' and Athabasca, ' Plenty of Narrows,' and Saskatchewan, ' Strong Current,' and Moosonee, ' Moose Deer Walk,' and Qu'Appelle, ' Who Calls ?' And I hardly see why ' Selkirk' should be deemed an inferior name to these."

Before Alaska was purchased from Russia by the United States Government in 1867, Fort Yukon was the centre of missionary activity of the Church of England along the Yukon River. It was visited by Mr. Kirkby from Fort Simpson, on the Mackenzie River, in 1862, and in the same year the Rev. Robert McDonald was placed in charge. Great was the work done by this latter noble missionary during the eight years he was there. No better testimony can be produced of the influence he exerted upon the Indians for many miles around than that of Archdeacon Stuck, of the Protestant Episcopal Church of the United States, thirty-six years after. Travelling in the winter of 1906, he reached the Chandelar village, sixty miles from Fort Yukon, and, in an account of these Indians, writes :

" And here I found a most interesting thing— that as long as thirty years ago the older ones among these people had been under the instruction of the men of the English Church Missionary Society,

* The name of the district was changed to " Yukon " in 1907.

257

and were furnished with Prayer Books, Hymnals, and complete Bibles of Archdeacon McDonald's translation, carefully treasured, and that one of their number conducted regular service. They were still praying for ' Our Sovereign Lady, Queen Victoria, and Albert Edward, Prince of Wales,' and I suppose are still ; for though I took a lead pencil and struck out these prayers, and tried to explain that they were living under the Government of the United States, and that Queen Victoria was dead, I doubt if my remarks made much impression against what they had been taught by Archdeacon McDonald, whose memory they revere. And I cannot blame them much ; they owe us little enough—I was the first missionary of the American Church who had visited them."

Bishop Bompas, before his consecration, had paid two visits to Fort Yukon, and travelled up the river to where another stream, the Forty Mile, joins the Yukon, the site of the mission started in 1887 by poor Ellington. To this spot the Bishop turned his attention in 1891 as a suitable site for his abode. Crossing the Rocky Mountains, he spent the winter of 1891 and 1892 at the lonely Rampart House.

Writing on April 2 to his brother George from this place, he tells of his great happiness in Scripture studies: "The symmetry of the construction of Scripture,' he continues, " presents ever new wonders, and is similar to God's works in Nature, the pencillings of summer flowers, the plumage of the birds, the harmonies of music. Nor need this

surprise, for Christ tells us that His words will
abide when heaven and earth shall pass away.
Again, He says : 'The words that I speak to you I
speak not of Myself'—that is, they were dictated
by the Holy Spirit, the Author of all Scripture, and
were thus measured by the cadences of that heavenly
music which we may suppose to be the speech of
angels, and which resounds in a thousand echoes by
the transposition of its letters. Our words are re-
echoed from the rocks, not because the rocks have
a mouth, but because the air has been created with
such an elasticity as to reverberate the words spoken.
So the words of God in Scripture are capable of a
million turns, because the language in which they
are spoken was arranged from the first to admit of
its secreting God's messages of love and peace, and
afterwards restoring them. Now that men can
bottle up the human voice, and cause its words to
be repeated at a distant time and place, they need
not deny to God the skill they have themselves,
when they know they cannot make so much as a
feather or a blade of grass."

On July 2 the Bishop wrote from the same place
to his sister, and says : "The last few days I have
been pleased with the following points. First, by
finding that there seems to be no word for ' danger '
in Hebrew or Syriac. Secondly, being scandalized
by the omission of the words ' and of an honeycomb' from the Revised Version of Luke xxiv. 42.
I thought the best way was to try the experiment of
eating dried fish with syrup. I found it so delicious

that I strongly recommend it to you, and think it will fully convince you of the genuineness of the words. Thirdly, I have been profited by noticing the frequency of the command to 'wait,' which I am trying to fulfil just now. You are perhaps aware that the common expression in the Psalms, 'Wait on the Lord,' really means, 'Wait for the Lord.' . . .

"I have just been for a short walk in the woods, and find a few flowers in even this Arctic clime, such as a pretty wild - rose, lupin, and bluebell. There are also berry blossoms, and plenty of the white blossom of what we call 'marsh tea.' These blossoms really make rather pleasant and aromatic tea. The leaves, when used for the same purpose, are rather bitter. Raspberry shoots, birch buds, and some other berry-trees, are also at times used to make tea in the absence of the genuine article, but they are rather medicinal. The west side of the mountains is, on the whole, more flowery than the east side."

In the spring he went down the Porcupine River to the Yukon. It was here he met Mrs. Bompas, who was returning from England. They had not met since 1887, and Mrs. Bompas vividly describes this meeting. After speaking about the trip up the river from St. Michael's, she mentions the great excitement which ensued on July 26, when "two Indians came on board, bringing news of the Bishop, who is at the next village, 'Showman.' But a delay took place owing to the boiler being cleaned, and it

A WINTER SCENE IN THE NORTH-WEST
From a photograph by Mr. E. J. Hamacher, of Whitehorse, Y.T.

was not until midnight that 'two bells' sounded, a signal for the boat to stop. I pricked up my ears, and then another bell, which meant 'stop her.' It must be for wood, of course; but I sprang from my berth, and looked out of my small window to see a pretty Indian camp, and—my husband on the beach, grey and weather-beaten, but in health better than I had expected."

Accompanying Mrs. Bompas were the Rev. T. H. and Mrs. Canham, the Rev. G. C. and Mrs. Wallis, and Mr. B. Totty. After the Bishop had joined them a conference was held, when it was arranged that the Bishop and Mr. Totty should occupy Forty Mile, Mr. and Mrs. Canham Fort Selkirk, two hundred miles up-stream, while Mr. and Mrs. Wallis should go to Rampart House, on the Porcupine. Mr. Wallis, it will be remembered, succeeded Mr. Sim at this latter place, and, having returned to England after several years of earnest labour, was returning, bringing with him his bride to the lonely post. Mrs. Bompas, speaking of their landing at Fort Yukon, to ascend the Porcupine River, says:

" Here the Wallises left us, and their great cargo of 100 pieces was put on shore. Mrs. Wallis's tent was pitched, and I fixed a few flowers and a verse on her tent-pole to cheer her up, as she was a little down-hearted."

Anxious days followed the Bishop's arrival at Forty Mile. The miners kept coming into the country, and there was no man at hand to work among them. Then the white men exerted a baneful influence upon his Indians, demoralizing them through drink, and in many other unlawful ways. He had to contend with the same difficulties as other missionaries in like circumstances. It was Hans Egede, the great apostle to Greenland, who, in 1730, said that while able in perfect security to sleep in the tents of the natives, he had to keep a watch, and fire-arms by his bed, as a protection against his fellow-Christians. Bishop Bompas remarked, after several years' sad experience with the whites among his little flock, that " the advent of white population strengthens the call for missions to the natives. While they are in the minority in population, they are not so in Church attendance. At Dawson, with a population of 4,000 or 5,000, no weekday services can be maintained, while at Moosehide, Klondyke, with only 500 inhabitants, frequently fifty attend daily Evening Prayers."

But notwithstanding the anxiety, work went on apace. The Indian school made fair progress, and steadily were the natives brought into the fold. The winters were times of great loneliness, and often eight months passed without hearing from the outside world. The miners had the law in their own hands, and, with rare exceptions, kept good order. Occasionally a disturbance would take place which worried the missionaries much. In 1893 Mrs. Bompas wrote :

" A terrible quarrel reported among the white men on Sunday night, resulting in one being shot

MRS. BOMPAS
From a photograph by W. Notman and Son, Montreal

through both legs, and another stabbed in the
breast. Oh, for some police, or anyone to keep
order !"

"I hope for the arrival of some Government
control," wrote the Bishop, "but the miners have
themselves now checked the drinking among the
Indians by deciding that the next person who gives
a drink to an Indian shall receive notice to leave
the country in twenty-four hours. As the alternative to obeying the miners' laws is generally a
revolver or a noose on the nearest tree, they are
pretty well complied with, and they might possibly
do the same with a policeman if he interfered with
their own drinking."

As the miners continued to arrive, vice and crime
increased. The Bishop realized that, if life and
property were to be safe, strenuous steps must be
taken. It was, therefore, largely through his efforts
and representation to the Dominion Government
at Ottawa that the North-West Mounted Police
were sent into the country, and then law and order
prevailed.

In January, 1895, the Bishop gave a description
of Forty Mile : " A town is laid down at Forty Mile,
and they have two doctors, library, reading-room,
debating society, theatre, eating-houses, and plenty
of saloons, as public-houses are called in the West,
besides two stores, or shops, and a few tradesmen.
One debate was as to which has caused most misery
in the past century—war or whisky ? It was decided
to give the enviable preference to whisky. This

was truly appropriate to a mining camp. They had a feast on New Year's Day, of which every soul in the neighbourhood was invited to partake, both whites and Indians.

" We have just now about twenty miners who attend our Sunday afternoon English service, and afterwards we lend them some books to read ; but I have not a very good selection for them. They mostly ask for history of travel, and this I do not possess. I have some magazines, and they have taken the *Leisure Hour* more than any other book."

And yet for the Bishop and his devoted wife the miners had nothing but the profoundest respect. Though many of them were indifferent to all things spiritual, still, they could admire nobleness when they beheld it, as they did every day in the two faithful soldiers of the Cross in their midst. As a token of their esteem, on Christmas Day, 1892, a splendid nugget of gold was presented to Mrs. Bompas, with the following address, signed by fifty-three miners :

" It is proposed to make a Christmas present to Mrs. Bompas, the wife of the Rev. Bishop Bompas (for which purpose a collection will be taken up amongst those who are willing to contribute), and that the present shall be in the form of a Forty Mile nugget, as most appropriate to the occasion, as a mark of respect and esteem from the miners of Forty Mile, irrespective of creeds or religions, and, further, that it be distinctly understood to be a personal present to the first white lady who has wintered amongst us."

From time to time we catch brief glimpses of the life in the mission-house. Occasionally Mrs. Bompas lets in a little light, which is most interesting. We see the Bishop turning from the cares of the diocese to provide for some Indian child, or do necessary work around the house. She tells how the Bishop " has been busy carpentering and devising a number of things for our comfort—a beautiful cupboard to hold the girls' clothes, shelves and brackets, new bench for dining-room, bedsteads mended, a new door for our little dining-room, frames for double windows, new dining-table, and old one repaired. This, with his self-imposed duty of waiting upon every one, superintending the kitchen, and doctoring any sick members, has filled up his time the last few weeks. I feel thankful when for a short time in the evening he retires to his study and takes up his beloved Syriac."

But, alas for " the beautiful cupboard and shelves " which the Bishop had so carefully made ! Boards were very scarce, not enough even to make coffins in which to bury the dead, and the shelves had to be taken down to make a coffin for an Indian who had been brought in from the distant hunting-grounds. Mrs. Bompas, who relates this incident, tells most pathetically of the trials they had in connexion with burying the dead on the Mackenzie River. The Indians would beg packing-boxes from the Hudson Bay Company's officers, and as these were generally too small, arms and legs would often be seen hanging out of the box as it was lowered into the grave.

Whenever the Indians arrived from some hunting-grounds, the Bishop was kept busy almost night and day attending to their wants, and instructing them in the faith, if only for a few days. This teaching was by no means lost, for out on the hills and mountains the Indians had their daily services, when appointed leaders would instruct the others. Occasionally there would be turbulent spirits among these natives, but the Bishop was always able to control them. One day two Indians became engaged in a serious fight close by the mission. One, Roderick by name, was determined to kill the other, and was making desperate thrusts with a long, sharp knife. The Bishop, observing the encounter, made for the contestants, and, taking Roderick by the collar, quietly said, " Come." But the Indian still fought and slashed with his knife, the Bishop all the time retaining his hold and saying, " Come, come with me." After much effort he succeeded in separating them, and, half leading, half dragging, drew Roderick to the mission-house. Then the Indian, completely exhausted, sank upon a large stone near by. Ere long he began to realize how he had been saved from committing murder, and, reaching out his hand, seized that of the Bishop to thank him for what he had done.

As the miners continued to arrive, the Bishop became much worried over the change that took place among his Indians, and sadly he wrote :

" Nothing could be of a greater contrast than the squalid poverty and want of all things in which the Indians here lived thirty years ago, and the lavish luxury and extravagance with which they now squander hundreds of dollars on needless food and dress, if not in a still more questionable manner. The Indians now place such high prices on any meat or fuel, or other things which they supply to the whites, such as leather or shoes, that it is hard for your missionaries to live with economy among them, and the worst of all is that the younger Indians are only too apt to imitate the careless whites in irreligion and debauchery."

Each spring was a season of anxiety to the Bishop and his household. The mission-house was on an island, and when the ice of the great Yukon was going out there was often great danger. As the mighty blocks of ice moved by, and then jammed and piled high, the water would rise and flood the building. Several times they were awakened in the night to find the water rushing through the house, and were forced to climb aloft till the waters subsided. Through these dangers they were mercifully delivered by Him who had preserved them so often before.

In 1893 the Rev. G. C. Wallis was compelled to return to England, owing to the ill-health of his wife, and this necessitated a change in the missionaries who remained. Archdeacon and Mrs. Canham accordingly went to Rampart House ; the Rev. B. Totty, who had been admitted to Priest's Orders on July 15, 1894, and who had spent the winter of 1893 at Rampart House, was sent to Fort Selkirk, while the Bishop and Mrs. Bompas remained at Forty Mile.

Thus the Bishop was left with only two men, and the outlook appeared very discouraging. But just at the right moment there arrived on the scene a young man who was destined to be of great service in the pioneer work of the diocese. This was Mr. R. J. Bowen, who had been in the preparatory institution of the Church Missionary Society at Clapham for a short time, and who volunteered to go to Bishop Bompas as an industrial agent. This was in 1895, and not long after new conditions arose in the diocese, which taxed the minds and energy of the mission-workers to the utmost.

CHAPTER XVI

THE FLOOD

(1896-1900)

" Thy hand, O God, has guided
Thy flock from age to age ;
The wondrous tale is written
Full clear on every page."

THE year 1896 marked a new era in mission-work
in the Diocese of Selkirk. Up to this time the
Bishop had been groping his way with a small force
at his command. Often he became much discouraged, though pressing bravely forward. But
upon the arrival of Mr. Bowen in 1895, the Rev.
H. A. Naylor and his wife and Mr. F. F. Flewelling
in 1896, sent out from Eastern Canada by the
Canadian Church Missionary Society, prospects
appeared much brighter.

Not only was the Bishop cheered by the addition
to his staff, but the arrival of the Right Rev. Peter
Rowe, the new Bishop of Alaska, filled him with
thankfulness. His joy, however, was somewhat
marred when he learned that the sister Church of
the United States had made no provision for the
spiritual care of the Indians in the northern diocese.

THE FLOOD

The great work of the Church Missionary Society among the Indians of Alaska, along the Yukon River, adjoining British territory, cannot be too strongly emphasized. From 1862, when the Rev. W. W. Kirkby crossed the Rocky Mountains and visited Fort Yukon, this post was held by the Rev. Robert McDonald till 1869, and a splendid work was carried on among the Indians for miles along the great river. When the United States Government purchased the territory of Alaska from Russia, the Indians had been left shepherdless but for the noble exertions of men of the Church of England, such as the Rev. V. C. Sim, the Rev. T. H. (afterwards Archdeacon) Canham, the Rev. R. J. Bowen in 1896, and the Rev. John Hawksley, who was stationed at Fort Yukon in 1897, having been transferred from the Mackenzie River Diocese. Bishop Rowe, upon his arrival, at once realized the condition of affairs, and sought to make an improvement. He was the right man in the right place. To him the Church was one, and national boundaries formed no bar when souls were at stake. He asked Bishop Bompas to care for his Indians till he could take over the charge himself. This he did a few years later, and now has an earnest band of men working among the natives.

Bishop Bompas, in 1893, had himself visited along the Yukon River to its mouth, holding services and baptizing a number of Indians. During the summer of 1896, in company with Archdeacon Canham, who was then on his way to England, he spent six

An Indian Village, with Totem Poles

weeks at Fort Yukon. Concerning this visit among the Indians, the Bishop wrote :

" It was a pleasure to me to hold a daily afternoon class of middle-aged men, at which several chapters of the New Testament were daily read by them, with intelligence and interest, in their own tongue, by way of exercise and at their own request. For the first two weeks I was mostly engaged in schooling from 8 a.m. to 8 p.m. Afterwards I was partly relieved by the arrival of the schoolmistress from Rampart House."

Little did the Bishop realize while at Fort Yukon that an event was taking place in his diocese which in less than a year would change the whole aspect of mission-work.

About fifty miles up stream from Forty Mile the Klondyke River joins the Yukon. From time immemorial this had been a favourite Indian fishing resort, and on various occasions missionaries had gone up from Forty Mile and held services for the natives. Little did they think, when pitching their tents at the confluence of these two streams, what a change would take place there in a few years.

In July, 1896, George W. Carmack, with several Indian associates, made the famous gold discovery, news of which soon travelled abroad and thrilled the world with intense excitement. At the very time this information was speeding far and wide the Bishop was calmly writing :

" There are about 500 miners now in this neighbourhood, and some few have gone out this summer with fortunes in gold-dust. The chief mining attraction just now is on the American side of the border, about 200 miles farther down the Yukon River at Circle City, where there are said to be nearly 1,000 miners."

This was in August, and with the opening of navigation the human flood arrived. The story of that great rush of 1897 and 1898 has scarcely a parallel in history. The Klondyke, a stream which a few years before geographers did not think worthy of notice, became a household word the world over. The Yukon River literally teemed with boats and rafts of every conceivable shape. Men poured in thousands over the frowning Chilkoot and White Pass summits, enduring untold hardships and dangers. Merchants left their stores, clerks their desks, farmers their ploughs, woodmen their axes, carefully nourished sons their homes of luxury, and rushed for the gleaming treasure. The city of Dawson sprang like magic into existence, and in the space of a few short months the Bishop found the civilized world thrust upon him.

In the following extracts from letters to his brother George in England we catch brief glimpses of those stirring days:

"BUXTON MISSION,
"UPPER YUKON RIVER,
"*April* 15, 1897.

"I think I will put on paper for you a few notes about the sudden change that is taking place in the course of a striking Providence in this region.

THE FLOOD

From being a poor, desolate, and neglected country, it is suddenly becoming a rich and populous one. This is the effect of the new and very valuable gold-mines discovered last year, about fifty miles south of us, at a place now called Klondyke, and Dawson City. These new mines are said to be as rich as any yet known for their size, which is at present very limited. Only about one hundred claims are yet found that are very profitable. . . .

" At the new mines last autumn any claim could be bought for a few hundred dollars. Now we hear that some have already changed hands for 50,000 dollars, and some are estimated to be worth 500,000 dollars. The owners of the richest claims are said to be leaving the country in spring, having already as much gold as they can carry, and being as rich as they care to be, and they will sell their claims at a high price to others.

"The miners of Circle City, about 300 miles below us, have been coming up all winter hauling their sleds of provisions, to the number of about 500, till the Yukon has become like a thronged thoroughfare. They have paid, I think, as much as 250 dollars for an Indian dog to help haul their sleds.

" Flour and meal have both been selling during the winter at from half a dollar to one dollar per pound, and the Indians here loan out their dogs at one dollar per day. The Indians, too, get some-what rich, but, of course, they squander their money.

THE FLOOD

"The temperature has been most singular. The winter set in very early, being severe in October, and partly so in November. Then three months, December, January, and February, were so mild that it was not like winter at all. This seems quite a providential favour to the numerous travellers.

"For myself, during the past winter I have enjoyed more ease and leisure than usual, from having more helpers around me, and I have devoted my days to digging the mines of God's holy Word, and have found, in my own estimation, richer prizes than the nuggets of Klondyke."

May 28, 1897.—"I hear now that the creeks are so winding as to make the gold streak extend 200 or 300 miles. I am told £4,000 was washed from the earth of one claim in one day. Another bought a claim for £10,000, and paid it all off out of the ground in two or three months. The richest claims are thought to be worth £100,000 to £200,000. (A claim is 600 feet of the creek, which each miner is allowed to pick for himself at the start.) . . . From one to two dollars per pan is reported to be a common rate there. This is something like taking your washing-basin, filling it with earth from your garden, and then, after washing away the earth with a little water, finding a silver crown or half a sovereign at the bottom. I suppose in such a case you might go again, and so do the miners. They next proceed to work with sluice-boxes, which is only a similar process on a larger scale. The earth is thrown into wooden boxes or troughs with a corrugated or uneven bottom, so as to retain the gold when the earth is washed out.

"An Irishman who was here yesterday is said to do his work so badly that his wife used to make from four to twenty dollars a day by picking up his leavings. She is now gone on a visit home with her earnings."

This new responsibility was a severe trial to the veteran of the North. So long had he laboured among the Indians that, as he sadly acknowledged, he was entirely unfitted for work among the whites. But, as has always been the case in the world's history, just when the need was greatest God raised up a man for the work. This was the Rev. R. J. Bowen, the young Clapham student, who had volunteered for service, and was ordained by Bishop Bompas. We see in his case the working of the Divine hand. Mr. Bowen at first intended to labour among the Indians, and, in fact, did make several visits to their various camps, with encouraging results. But, finding that the Colonial and Continental Church Society had made a grant for a mission to the miners, and being asked by the Bishop to take up this special work, he did so, and thus became the first missionary among the miners in the diocese. For a time the work consisted chiefly in visiting the creeks where the miners were scattered, and their cabins when in town, holding services when possible, and in every way endeavouring to win them to Christ. During the spring of 1896 he began to hold services at Forty Mile,

" in the first mission building that was wholly devoted to the spiritual welfare of the miners." Thus, when thousands of men poured into the country, the Bishop had a man tested in pioneer work to send among them.

At once Mr. Bowen started up the river to plant the standard of Christ in that excited camp of gold-seekers. It must have seemed a forlorn hope to the young missionary as he drew near the new town. Almost two years before he had visited that place, and on the very site where his camp had then been pitched large buildings were now erected, and a hurrying crowd thronged the streets. The great cry was gold ; for that the people had come, and not for religion. Yet among them Mr. Bowen began to work, and through his earnestness won the hearts of the miners, and induced many of them to attend service.

These men were not miners in the ordinary sense of the word. Many had never handled a pick or shovel, but had been reared in ease in comfortable homes, sons of noble families, who had joined the mad rush to win a fortune in a short time. Such men were not slow to see the efforts the Mother Church was making for their spiritual welfare in the great north land. They saw the earnest missionary valiantly standing in their midst, pleading the Master's cause. Their hearts were touched, and around him they rallied.

A church building was the next important consideration, and towards this the miners gave what they could in labour and money. But even a modest log edifice meant much in those days. Wages were $15 a day, and lumber 25 cents a foot. Then the Bishop cast about for some plan to help on the work. In 1896 he had applied to that noble handmaid of the Church, the Society for Promoting Christian Knowledge, for money towards the building of a church for the miners at Forty Mile. A grant of £250 was therefore made according to the rules of the Society. But when the sudden change took place, and the miners left Forty Mile and flocked to the new city of Dawson, the Bishop in 1897 wrote an urgent letter to the Society for Promoting Christian Knowledge, asking permission " to remove the site of the proposed church from Forty Mile Creek to Klondyke Creek, where a greater need for it now exists. The stay of the miners at the rich Klondyke mines," he continued, " is likely to be permanent for ten years at least, and in case the whites should leave, there has always been a band of Indians at Klondyke, for whom the church would be available."

The society accordingly acceded to the Bishop's request, and the money was transferred to the erection of the new church at Dawson. This building, composed of logs, was ere long erected under the name of St. Paul's, and a few years later was replaced by a large frame structure of imposing appearance.

Two great societies of the Church had mission agents at work in the diocese : the Church Missionary Society for the Indians, and the Colonial and Continental Church Society for the whites, while the Society for Promoting Christian Knowledge aided in erecting churches and providing scholarships for the Indian schools. In 1892 the Society for the Propagation of the Gospel was appealed to by the Bishop for a man to labour among the miners, as the Church Missionary Society considered this beyond its scope. It was not, however, till the opening of the Klondyke goldfields that an offer came to the Society for the Propagation of the Gospel from the Rev. G. W. Lyon for this special work. The Society at once made a grant of £200 for the purpose, and Mr. Lyon was sent out. He climbed the rugged Chilkoot Pass, and ministered to the people stationed at Lake Bennett, and upon the opening of navigation in 1898 started down to Dawson with a servant, Montegazza by name. While crossing Lake Laberge, both Mr. Lyon and his servant were drowned. Their bodies were recovered by the North-West Mounted Police, and buried on the shore of the lake.

Considering the fact that other societies were already in the field, the Society for the Propagation of the Gospel did not renew its offer. But at Lake Bennett, Tagish, and Caribou Crossing, for convenience, the work for a time was under the superintendence of Bishop Ridley, of the Diocese of Caledonia. When Bishop Bompas took charge of these two latter places the Society for the Propagation of the Gospel withdrew from the field entirely.

THE FLOOD

When the Church work was well under way at Dawson, the Bishop for a while relieved Mr. Bowen, who returned to Forty Mile, and was united in marriage to Miss Mellet, who had been labouring in the diocese for some time as schoolmistress. At Dawson the Bishop was out of his element. So long had he laboured among the Indians that work among the whites was very hard. In his letters of that time he draws a pathetic picture of the condition of affairs : the dwindling of the congregations, and the frank acknowledgment of his own inability to do much among the miners. " But Christ reigns," he wrote, " and the work is His, not mine, and let us trust and hope."

This worry, together with improper food, brought on a severe attack of scurvy, and when he went back to Forty Mile in April he was in a very weak condition. Yet, notwithstanding his illness, he persisted in conducting the Indian school and attending to his correspondence.

" I cannot move," he wrote, " without losing my breath, nor walk a few steps without great pain. If I can hold on till I obtain green vegetables, they may benefit me."

After a time " green vegetables " reached him from Dawson, and at once an improvement took place. To these the Bishop declared his recovery was almost entirely due.

Mrs. Bompas, during this trying season, was at Fort Yukon, unable to reach the Bishop. She had been summoned to England, to the bedside of her sister, who was dangerously ill. On her return to San Francisco, after a few months' absence, she found that wild excitement reigned, owing to the Klondyke gold discovery.

"The whole of the great city," so she writes, "was gathered on the wharf to witness the departure of the first steamer for Klondyke. On the boat itself the crowd was no less conspicuous. Men and women seemed locked together in frantic excitement. Shouts and cries were heard on all sides. Parting gifts were thrown on board, hats and handkerchiefs waved with enthusiasm, and in a few instances with wild sobs of pain. Then the anchor was raised, and the vessel started for St. Michael. Such a motley crowd is not often seen gathered together in one vessel. The Company did its best to accommodate all, but the attempt was but partially successful. Seven men were often the occupiers of one state-room, and the chief number of passengers were of the roughest kind of miners. On reaching St. Michael, the same number of passengers were moved on to the smaller steamer. Here our discomforts were considerably increased."

After a tedious voyage up the river, Fort Yukon was reached. It was a memorable day on which they arrived at this place.

"The miners," continues Mrs. Bompas, "were looking eagerly forward to the gold-mines of the Klondyke, when the whole load of passengers were set ashore, and the captain announced that he was not going a step farther. Prayers, entreaties, and remonstrances were unavailing. He gave no excuse for his conduct but that he was going back immediately to St. Michael—it was supposed to lay in a cargo of whisky."

And at Fort Yukon Mrs. Bompas was stranded for eight long months, thirty miles within the Arctic circle. Fortunately, the Rev. John Hawkesly and family were stationed here, who did what they could for her comfort. But to the Bishop at Forty Mile, in feeble health, disturbing news arrived of the riotous times among the miners at Fort Yukon, and their desperate efforts to overpower the American soldiers. Such information caused him much anxiety, and most thankful was he when at length the ice ran out of the river, and Mrs. Bompas was able to continue on her way after the long delay.

The following summer the Bishop turned his attention to the southern part of his diocese. Word had reached him of stirring towns on Lake Bennett and Lake Atlin. Thinking them to be in his jurisdiction, he made the long and difficult journey up stream to view the land. Reaching Bennett during the summer of 1899, he was astonished to see a flourishing city containing thousands of people. But greater still was his surprise to find that Bennett and Atlin were in British Columbia, and that he had gone several miles beyond his diocese. His stay was very brief at Bennett, and on his return trip down the river he spent two days among the Indians at Tagish, gaining much information concerning these natives and their language. One week later Bishop Ridley arrived at Bennett, and, writing of the visit of the Bishop of Selkirk, he says:

"Dr. Bompas has the full tide of civilization forced upon him to his sorrow. . . . A week before my arrival he stood where I now write. Would that he had waited the few days, that I might have had the honour of welcoming him to my diocese. He thought Bennett and Atlin were within his, and therefore ventured so far. Arriving here, he found that he had trespassed beyond his jurisdiction no less than fourteen miles. The newspaper man who reported an interview with him states that he hurried northwards and buried himself once more in the frozen north, that no other man loves but for the sake of its gold. This report, copied into an American paper, added striking glosses to the account. What would the dear Bishop think if he saw himself described as the most devoted of Catholic (meaning Roman Catholic) Bishops in the wide world? This gloss was evidently by a Roman newsman, who covertly hit at the snug and comfortable lives of Protestants who assumed episcopal authority. Bishop Bompas, says the paper, was so modest that he would not talk of the countless hairbreadth escapes from awful peril and death, treating them as phases of everyday life not to be counted worthy of notice."

The following winter Bishop Bompas remained at the Indian village of Moosehide, and, amidst school labours and diocesan cares, formed plans for important extension of the mission-work.

CHAPTER XVII

"FAINT YET PURSUING"

(1901-1906)

" Plain patient work fulfilled that length of life."
ARTHUR HUGH CLOUGH.

WHEN on a visit to one of his mission-stations during his later years, the Bishop was asked to write a few lines in an autograph album. He at once complied with the request, and wrote the words, which he felt applied to him as they did to Gideon and his 300, " Faint yet pursuing."

Years of strenuous work were telling upon his gigantic constitution, and he began to realize that ere long he must lay down the staff of office. For some time he had his attention turned towards the southern portion of the diocese, to the Indians who were gathered at Caribou Crossing, which had become quite an important railway centre. In August, 1901, he and Mrs. Bompas bade farewell to all at Forty Mile, and started on their journey up the river. Whitehorse was only in its infancy, and the Rev. R. J. and Mrs. Bowen had just returned from England to take charge of the Church work. In

289

the little tent they received the venerable couple, and did all in their power to minister to their comfort. The accommodation at Caribou Crossing was most meagre. A tent which belonged to Bishop Ridley gave them shelter for a few hours, when, hearing of a bunk-house across the river, they at once rented it, and afterwards purchased it for 150 dollars. It was dirty and uncomfortable, but the Bishop placed a rug and blanket on the big table for Mrs. Bompas to rest on, while he went to explore. The house was infested with gophers, which ran along the rafters, causing great annoyance. But notwithstanding the toil of the day, Evening Prayer was held in Bishop Ridley's tent. Here services were conducted till the fall, when the weather grew so cold that Mrs. Bompas's fingers became numb as she played at the little harmonium, which she had brought with her. After that services, morning and evening, were held at the mission-house, "which," as Mrs. Bompas tells us, "had been used as a road-house and post-office, and possessed one good-sized room, over the door of which there still exists the ominous word 'Bar-room' (now hidden behind a picture); and in this room we had to gather, Indians and white people, for Sunday and weekday services, for baptisms, marriages, and funerals, for school-children and adult classes, etc."

In 1903 Bishop Ridley, of Caledonia, paid a visit to Caribou Crossing on his way to Atlin. His description of the episcopal residence and the life

290

THE BISHOP AND MRS. BOMPAS AND AN INDIAN GIRL
AT THE BISHOP'S HOUSE, CARCROSS

of the venerable occupants is most interesting, and a few extracts must be given here.

"There on the platform stands the straight and venerable hero of the North, Dr. Bompas, the Bishop of Selkirk. I jumped from the train, and, though I had never met him before, I grasped his hand and exclaimed: 'At last! at last!' We knew each other well by letter only. He was as placid as the mountains and the lakes they embosom."

Then a glimpse is permitted of the "Bishop's house, built of logs, on the sand. The flooring-boards were half an inch apart; so shrunken were they that it would be easy to rip them up and lay them down close together. Then the roof: it was papered, with battens across the paper. I was anxious to see inside less of the light of heaven through the rents. Ventilation is carried to excess. Everything around is as simple as indifference to creature comforts can make it, excepting the books, which are numerous, up to date, and as choice as any two excellent scholars could wish.

"The question that has often sprung from my heart has been this: if this poor £30 affair is by comparison delightful, what of the contrivances that have sheltered them in the past forty years?

"Never in my life did I value hospitality so much, or feel so honoured, as here under the roof of these grand apostles of God. Two septuagenarians of grace and broad culture, whose years have been spent nobly in God's eyes, have deliberately chosen an austere type of service, not for austerity's sake, but for Christ's sake, under circumstances the average citizen of the Empire would feel to be past endurance. They are as happy as heroic. She, accomplished far beyond the standard one meets with in London drawing-rooms, unless among the most cultured circles ; he, a fine scholar, steeped in Hebrew and Syrian lore, as well as in the commoner studies of the clergy, live on, love on, labour on in this vast expanse, little trodden but by the Indians for whom they live and will die.

" If such lives fail in Christ's cause, that cause is doomed. Let those who criticize cease their cackling, and try to imitate by self-sacrifice such lives as those I have just touched on, and they, too, may have some share in the betterment of mankind, the expansion of Christ's kingdom, and the eternal welfare of humanity."

Bishop Bompas notes in one of his reports that Caribou Crossing " forms the centre of a hitherto unoccupied area, and forges, perhaps, one of the last links of the chain of the Church Missionary Society stations which girdle the world."

Anxious days followed the Bishop's removal to this place. Clergy were scarce in the diocese, and when Mr. Bowen left Whitehorse earnest appeals were sent " outside " for men. Then it was, upon the Bishop's earnest request, that the Rev. I. O. Stringer arrived in November, 1903, to take up the work laid down by Mr. Bowen. Much pleased was

the Bishop to have Mr. Stringer so near, and at
once marked him as his successor.

Then followed the death of his old friend Archbishop Machray, and as senior Bishop of the
province of Rupert's Land he was summoned to
Winnipeg. A message reached him from Mr. John
Machray, nephew of the late Primate, telling him
of the Archbishop's death, with the addition : " As
senior Bishop it is important that you should attend
a conference of Bishops in Winnipeg to select a
successor."

Though the Bishop shrank much from leaving
the north to mingle with the bustling world, yet,
after a few minutes' thought, he sent back the
following answer:

" I will try to be with you by Easter."

And on Easter Eve, April, 1904, with Mrs.
Bompas, and Susie, a little deaf-and-dumb girl,* he
was met by several of the clergy at Winnipeg, and
was present at St. John's Cathedral on Easter Day,
though only as one of the congregation, being too
much overcome by the crowd and bustle of the city
to take any active part in the service.

On the following Sunday he was able to preach
in St. John's Cathedral. "His sermon," so Mrs.
Bompas tells us, " was in his usual earnest and unembellished style, referring to the last time he had
officiated in that church, nearly thirty years before,

* This girl was placed in the Deaf and Dumb Institution
at Winnipeg. She died on February 26, 1907, of tuberculosis, aged ten years.

alluding with pathos to the many who had left the busy whirl of life during that period, and expressing his great pleasure that, among the many changes that were taking place in the Church, the services of St. John's Cathedral still retained something of their old, almost austere, simplicity."

Many and varied must have been the thoughts which surged through the Bishop's mind during his visit to Winnipeg. He was on historic ground, made sacred by the names of noble men who had toiled so hard for the Master's cause. There was John West, the pioneer missionary of the Church of England in the country; Archdeacon Cockran, the " sturdy Northumbrian from Chillingham," who did such a great work for the Indians and half-breeds; Archdeacon Cowley, of undaunted courage and determination, able " either to build a stone wall or to go through one " as occasion required ; and the noble Dr. Anderson, first Bishop of Rupert's Land, " whose heartiness and practical good sense were conspicuously manifest for sixteen years in the forests and over the snowfields of Rupert's Land."

But there was one figure which the veteran from the North most sadly missed, and whose absence was the cause of his visit to Winnipeg. It was his firm friend and adviser of long years, the venerable Archbishop Machray. He saw him for the last time in 1874, standing on the Red River bank, near St. John's College, waving his hand in adieu to him and Mrs. Bompas as they proceeded northward.

They had been set apart the same year in England

for work in the Canadian North-West, and while one
bravely upheld the standard of the Lord in the far
North, and ministered to scattered bands of Indians
and a few white people, the other laid the strong
foundation and planned for the welfare of the
Church over the vast diocese. No more fitting
tribute could be given to this great Bishop than that
made by the Ven. Archdeacon Ker, in St. George's
Church, Montreal, March 13, 1904, a portion of
which must be included here :

" As the great Hebrew captain (Joshua) was permitted to see the twelve tribes of Israel encamped
around him in peace, according to their lots, so in
like manner the Archbishop of Rupert's Land was
permitted to see the Israel of God encamped and
entrenched around in their dioceses, Saskatchewan
and Moosonee, Mackenzie River and Athabasca,
Qu'Appelle and Selkirk, Keewatin and Calgary—
each diocese according to its boundaries. . . . He
lived to see all this—to see towns and cities spring
up magic-like while he gazed; to see his college
grow into a university, and the clergy of his diocese
increase by scores and scores ; to see the Church of
England in Canada united in one bond of faith and
love, working with one heart and one mind for the
universal extension of the kingdom of God. All
this he witnessed ; and long years before, when he
stood the lonely missionary at Fort Garry, his
master mind saw and saluted the coming glory.
And when at last the silence of the desert was
broken by the tramp of the hosts carried thither in

search of new homes and new hopes, the Archbishop
was ready, and, so far as he could prepare her, the
Church of England was ready to deal with the
manifold difficulties presented by the new conditions.

" The memory of such a life, such an example,
is the splendid heritage of the Canadian Church.
It is many-sided, and suggests many thoughts
worthy of consideration. The dignity of personal
self-sacrifice for Jesus Christ's sake ; the dignity
of the lonely watcher, who in the kingdom and
patience of Jesus Christ waits for the dawn ; the
dignity of the labourer in the Master's vineyard
who toils at his task, whatever or wherever it may
be, in blazing summer and frosty winter, all through
life's weary day, only ceasing his labours when
the sun has gone down in the west for the last
time, when the sight has gone for ever from the
eyes, when the hands are folded in death, and the
great soul has been summoned to its kindred in the
Paradise of God."*

The Bishop's time was fully occupied during his
stay in Winnipeg. There were old friends calling
upon him, reporters seeking interviews, meetings to
attend, and addresses to deliver, which wearied him
very much. His voice was feeble, and could not be
distinctly heard at the gatherings where he told of
his northern diocese. But what did that matter ?
The people thought rather of the man—the man of
whom they had heard such wonderful things—and
cheered him heartily.

* *The New Era*, May, 1904.

"FAINT YET PURSUING"

The Archbishop of Rupert's Land, in an address at the 107th Anniversary of the Church Missionary Society, at Exeter Hall, London, April, 1907, thus referred to the visit of Bishop Bompas to Winnipeg:

"Dr. Bompas, that splendid veteran missionary, who came down at the time of my election—he was as humble as a little child—when he stood on the platform at a great missionary meeting, and when I, introducing him, spoke of the hardships he had gone through, corrected me thus when he started to speak. He said : 'It is you men at the centre, with your telephones and your telegrams, who have the hardships. We have a soft time in the north. Nobody ever worries us.' That is all that he said about his hardships. Then he told the story of his work in a simple childlike way."

But the city life did not agree with him. He longed for his northern flock, and the quietness of his little log house at Caribou Crossing. A doctor was consulted, who strongly advised him not to return to his diocese for some time. Before this the Bishop was uncertain when he would return ; but after the doctor's verdict had been given he hesitated no longer, but fixed a date for his departure. Only three weeks did he stay in Winnipeg, and then started northward. Acts of kindness were showered upon him on every hand. All delighted to honour the noble missionary in their midst. As he stood on the platform before leaving Winnipeg, an unknown friend, knowing that the Bishop would not afford himself the luxury of a good

berth, slipped into his hand a ticket for one in the
Pullman car.

When once again in his own diocese, the longing
grew stronger for rest, and he became impatient
for the time when his successor would be appointed.
Then, the delay in the election of the new Archbishop gave him much concern. He felt it was
his duty to go once more to Winnipeg to hasten
matters, and many were the letters written and
received before everything was finally arranged.
His annual trip down the river to visit the various
mission-stations became more and more of a burden,
and he wished to stay quietly in one place to carry
on his desired work.

And that desired work filled him with gladness.
" The daily round, the common task," was all that
he asked for. Praise might go to others, he wished
for none for himself. The Indian school occupied
much of his time, and part of each morning was
given up to it. The building over the river, which
at first had been used for the school, was exchanged
for the log police-barracks, quite close to the
mission-house. It was an interesting sight to
observe the venerable, grey-haired teacher among
a number of stirring young Indian pupils. Gladly
did he leave his beloved translations to be awhile
the teacher.

> " Freely the sage, though wrapped in musings high,
>   Assumed the teacher's part."

Though the Bishop used to say that to teach
Indians was a very difficult task, " like writing in
300

THE MISSION SCHOOL AT CARCROSS

the sand, instead of graving in the rock," yet he never gave up, but went bravely on till the last.

A portion of his time was devoted to letter-writing and translation work. He was always an early riser, and his letters were written in the early morning in the quietness of his study. Letter-writing he seemed to love, and seldom did he pen less than six or seven missives a day. It was in this manner he could express himself most freely, and sometimes, when wishing to convey a message to a member of his household, he would do so by letter, at times leaving it at the post-office to be delivered later in the day.

Rarely did he miss meeting the train on its arrival at the settlement, that he might be at hand to receive his mail as soon as possible. His tall, erect figure, with the leather travelling-bag slung across his shoulder, walking up and down the platform, was a most familiar sight. Strangers would gaze with curiosity upon the veteran of the North, of whom they had heard so much, and often snapshots were taken, to be reproduced in books, magazines, or newspaper articles. This latter the Bishop bore with good-natured tolerance, considering it a necessary evil, and one of the discomforts of modern civilization. He told one of his clergy—him who now wields the episcopal staff—who was busy taking a number of pictures of the Bishop and his Indian school, that he did not wish to see *him* go, but he would like to see the *camera* make a hasty departure.

For some time the Bishop wished to change the

Q 2

name of Caribou Crossing, as his letters often went to
other places of a similar name, and thus caused much
delay and confusion. After careful consideration,
he chose the name of " Carcross." Many objected
to the change, and strongly worded articles were
written in the local paper condemning the " mongrel
name of Carcross." The Bishop remained silent,
replying to none of these attacks. At length a
letter appeared, addressed to the Bishop, from the
Secretary of the Geographic Board of Canada,
stating that at a meeting of the Board " the name
' Carcross' was approved instead of ' Caribou ' or
' Caribou Crossing.' " The Bishop smiled, but said
nothing. Since then the new name has steadily
won its way.

Notwithstanding the school work and study,
ample time was found for other duties which devolved upon him. There were Indians calling at
most unseasonable hours for assistance in some per-
plexing question. The advice thus freely given
was often interpreted in most unexpected ways.
On one occasion he had a long talk with an Indian
who had taken a young woman as his second wife,
having wearied of the first. The Bishop told him
it was wrong to have two wives, and that he should
only have one. The Indian seemed much surprised with these words, and promised to obey ;
but, to the astonishment of all, he put away his
old, faithful wife and kept the younger.

Once at a wedding of two Indians the Bishop
repeated very carefully the words, " for better, for

worse, for richer, for poorer, in sickness and in health," etc., and told the groom to repeat them after him. The Indian was much puzzled. He could not repeat the words, neither could he understand their meaning, and looked vacantly around. After a time a light illumined his face, and, turning to his passive, dusky bride, he said :

" Me sick, you take care me ; you sick, me take care you—eh ?"

The building of the new church at Carcross was a great comfort to the Bishop. Services had been held in the mission-house, which was much too small to accommodate all who attended. The cost of building was met almost entirely by kind friends outside the diocese. In 1904 Mrs. Bompas visited Eastern Canada, and addressed the Women's Auxiliary at Montreal, Toronto, Ottawa, and Quebec on mission-work in the North. Great was her surprise when, at the Annual Meeting of this noble handmaid of the Church, at the cathedral in Toronto, she was presented with the generous gift of $800 towards the church building fund for St. Saviour's, Carcross. Other gifts came steadily in, and the success of the church was complete.

In the erection of this little building the Bishop was most active, not only superintending the work, but doing much manual labour himself. It was a happy day when at last it was opened for service. It was consecrated on August 8, 1904, after Mrs. Bompas's return to the diocese.

The services were of a very simple nature, for

the Bishop seemed to have an almost complete dis-
regard for external things. Seldom did he wear his
episcopal robes, not even when visiting the different
mission-stations in his diocese, being content to use
the long white surplice, with the black stole, and
without his Doctor's hood. This was a cause of worry
to Mrs. Bompas, who rejoiced to see all things done
" decently and in order." Once on the Mackenzie
River, when starting to hold a Confirmation service
some distance away, he was urged by Mrs. Bompas to
take his episcopal robes. He refused to do so, saying
that the surplice was sufficient. On that trip his boat
was swamped, and everything was lost, and only with
difficulty were he and his companions saved.

Though caring little for the outward observances
of worship, he had a jealous regard for his episcopal
office, as an extract from a letter to one of his
clergy will show :

" As the Epiphany appeals were sent direct to
the clergy this year and not to me, I have not yet
notified you on the subject. I think the Mission
Board rather wrongs the episcopal office, and makes
the other Bishops also interlopers in all the dioceses.
Any request to the clergy ought to come from their
own Bishop only. No Bishop has any other
authority than over his own see, and any request
from the Mission Board should come through their
own Bishop to the clergy.

" However, we need not quarrel with them, as it
is well meant, and they are not likely to put my
name to any future letters or addresses without my

BISHOP BOMPAS

seeing them. It is a good address, and I read it last night.

"I think the modern idea must be that in ecclesiastical matters all irregularities, however grave, and of whatever kind, are quite reasonable and proper."

Great was the Bishop's pleasure when a message arrived summoning Mr. Stringer to Winnipeg for consecration. Anxiously he awaited his return to take over the work. For some time his heart had been set upon going to Little Salmon, on the Yukon River, to start a mission among the Indians at that place, and he discussed plans with the enthusiasm of youth. This idea filled him with happiness, and the following words, penned on December 29, 1905, express the state of his feelings:

"We are fast approaching the close of the year, and I am very thankful to find it ending so tranquilly, with such fair prospects for the future. Things have assumed a much brighter prospect for myself since Christmas."

During the month of January the cold was so intense and the storms so severe that the trains were unable to run. The Bishop became impatient at the delay. He longed to hear when Bishop Stringer would leave for the North, that he might be free once again to go down the river to work among his dusky flock.

"It has been dull times for us this week," he wrote, "without trains."

But at length his successor arrived, and with great eagerness he handed over the charge of the diocese.

CHAPTER XVIII

LIGHT AT EVENTIDE

(1906)

" God's finger touched him and he slept."
TENNYSON.

In a famous picture an old warrior, scarred in many
a fierce battle, is seen hanging up his sword ; his
work ended, he could afford to rest.   But not so
with Bishop Bompas, the faithful soldier of the
Cross.   No thought of ease entered his mind, but
only more work for the Master.   As St. Paul of
old handed on his commission to St. Timothy, so
did this veteran apostle of a later day pass on the
torch to a younger son in the faith, that he might
be free for other work.   Then came the end, the
last scene in the life of this noble man.

Far away in dear old England, 7,000 miles from
a quiet grave in the great Canadian north land, the
following account of those last days has been
beautifully written as a loving tribute by her, the
faithful wife, who for long years bore with the
devoted Bishop the burden and heat of the day :

" The storms on Lake Bennett, on the shores of

Carcross, with the Bishop's House, St. Saviour's Church, and the Mission School

which Carcross is situated, are at times pretty severe. The winds blow in gusts down the steep mountain gullies, and toss into fury the waters of the lake. The depth of that lake between Carcross and Bennett is very great. It has often been sounded and no bottom reached. Many a hastily run-up scow, full of brave, enterprising miners, has been wrecked on these waters, and many a nameless grave in the white man's territory marks the resting-place of some poor fellow who was strong to venture, but had not learnt to realize the many dangers and vicissitudes of a miner's life. But the lake has its periods of calm no less than those of turmoil and unrest. Mark it on some evening of summer, when scarcely a ripple stirs its surface. The reflection of the mountains on the water is so clear and vivid that one is tempted to doubt which is the reality and which is the shadow.

" Such a calm, such a change from turmoil into peace, marked the evening of the life we have been considering. We believe that God's servants have been given a premonition of the approach of death. The Bishop had laid his plans some months ahead, and made necessary preparations for a winter down the river. He had always been remarkable for physical strength and energy. For his winter travelling he was always seen running, with the jaunty pace of the northern tripper, ahead of his sledge. He was ever ready to help the men hauling up a boat at some of the portages, or in pushing it down the bank into the river. Among our party it was always the Bishop who insisted on charging himself with the heaviest articles, and it was only within the last two years that he abstained from hauling water from the lake for the whole of our household. But symptoms of some diminution of strength and vigour in this strong man were beginning to show themselves. The eyes that had pored so long with imperfect light over the pages of Hebrew and Syriac, in which he so delighted, were failing, and had to be strengthened by glasses stronger and yet stronger still. Since his last attack of scurvy he had lost all sense of smell or taste. No one could be with the Bishop many hours without observing an expression of weariness and dejection in his countenance, which was as intense as it was pathetic. He was often heard whispering, ' Courage, courage.' To more than one of his friends he had given his impression that he had not long to live. To his brother he wrote just a year before his death : ' For myself, I am most thankful to be in this happy retirement. When the time comes, I hope for as tranquil an earthly ending as that of our brother George, though perhaps mine may be more sudden, and possibly not even in my bed.'

" The Bishop's burden of responsibility had of late years been greatly increased by the advent of the white men. The population of the diocese had increased sevenfold and at rapid strides. The problem of providing for the spiritual needs of these people, and especially of keeping the Indians

CHURCH BELL AT CONRAD WHICH FORMERLY HUNG ON
THE HOUSE OF BISHOP BOMPAS

HAULING SUPPLIES TO CONRAD. THE BISHOP HELPED TO
LOAD THE SLEDGE

from the allurements of the whisky traffic and the
snares of the gambling-table, was weighing heavily
upon him. But the darkest hour is the hour before
the dawn ; the labourer's task was nearly accomplished. The Rev. I. O. Stringer had been
nominated by the Bishop and approved by the
Church Missionary Society and the Canadian Board
of Missions as successor to Bishop Bompas in the
See of Selkirk (Yukon). He was a good man and an
earnest Churchman, and had had some years' experience of mission-work among the Indians of Peel
River and the Esquimaux of Herschel Island, at the
mouth of the Mackenzie. Mr. Stringer was consecrated Bishop in St. John's Cathedral, Winnipeg,
December 17, 1905, and his arrival in Selkirk
Diocese was ardently looked for. With him was
expected the Rev. A. E. O'Meara, of Toronto, to
be placed in charge of the newly started mission at
Conrad, twelve miles from Carcross, the centre of
a new mining camp.

"And so, with the mission staff a little better
equipped, with the work of the diocese passing
into younger and less toilworn hands, our Bishop
could now turn his thoughts to his own plans for
the coming months. The Church Missionary
Society had suggested to him a retiring pension, but
this he declined to accept, unless he continued in
some department of the work of the mission. His
great desire now, and one which had for a long
time past occupied his thoughts, was to start a new
mission on Little Salmon River, where there are

often congregated together 200 Indians who have seldom come within sound of the Gospel. But Bishop Stringer and others dissuaded him from the new venture, thinking that the work of starting a new mission, with the prospect of having to build a house and get in supplies for the coming winter, was one for which neither the Bishop himself nor his wife, at their advanced age, were fitted. Accepting this disappointment as God's will, Bishop Bompas prepared to go down the river to Forty Mile, below Dawson. Now was there bustle and unrest on the mission premises at Carcross preparatory to the departure.

" A passage for the Bishop and Mrs. Bompas and two Indian girls had been secured on one of the river steamers to sail on Monday. This was Saturday, June 9, a day calm and bright as our summer days in the far North mostly are. The Bishop was as active as ever on that day. Twice he had walked across the long railway-bridge, and his quick elastic step had been commented on as that of a young man. Later he had been up to the school, and on to the Indian camp to visit some sick Indians. Then he went home, and remained for some time in conversation with Bishop Stringer, into whose hands he had already committed all the affairs of the diocese. Then the mission-party dined together, and at eight o'clock they all reassembled for prayers. After prayers the Bishop retired to his study and shut the door.

" Was there, we wonder, any intimation of the

FUNERAL OF ELLEN, DAUGHTER OF THE CHIEF OF THE FORTY MILE INDIANS

The last funeral at which Bishop Bompas officiated.

coming rest in the breast of that stalwart warrior, whose end of life was now so near as to be reckoned, not by hours, but by minutes only ? Was there any consciousness of having fought a good fight, and finished his course ? We know not. Sitting on a box, as was his custom, he began the sermon which proved to be his last. Presently the pen stopped : the hand that so often had guided it was to do so no more. Near him was one of his flock, an Indian girl, who needed some attention, and as he arose he leaned his elbow on a pile of boxes. And while standing there the great call came ; the hand of God touched him, and the body which had endured so much fell forward. When Bishop Stringer reached his side a few minutes later, the Indian girl was holding his head in her lap. Nothing could be done, and without a struggle, without one word of farewell, the brave soul passed forth to a higher life.

" And so the tale is told, the chapter ended, of that life begun seventy-two years since. A suffering, quiet, uneventful life, and yet, we hope, not all unfruitful of God's glory, and of souls won for the fold of the Good Shepherd. Most aptly do the words of the poet apply to him :

" ' O good grey head which all men knew,
O voice from which their omens all men drew,
O iron nerve to true occasion true,
O fallen at length that tower of strength
Which stood four-square to all the winds that blew.
Such was he whom we deplore.
The long self-sacrifice of life is o'er.'

LIGHT AT EVENTIDE

" The awe and silence which overspread the camp and school and mission that night and the following day were very striking. By the morning of Sunday, tidings of the Bishop's death had been flashed to Ottawa and London and all down the river. On Tuesday morning notices of the Bishop's life and work were in many American and Canadian newspapers, with his portrait.

" The funeral had to be on Monday, June 11, the Festival of St. Barnabas (the Son of Consolation). Messages came from the Indians down the river, as well as from friends elsewhere, expressing deepest sympathy with Mrs. Bompas in the terrible shock she had sustained. The Indians heard with extreme satisfaction that their friend and Bishop had once expressed a wish to be buried among them. Two of them came and offered to dig his grave, adding, ' You no pay me.' In the Indian cemetery, therefore, beautifully situated less than a mile from Carcross, was the grave made ready. The mountains, clad with their dark pine-woods, looked down grave and solemn on the Indians' burial-ground. There were not many graves, but they were well and carefully kept and tended, for they were all friends who lay there, and we knew the life and history of each one. Below the cemetery were the waters of the lake, in summer ever studded with swift canoes or white man's row-boats, or the steamer *Gleamer* and smaller vessels. But on this day there was no movement on the lake. All vessels had their flags

The body of Bishop Bompas taken in a Boat from the Church to the Graveyard

half-mast high, and deferred their sailing that their captains and men might attend the funeral. It took place at five o'clock. On account of the distance, only two of the Bishop's clergy were able to take part in the solemn service, Mr. O'Meara, of Conrad, and Mr. Cody, of Whitehorse.

" The little church of St. Saviour's was now filled with all the white population of Carcross and all the Indians who had come to do honour to the great man who had fallen in their midst. The two hymns chosen from the Hymnal Companion were most appropriate—one, 'For all the Saints,' telling of the triumph of the saints of God after earth's hard fight ; the other, ' Jesus lives,' breathing forth the blessed hope of victory over the grave and a glorious resurrection. The service was conducted by Bishop Stringer, assisted by the two clergymen, and then the dear Bishop's body was lifted into a boat waiting at the foot of the bank, and rowed by two natives over water as smooth as glass to the cemetery. Three white men and three Indians carried the body from the shore to the grave, and, after the beautiful service had been read, the children of the Indian mission-school came one by one and dropped into the grave their little offerings of wild flowers, which had been gathered for the occasion.

" There is a humble grave in one of the loveliest and most secluded spots in the Yukon territory. Dark pine-forests guard that grave. During the winter months pure untrodden snow covers it. It is enclosed by a rough fence made of fir-wood, which an Indian woodman cut down and trimmed, leaving the bark on, and then fixed strong and stable around the grave. But none will disturb that spot, no foot of man or beast will dishonour it ; the sweet notes of the Canadian robin and the merry chirp of the snow-bird are almost the only sounds which break the silence of that sacred place. The Indians love that grave ; the mission children visit it at times with soft steps and hushed voices to lay some cross of wild flowers or evergreen upon it. There is a grey granite headstone with the words, 'In the peace of Christ,' and the name and age of him who rests beneath. It is the grave of Bishop Bompas."

" On the night of the Bishop's death," says Bishop Stringer, " one group of Indians after another came to the Bishop's house, with sorrow depicted on each face as they asked at first if the sad news were true, and then other questions, showing their deep concern. In the morning they came one by one to look for the last time on the face of him who was always their friend. Never more could he listen patiently to all their troubles—never again would he get up from the midst of his work and tramp off half a mile to their camps to see a sick person, and give all the relief possible in medicine, food, and clothing, and, above all, advice in their many adversities and, oftentimes, complicated troubles.

" The day after the funeral an Indian and his wife arrived on foot from Skagway. As Mrs. Bompas went out to shake hands with them as old

The Grave of Bishop Bompas at Carcross

friends, she said, 'Bishop has gone.' The woman looked interested, thinking she meant he had gone to visit some of the other missions. Mrs. Bompas tried to explain. 'Bishop dead three days,' she said. Then the truth seemed to dawn on the Indian woman, and she repeated, with rising inflection, 'Bishop dead? Bishop dead? Bishop dead?' at the same time giving vent to such a wail as I scarcely ever heard from a human being. I then realized more than ever how much the loss of our dear Bishop meant to his own people, the Indians."

All men had a profound respect for Bishop Bompas, especially the hardy prospectors. They had endured so much on the lonely trails that they looked upon him as one of themselves, who had not spent his life in ease and luxury, but struggling with Nature at her sternest. In speaking of the late Bishop, a prospector at Carcross said:

"I feel as if I had lost my best friend. Sometimes some of us were hard up, no funds and no food; but we always felt we could turn to the Bishop for help. We knew that to knock at his door and ask him if there was any odd job we could do meant always, and especially if the Bishop knew we were hard up, that he would find something for us to do—now some wood to get, or, again, some stove-pipe to fix, or a few nails to drive for Mrs. Bompas, or some other work that would give him the opportunity to pay us sufficient to keep soul and body together."

Bishop Stringer, who records this conversation,

also mentions that on the Mackenzie River he once met a miner who had been in Dawson in the early days. " When asked if he knew Bishop Bompas, he said he thought he had not seen him. When he was described as a pioneer in the land, he suddenly exclaimed, ' Oh yes ; that's the man who wrote the book. I have often seen him and spoken to him. Many of us have read his book. The miners know him as " the man who wrote the book." ' He referred to the ' History of the Mackenzie River Diocese,' which contains much matter of interest to the miner about the North."

The letters received by Mrs. Bompas were full of the sincerest sympathy. Some were from the men of the " Old Brigade," who had stood shoulder to shoulder with the Bishop in his great fight against the powers of darkness. Beautiful as well as pathetic are the words of the Venerable Archdeacon McDonald, from Winnipeg :

" He was a man dear to me, and I thank God for the abundant grace that was bestowed upon him, enabling him to labour patiently and persistently among the natives, for whose sake he became a missionary. I cannot forget that it was to replace me he first came to the North, when, as it was thought, my earthly course was nearly run, and I would have to lay down the Banner of the Cross. Nobly has he borne the standard; he has fought the fight of faith, he has finished his course, and has gone to receive, with the Apostle Paul and all who love the appearing of our sweet Saviour Christ, the

THE BISHOP'S HOUSE AT CARCROSS

crown of righteousness which shall be bestowed upon them. . . . Thus another landmark has gone. Bishop Bompas achieved a great reputation for devotedness and saintliness and the most heroic courage. Like our great Pattern, he constantly went about doing good. He counted not his life dear unto him, but exposed it many times in his great Master's cause. He has left a splendid record and example for all Bishops and clergy. You and the Bishop have done a magnificent work in that northern region—a work that has blessed not only the Indians, but, in an indirect way, the entire Church of God."

Dr. Matheson, Archbishop of Rupert's Land, wrote :

"On my arrival from England yesterday I was met with the sad news of the death of my very dear friend. I am deeply pained, as he was a lifelong friend, and I loved him. He was so loyal and true to his friends. How we ought to thank God for giving to the Church such a man as Bishop Bompas! Even without his great work, the very example is such an inspiration. Humble, unselfish, devoted, great in simple-mindedness—these are the words which seem to come to one when thinking of our departed brother. . . . Accept my heartfelt sympathy. With frail body, yet dauntless spirit, you have shared in all the trials of that great missionary hero's life, and now you are alone, and yet not alone. Oh no. God does seem to come so near to us at these times."

LIGHT AT EVENTIDE

From Alaska, Bishop Rowe sent the following
message :

" The passing away of your good husband was to
him a euthanasia, a translation into the rest and joy
of Paradise, for which his heroic life and work had
ever pointed and aimed. To him the translation
from warfare into peace, from the sight that is dim
into the perfect light and presence of the King in His
beauty, is a joy beyond all other joys. . . . The world
has lost one of the greatest missionary heroes of the
age, and his beautiful life of service and unselfish
labours will long continue as an inspiration and
blessing to many who, through the dear Lord, have
looked to your husband, and seen in him an
exemplar of the faith such as, God helping them,
they fain would be."

One more letter must be given of the many
testimonies sent, and this is from the Rev. A. J.
Doull, of Westmount, Montreal.

" You have this comfort, that not only has the
noble Bishop passed to the rest and joy of Paradise,
but that he has left behind a name and an example
that cannot and will not be forgotten so long as the
Canadian Church remains in our land, and her
history is read by those who come after us. God
never leaves Himself without witnesses, and it is a
great encouragement and help to feel that an age so
prone to worldliness and indifference has also been
the age which has produced Bishop Bompas, a man
truly Apostolic in self-denying work, fervent zeal,
and devoted consecrated love. The Church in

LIGHT AT EVENTIDE

Canada has a tremendous work to do, and she needs the brightest examples that can be put before her sons and daughters to inspire them to go in and possess the good land. Truly may we bless God that such an example has been provided at this crisis in her history, the example of the first Bishop of Selkirk."

CHAPTER XIX

THE STUDENT

"The best of thoughts which he hath known
For lack of listeners are not said."
                                    JEAN INGELOW.

SOME there are who assert that missionary work in
the far North is detrimental to all study, owing to
the unsettled life and the want of kindred spirits.
But Bishop Bompas believed just the reverse, and
contended that in the quietness of the great wilds
a person, freed from the bustle of the city, could
pursue his studies undisturbed.

To the travelling missionary life the Bishop
added that of an indefatigable student of no mean
ability. An old manuscript note-book which belonged to him gives food for much thought. It is
rude and worn, showing most plainly hard usage
when brought forth by some Indian camp-fire that
he might write down the new words he had
acquired during the day. The cover is only a thin
piece of oil-cloth, and how often it has shed the
rain or snow from the pages beneath ! As St. Paul
carried about "the parchments" from place to

336

place, so did this faithful apostle of a later day carry with him his rude note-book.

As soon as Mr. Bompas reached Fort Simpson, on that Christmas Day, 1865, he began the study of the Indian language spoken thereabouts, jotting down words here and there, and, according to Mr. Kirkby's testimony, by summer he had made such progress as to be able to converse quite fluently with the natives.

There were several dialects in the region over which he travelled, and to learn these in a short time is proof of no ordinary linguistic ability. Yet we find that between 1870 and 1880 he put forth four Indian primers in as many dialects—the Slavi, Beaver, Dog-Rib, and Tukudh—which were printed by Gilbert and Rivington, of London, and a portion of the Prayer Book (syllabic), in Chipewyan, in conjunction with the Rev. W. W. Kirkby, which was published by the Society for Promoting Christian Knowledge. Then followed a long list of publications showing steady work. In 1880 came forth a " Manual of Devotion, Hymns, Prayers, Catechism, etc.," in Beaver, and in 1882 " Portions of the Prayer Book, adapted to the Slavi," prepared in co-operation with the Rev. W. W. Kirkby, and published by the same society ; in 1883 " The Gospels in Slavi," published by the British and Foreign Bible Society, and a vocabulary in manuscript ; in 1886 and 1890-1891, with Bishop Reeve, " The Four Gospels, and Acts to Revelation " (syllabic), published by the Bible Society. Besides these, the

Bishop produced the Epistles and Revelation, Acts of the Apostles, a hymnal, the New Testament, and Prayer Book, all in Slavi. Though some of these have been revised, yet they show the labour performed by this missionary as he travelled from place to place, studying by camp-fires in mid-winter, and in canoes on the great northern streams in summer, contending with the myriads of insects which surrounded him.

But while working at the Indian languages the Bishop was patiently observing everything which came under his notice, and collecting a fund of information concerning the country in general and the customs of the natives. This work was carried on quietly and steadily, and when occasion arose the treasure was stored up ready for immediate use. Whether he intended at first to use his data for publication is not known, but the proverb that necessity is the mother of invention proved true in his case.

Money was needed for the diocese, and he was urged to make an effort to raise funds. To go to England for the purpose was most repugnant to him, on account of the publicity to which he would be exposed, and he mentioned time and time again that this was one of the reasons why he did not wish to leave his field of labour. Then the thought occurred to him that he might " raise money by publishing some account of the country." Even this idea caused him much doubt, for he said : " It is hardly likely that I could write in a style acceptable to a fastidious public, after my long isolation, though I think to try the experiment, which I hope may be a harmless one."

And " try the experiment " he did, with the result that in October, 1888 the Society for Promoting Christian Knowledge brought forth his " Diocese of Mackenzie River." This book of 108 pages, containing ten chapters, shows careful observation, and is written in a pleasing style, though one longs for more information concerning the mission-work in the diocese than that contained in one chapter. The book treats of the early explorers, and the work of the Church of England ; the inhabitants, their language, dress, and habits ; geography, meteorology, fauna, and flora ; and closes with a chapter on resources and prospects. Though the book was reviewed in over twenty leading English papers and magazines, for the most part favourably, the sale was not large. By permission of the Society much use has been made of it in this Memoir.

This work was followed in 1892 by " Northern Lights on the Bible," published by J. Nisbet and Co., London, which will be referred to at length in another chapter.

But the Bishop's steadiest and most thoughtful work was the study of the Bible. He maintained that " Scripture studies may be the easiest and most profitable to pursue in the North, as the Bible is oftener close at hand than any other book. It is right also that the far North, as well as every other land, should contribute its quota towards the elucidation of the Sacred Volume."

Here was a man far from refined society, and yet through the pages of Scripture he lived and communed with Kings, Princes, Apostles, and Martyrs ; and what greater society could he have ? Truth was what the Bishop thirsted for, and the more he studied, the greater became his desire for further knowledge. Greek gave him a thirst for the study of Hebrew, and through these he probed deep into the sacred mine. But still he was not satisfied. He longed for something more, and not until he began the study of Syriac did he reach the haven of his desire. In this new field he revelled, and lost a taste for lighter reading. He wrote enthusiastically to Mrs. Bompas in England :

" I shall bless the day you were born, for two things you have done for me. You sent me my first pair of spectacles when I was getting blind, and so imparted new strength to my bodily eyes ; and you sent me the Syriac Testament with Lexicon, and so have let the light of heaven into my darkening mind. I find the Syriac text leads me nearer to God than all the commentaries I have ever read."

The more he studied, the greater were the wonders he discovered, and, writing again to Mrs. Bompas, he said : " It is now almost 400 years since the *Nina*, with Columbus on board, brought to listening Europe the tale of the discovery of a new world in the far West, and it may in God's

providence be reserved for you to tell the tale of
the discovery of a new world of wonders in God's
Holy Word, which will, I think, prove the delightful
study of God's people for a thousand years to come,
and perhaps for a thousand generations. As you
sent me the Syriac Testament, which was the seed,
you ought first to partake of the fruits. . . . If
spared to next winter I may (D.V.) be sending
home some matter to be printed."*

" I once told you," he wrote on another occasion,
" that the name of your natal saint, Matthias,
means 'Faith,' and so it has been explained in
Hebrew; but in Syriac it appears to mean 'Advent,'
or arrival. This is, doubtless, the better explanation, of which I was ignorant till I saw the Syriac
Testament you sent me, and therefore I misled you.

" I trust that the wonderful things now coming to
light in His Word may be taken to harbinger our
Lord's approach and the extension of His kingdom.
I trust, also, the pleasure I have been having in these
studies may be taken as harbinger for me of the
joys of heaven, which I feel must follow them
speedily, if ever at all."

There is something grand in the thought of this
man, away in the great North in some rude log
building, or by a camp-fire, with hardly the bare
necessities of life, perfectly indifferent to his surroundings, rejoicing in the Sacred Volume, and
discovering so many wonderful things therein.

* Mrs. Bompas's name is Selina, shortened by her relatives
to " Nina," which fact gives point to the Bishop's illustration.

THE STUDENT

In 1896 James Pott and Company, of New York, brought forth " The Symmetry of Scripture," a volume of 350 pages. The book contains " Passages of Scripture with Notes," and portions of Scripture systematically arranged from the Old and New Testaments and the Prayer Book. Though most of the work is taken up with translations and re-arrangement of texts, yet in the first few pages the Bishop sets forth his discoveries, which gave him such pleasure during the long Northern nights.

Few realized the extent of the Bishop's Biblical labours till after his death, when an old wooden box filled with a mass of manuscripts revealed the secret. It seemed almost irreverent to disturb the collection, and the sight of those old, worn papers tempted the imagination to stray far afield. And what did the old box contain ? First, a complete translation of the New Testament from the Syriac, the whole of Genesis, portions of the Psalms, Proverbs, and the Apocrypha, besides a second translation of all the Epistles and Revelation, and much of the Gospels and Acts.

On the left-hand side of each page is the Syriac in English characters, with the translation opposite. This latter is rendered in most literal English without note or comment. The following will serve as examples :

ST. MATT. i. 1-4.

" A book of history of the Sovereign Saviour,
Son of Darling, Son of Choice-crowd.
To Choice-crowd was born Smiling,
To Smiling was born Heel.

342

" To Heel were born Confessor
And his brothers.   To Confessor were born
Outburst and Sunrise from Palm-tree.
To Outburst was born Fold,

" To Fold was born Height,
To Height was born Bounty,
To Bounty was born Divining,
To Divining was born Peaceful."

St. Matt. ii. 1-2.

" And while the Saviour was born
In Bread-home of Confessor's land,
In the days of Hero the King,
Came Astrologers from the East

" To Peacesite, and were saying, ' Where
Is the King of the Confessors, who was born ?
For we saw His Star in the East,
And we come to bow to Him."

Next, the box contained two complete works in manuscript, showing great labour, prepared for publication.   " Scripture Acrostics and Texts of the Bible Reversed and Transposed " is a mass of material closely written on 287 pages of 8 by 10 paper, with directions to print " 500 copies in limp cloth, thin paper, to be printed and published at a total cost not exceeding $250.00."   It is divided into seven sections dealing with various subjects. First there is a comparison between the Syriac and Greek of the New Testament, with eight arguments in favour of the former.   Then follows in alphabetical order lists of ordinary and rare words in the new Testament, with detailed explanations and copious references, showing most careful research.

Section 4 treats of Bible history, while the remaining three consider very fully impugned texts and acrostics of Scripture.

"Scripture Analysed ; or, Investigations in the Original Text of the Holy Bible," to which the date 1894 is attached, is a work of 168 pages, divided also into seven sections. "The object of this publication," so runs the preface, "is to establish the fact that the original text of the New Testament is to be found, not in the Greek, but in the Syriac tongue, which was actually spoken by Christ and His Apostles. . . .

"This present publication proceeds to establish that this original and inspired text of the New Testament is found in our present Syriac text, commonly called Peschito, or untranslated text."

The table of contents shows the subjects considered in this book : "Scripture Analysed," "Parallel Passages in the Gospels alike in Syriac and Varied Greek," "Alliterations Initialled," "New Testament Words in the Syriac," "Texts Reversed," "Old and New Testament Texts Analysed."

Such independent research on the part of the Bishop made him rather a severe critic. He had little patience with the popular theological writers of the day, saying that "they pulled the Bible to pieces too much." The Revised Version of 1885 received a share of his severe denunciation. He had waited with much expectation, mingled with anxiety, for the production of this work, and when Mrs. Bompas sent him a copy from England he was much delighted. But, alas ! his joy was of short duration, and sadly he wrote :

" I do not write more on the Revised Old Testament, for I dislike it too much to consider longer its dissection, and the most painful part is that I feel it must be taken as an index of a defection from purity. Many of the prophecies are rendered as historical, and some of the most important prophecies of Christ are diverted from application to Him."

It is remarkable, considering his isolation, how the Bishop was conversant with the great Biblical questions of the day, and the arguments of leading scholars. He wielded the pen with great facility, and at times wrote learned articles to Biblical magazines. His essay, written for *The Expositor*, on his favourite subject, a plea " for a wider study of the Scripture in the Syriac tongue," is written in a pleasing style, and shows most plainly the skill and strength of the master in its execution.

No matter what subject he handled, the standard was always the Divine Word, and every idea had to be squared and fitted to that, or else he would none of it. Through long years of patient study he had " straight got by heart that book to its last page," and knew his ground. In 1900 the Bishop wrote an answer to a pamphlet on " The Unlawfulness of War." In this he gives an exhibition of his strength and versatility in handling the Word of God. We can almost imagine a smile flitting across his face as he proceeded, clearly and logically, to deal with the arguments of his opponent, bringing forth from the great armoury things both new and old to serve his purpose.

This, then, was the man who, steeped in Hebrew and Syriac, and with natural endowments which would have graced a professor's chair, yet was content through long years to minister faithfully to his little flock of untutored Indians. To them he could impart nothing of his grand thoughts, neither did he think to do so. His sermons, whether to Indians or white people, were full of simplicity and beauty. Love formed the warp and woof of each address, a language all could easily understand. Few of his sermons have been preserved. He always spoke from notes, written on a small slip of paper, which, as a rule, served to light his fire on Monday morning. Occasionally he would consider his notes worthy of preservation, and just two months before his death he forwarded those of his sermon, preached on the fifth Sunday in Lent, to the London Society for Promoting Christianity among the Jews, with a view to their publication.

The Bishop was fond of giving expression to his thoughts in verse, and he produced several poems of much beauty. In 1873, while travelling with the Indians in the North, he composed 200 lines on " The Loucheux Indians." Not only are these verses very descriptive and clothed in simple language, but a yearning strain pervades the whole poem. He had been labouring among these natives, walking and camping with them for eighty days.

THE STUDENT

He had learned to love them, and in this manner expressed some of the affection he felt. One extract must suffice here as typical of the whole :

> " 'Neath skies with stars that never set,
> But round the pole still circle yet ;
> Where streamers of magnetic light
> Enliven winter's lengthening night ;
> Where niggard suns must stint their ray,
> To spend on climates far away ;
> There Christian brethren bend their knees
> In shelter of the forest trees.
> Hearts that with heavenly fervour glow
> Are found amid the Arctic snow ;
> And in the dreadful day of gloom,
> When all the world to judgment come ;
> When, worldly sentence all reversed,
> The first are last and last are first ;
> What if these tribes of sallow face,
> Hindermost now of human race,
> Their want and poverty lay by
> For robes of immortality ?"

Twenty years later the Bishop again made a passionate appeal for these Loucheux Indians in a poem entitled " A Plea for the Wild Sheep of the Rocky Mountains." He was Bishop of the Diocese of Selkirk at the time, and longing for workers to man the field. He alludes to poor Sim's death, and the heroic efforts of Archdeacon McDonald, and draws a vivid picture of his own position :

> " A Bishop and his flock,
> Two thousand zealous converts,
> Walled in with mounts of rock,
> No churches and no clergy.
> Was ever such a sight ?
> But one chief pastor merely,
> In solitary plight."

THE STUDENT

This poem of twenty-four verses of eight lines each was published in the *Church Missionary Gleaner* of November, 1893.

Other poems were put forth by the Bishop from time to time. " A God of Stone" is a modern development of Bishop Heber's well-known hymn " From Greenland's icy mountains," and draws a sad contrast between the simple faith of the Christian converts in heathen lands and the agnostic tendencies which prevail so widely in Christian England.

"One of great length, entitled ' The Critic,' deals quaintly, yet forcibly, with the modern criticism of the Bible ; another, upon Lot's wife, contains a solemn warning against tampering with ' the pleasures of sin,' and the remainder consist chiefly of parables and leading events recorded in the Gospels, rendered in a versified form."*

With this brief sketch we must turn from these " monuments of pathetic labour, tasks patiently fulfilled through slow hours," when, as the Bishop tells us, " it seemed almost as though I saw an angel's hand tracing for me Hebrew sentences, as on the wall of Belshazzar's house." The joy of the scholar was great as he sat in his rude log building soberly among his papers, unheeding the loneliness around him. Some day a worthy and loving hand may arrange that mass of material, and bring it forth for the benefit of mankind. In the meantime the best that those old papers can do for us " is to

* *Church Missionary Intelligencer*, June, 1894.

bid us cast a wistful and loving thought into the past, a little gift of love for the old labourer who wrote so diligently in the forgotten hours, till the weary, failing hand laid down the familiar pen, and soon lay silent in the dust."

CHAPTER XX

" NORTHERN LIGHTS ON THE BIBLE "

" Blessed is the man whose strength is in Thee ; in whose
    heart are Thy ways.
Who going through the vale of misery use it for a well,
    and the pools are filled with water."
Ps. lxxxiv. 5, 6.

IN the far northland there are two books the
missionary always has with him : one, the great
volume of Revelation, the other, the book of
Nature. No matter where he goes, over what
lonely trails he winds his devious way, his companions may be the squalid savage, his dwelling-
place the rude lodge, snow-house, or log hut, his
library is ever with him.

These two books Bishop Bompas studied in no
ordinary degree, and when we consider the delight
he found in the work, we begin to understand why
the northland was so dear to him.

For years he had studied the Bible in English,
Greek, Hebrew, and Syriac. In early days he
loved the sacred volume, and ever found pleasure in
discovering new meanings. As he wandered over
the vast regions of the North, he realized how much

the country might produce in the way of illustrating many passages of Holy Scripture. If he could not tell his discoveries by word of mouth, he could write them down for the benefit of those who would come after.

For twenty-five years, as he moved about, he gained new light and wonderful lessons. These he embodied in a most fascinating little book, which he aptly named "Northern Lights on the Bible." This book, of 207 pages, is an interesting commentary on fifty passages of Scripture, retouched by illustrations from the far North. Though a record of the Bishop's experiences, yet he never once mentions himself in the book, but remains ever in the background with that humility so characteristic of the man. If he wishes to tell of some event in which he took part, it is always in the third person.

Taking such subjects as "rivers," "gold," "storms," "skins," and "pine-trees," and beginning with an appropriate verse from the Bible, he weaves beautiful patterns from his rich storehouse of knowledge. We walk among richly-scented pines and cedars, but instead of a lonely forest, pictures of "an ark of gopher wood," and King Solomon's stately temple, adorned with the cedars of Lebanon, rise before the mind. Then, while lost in admiration, we are suddenly aroused, reminded that the trees teach lessons of strength, security, growth, and freshness for those who wait upon the Lord.

The following extracts will serve to show the

"NORTHERN LIGHTS ON THE BIBLE"

Bishop's method of handling his subjects in this interesting book :

"MOCK SUNS.

"' Sun, stand thou still upon Gibeon.'
JOSH. x. xii.

" Without the slightest wish to invalidate the miracle here recorded, or to diminish its stupendous character, it may not be uninteresting to suggest some modes in which it may have pleased the Almighty to accomplish the effect without a suspension of the laws of Nature.

" It may be rightly held to enhance the power and glory of Almighty God, if it can be shown that He is able to compass the most surprising results without travelling outside of the ordinary routine of His work.

" It appears most unreasonable to attempt a denial that the Author of what are called Nature's laws can dispense with them on occasion, but it may be more allowable to suppose that He may have seldom occasion to do so, in order to effect His every volition.

" To use common and unworthy illustrations, the owner of a watch can move its hands at will without disturbing its works ; the master of a power-loom may introduce a new pattern without arresting the machinery ; or the driver of an engine may reverse its action on an incline without retarding the train.

" In Arctic regions it is well known that the cold

352

and mists of the air produce singular appearances of
displacement of the sun and moon by reflection or
refraction in the air, which are not easily explained.

" By refraction the Arctic sun may remain visible
above the horizon for some time after that calculated
for its setting ; and by a parhelion, or mock sun, it
may be seen in mid-heaven when near its setting.

" Now, it would appear from the account in Joshua
that through some deflection of the polar current of
the upper atmosphere, an Arctic temperature was
produced for the time in the region of the clouds,
and not far above the surface of the earth. This is
implied in the congelation of the atmospheric vapours
so suddenly into huge hailstones before the moisture
had time to be shaped into drops.

" This cold, adjacent to the almost tropical heat of
a Syrian sun, must produce such evaporation and
mists as would be highly conducive to the formation
of a parhelion, and all the phenomena of a highly
refracting atmosphere, if not to an actual reflection,
as seen in the mirage.

" It does not seem useless to suggest that any who
find their faith stumbled by Joshua's surprising
miracle, from being unable to imagine the means by
which it was wrought without subversion of astronomical science, may find a stumbling-block removed
from their way by being reminded how often without
miracle an Arctic sun is apparently displaced.

" Hailstones of dangerous size, as described by
Joshua, are not unusual in the Western Saskatchewan. In Arctic regions hail is infrequent, as the

cold of the upper air forms the vapours into snow
before they condense into water.

" It is singular that in Arctic latitudes the winter
temperature on a mountain height is milder than on
a lower level. This, again, may be owing to upper
equatorial currents of air.

" Mild weather is associated in Arctic climes, as
elsewhere, with a cloudy sky, and intense frost with
a clear atmosphere, but it is not so certain how they
are connected.

" It seems most probable that the casual deflection
downward of a warm current in the upper air, both
deposits its moisture in the form of cloud, and raises
the temperature on the earth's surface. A clear sky,
on the other hand, shows that the air is dry and
deficient in moisture, the suction of which by
evaporation intensifies the cold.

" The old explanation of the nightly radiation to
a clear sky of the heat acquired by the earth the
previous day appears quite inapplicable to polar
regions, where, in the sun's absence, there is no daily
accession of heat to be radiated, and the covering of
snow and ice seems impervious to radiation from
below.

" Somewhat similar considerations may apply to
the surprising miracle recorded in 2 Kings xx. and
Isa. xxxviii. 8, as have been ventured on in regard
to that of Joshua x. In the case of Hezekiah's
miracle, we have also a hint of an unusual rarefac-
tion of the air. For the miracle of the sun-dial
appears to have immediately preceded the deadly

simoom by which 185,000 of the Assyrian army were slain in one night. It may be thought that an apparent elevation of the sun, either by refraction or reflection, produced, in obedience to the fiat of the Almighty, the stated effect on the sun-dial; and the agent employed may have been a mist or fog in connexion with that peculiar state of the atmosphere which presages a coming storm. In Hezekiah's time it would seem to have been the rising, and in Joshua's case the setting, sun, that was apparently retarded for a time, though it is not definitely stated in either case that the day was in the end actually lengthened.

"NAMES.

"'Oreb and Zeeb.'
JUDG. viii. 3.

"These two marauding chiefs of the Midianites come before us in the history of the Judge Gideon. They were truly dwellers in the wilds, and came up with their numerous bands to prey upon the harvests and stores of the defenceless Israelite.

"Such forays have been often made in modern times by wild tribes of North-American Indians, but the natives of the extreme North are at present inoffensive.

"It may be worth while to notice how well the names of the Midian chiefs would befit a modern Indian brave. Translated, they are the Raven and the Wolf. The reference is to the feasts provided for birds and beasts of prey by these plundering chieftains, who almost exhibited the same spirit as those greedy animals. Many a modern Indian has a similar appellation. The Crow or the Fox, and other such names, borrowed from animals, are frequent among present Indian chiefs.

" Zebah and Zalmunna, the kings or leaders of Midian, had similarly significant names. These may be rendered 'Slaughter' and 'Wandering Shade.' So a recent Indian chief in the Saskatchewan plain was called 'Wandering Spirit,' an idea very similar to that of Zalmunna, both implying the consignment to the shades of death of the victims of their fury.

" It may be noted also that it is now generally the custom to translate into English the native Indian names, both for the preservation of their significance and for avoiding the uncouth syllables of a barbarous tongue.

" It might be well if the Hebrew names, which are all significant and appropriate to the occasion of their occurrence, were also translated for a like reason.

" Places in the North-West have also generally their Indian names translated into English when spoken of by Europeans, such as Flint River, Axe Lake, or Stony Mountain. Scripture names are similar, only buried for us in unattractive Hebrew, as, for example, the rivers of Paradise might be called Spreading, Coiling, Gladness, and Fertile. . . .

" Even an inanimate object, when seen for the first time by an Indian, will be named readily, according to its use. So a table is a thing to eat on, a chair a thing to sit on, and so forth. These became the permanent designations of those objects in the Indian tongue. . . .

" The names of the Hebrews appear to have been mostly given to them at birth, and to have been bestowed by the mother in commemoration of joy and gratitude at the birth of offspring. The names of the kings above mentioned may have been possibly assumed in after life.

" The Indian children are also generally named by the mother, and called from some characteristic of the infant, or from some circumstance attending the birth. They have not been taught till recently the feeling of gratitude to God on such an occasion, and the Christian converts, of course, give their children usual Christian names.

" Among the Hebrews many names were patronymics, that is, the son is called by his father's name, as Bartimæus, the son of Timæus (Mark x. 46). In the far West, somewhat strangely, the habit is just the contrary, and as soon as a son is born both father and mother drop their previous names, and are thenceforth known by the name of the son, as William's father or John's mother.

" An Indian has great shyness in mentioning his name, and if he wishes you to know it he will ask his friend to tell you. If you wish to know an Indian's name, it is needful to ask this, not of himself, but of his companion, when you will obtain a ready answer.

"NORTHERN LIGHTS ON THE BIBLE"

" Modern critics are apt to indulge in some display of learning, by deciphering from the hierogylphics of some ancient Egyptian papyrus a name which is supposed, by its similarity, to illustrate some Scripture appellation, or even to be its source or derivation.

" A readier match for the Hebrew names might be found among the present Indians of the North-West. The father of King Saul was named Fowler or Snarer (1 Sam. ix. 1). A modern Esquimaux chief was named Grouse-snare. An Indian chief's name, Large-foot, may be compared with the patriarch Israel's first name, Heel. More exact parallels might be found, for there is hardly a common object or a living animal, but what has furnished a name to a Hebrew of the Old World, or to an Indian of the New.

" AURORA.

" ' Nor the moon by night.'
Ps. cxxi. 6.

" In expounding this text, commentators have been at some pains to discover tradition and examples of the injurious effect of the moon's rays on a sleeper exposed to their glare. The words lunatic, mooned, moonstruck, betray the same idea. On the other hand all travellers in the North are accustomed constantly to sleep exposed to the moonbeams without being conscious of any injurious effects from them. It may be suspected that night-dew and

malarious vapours are more noxious than moon-
shine.

"The promise of the text may also be held to
have a fulfilment to the Arctic traveller in that
Aurora, or Northern Lights, which, when there is no
moon, frequently tempers for him the midnight
darkness. . . .

"The shape and apparent height of the Aurora
varies much. It does not seem to appear without
some kind of a cloud, mist, or vapour on which to
exhibit itself. It seems often, therefore, to follow
vaguely the course of some river or frozen lake, or
the direction to which the wind may drive the
exhalations rising from such a source. After a
brilliant display of the Aurora, as morning dawns,
a slight cloud will mostly be seen remaining in the
position from which the chief coruscations appeared
to emanate.

"At times the Aurora descends till it is very
close overhead, just as clouds sometimes do. The
movements of its gleams are then very rapid,
and resemble the foldings of a great fiery pennon
waving in a strong breeze. It is, however, hard to
compare the Aurora's display to anything earthly,
unless indeed to the 'brush' from an electrical
machine.

"It has been much questioned whether the Aurora
is audible. Those who think they have heard it,
describe the sound as being like the rustling of silk
drapery. This calls to mind the expression of St.
Peter, that when the heavens, being on fire, shall

dissolve, they shall pass away with a rustling noise (2 Pet. iii. 10).

" In severe frost the listening ear will always detect some sound caused by congealing moisture, and even the human breath makes a sort of sawing sound in condensing and freezing from the lips. These sounds may have been attributed by some to the Aurora.

" Certainly a vivid display of the Aurora over the whole sky helps us to picture the day when the heavens shall be on fire, as the blazing of an extensive forest feebly portrays the day when the earth also, and the works that are therein, shall be burned up.

" Most of the Arctic winter travelling is made at night time, because the day is so scanty, and the Aurora is then a pleasant and salutary guide and companion. It cannot fail to remind a devout Christian of Israel's pillar of fire of old, which may have resembled the Aurora in its flash.

" When the light of the Aurora breaks out in the night time with a cloudy sky, it is difficult to distinguish the light from day-break, and an unwary traveller may thus be deceived in the hour. We may then say with David, ' The Lord my God will enlighten my darkness ' (Ps. xviii. 28).

" It may be remarked that in the snowy regions of the North, the winter nights, even without the Aurora, are by no means of pitchy darkness. The reflection from the white carpet of snow is enough to make visible trees, rocks, etc., for some short distance, and the traveller needs not to grope his way in the forest, though care is requisite that his face be not cut at night with a random branch.

"The twilight also is so long, that even when the sun does not rise at all, a slight streak of day dawn will be visible in the south-east, in a clear sky, soon after 7 a.m., and the last streak will not expire till nearly 5 p.m.

"The constant displays of the Aurora are associated in the North with a highly electrical state of the air, so that clothes, blankets, and furs will crackle and sparkle at night when removed or disturbed, and the human hair scintillates in the dark.

"The force of the earth's magnetism is also strong, but the use of a mariner's compass needs care, as within the Arctic circle the compass may point as much east as north, until in approaching the magnetic pole the attraction is so nearly perpendicular as to render the compass useless as a guide for direction.

"BURIAL.

"'Bury thy dead.'
GEN. xxiii. 6.

"The anxiety, which Scripture shows to have existed from the earliest times, for the suitable interment of deceased relations is a natural one, especially in places where unclean animals prowling for prey are likely to disturb the remains.

"In the great North-West, where the ground

throughout the long winter is frozen to a considerable depth, the interment of the dead is no easy matter. The grave has to be chopped, rather than dug, either with the axe or pick, if the latter tool is at hand, which is seldom the case. The work is laborious, and sometimes beyond the power of the relatives of the deceased Indian.

" Probably for this reason the original custom of many tribes of Indians, before the introduction of Christianity among them, was to suspend their dead on high stages elevated on poles from the ground, and thus beyond the reach of predatory animals. By this means the need of hewing the frozen ground was avoided.

" It was customary also to place with the body of the deceased the articles he required for daily use in life, his bow and arrows, or in later times his gun and hatchet, his pipe and fire-bag. These customs have waned before the light of the Gospel, but it is still difficult to wean the Indian from all superstition regarding the dead, or to convince him that the corpse does not retain some life or consciousness, that it is no longer the dwelling, but only the forsaken shell of a spirit, that has winged its flight elsewhere.

" The wailings of an Indian over his lost relative, and especially of a mother over her lost children, are piercing and heartrending ; but it is pleasant to see the contrast in this respect between those who are still ignorant of the Gospel, and such as have received it. The Christian converts have now learned to accept their bereavements as from God's hand in silence and submission, and their mute grief is more impressive than the loud lamentation of the heathen.

" If a conversation is begun with an elderly Indian female, she will generally turn the subject to the number of children she has lost, and these she will count on her fingers. It often takes the whole ten to number her little ones deceased. The severe climate and constant removals, with uncertain food, are very fatal to infant and child life in the North, and the only comfort is to trust that such little ones are gathered by our gracious Saviour to His arms, before they have become the prey of vice and sin, either among heathen, or, what is perhaps worse, among only nominal Christians.

" In some instances the Indian mothers literally cry their eyes out ; and if you ask a blind woman how she lost her vision, she may answer that it was by weeping too hard for her lost relatives, and dimness of sight is attributed to the same cause.

" Some Indians cling tenaciously to a love of life, others exhibit great indifference about it. If a sick Indian despair of recovery, he may die of mere hopelessness. A medicine man may also take the life of an Indian by telling him that he is going to die. The Indian may go home and sicken, and expire from the very expectation of it.

" Sometimes an Indian will carry about with him the corpse of a deceased child half the winter, waiting for the thawing of the ground in spring to bury it suitably. It is, however, more common to notice unseemly haste in disposing of the remains of one deceased. In Scripture we have instances of hasty interment, as in Acts v. 6-10, where the burial followed immediately upon the death. With the Indian, what is termed in that chapter the winding up of the dead, or the wrapping round of the body, sometimes takes place before the breath has left it. The relatives may have a superstitious fear of touching a corpse after death. There is no fear of resuscitation in a climate where the frame is stiffly frozen as soon as removed from the camp fire.

" On the Pacific coast it is the custom for the chiefs to be buried each at the door of his house, and they are careful not to disturb the remains. An Indian in the North is often buried under the place occupied by his camp fire, because the ground there has been softened by the heat. The Indians will remove at once from a place where one of their camp has died, and will avoid the place in future.

" As the natives have such a superstitious dread of a place of burial, it does not seem well to follow in that country the European custom of placing the graves round the church.

" A body interred in the constantly frozen ground of the extreme North might remain unchanged till the world's end, so complete is the action of frost in arresting the decay of substances congealed by it. It is possibly this idea that makes the Indian more superstitious about the place of his dead."

CHAPTER XXI

RESULTS OF MISSIONS IN THE NORTH-WEST

" God spake, and gave us the Word to keep;
    Bade never fold the hands nor sleep
    'Mid a faithless world ; at watch and ward
    Till Christ at the end relieve our guard."
                                    ROBERT BROWNING.

WE have thus followed Bishop Bompas in his long
and noble course of over forty years in the great
northland, and the question naturally arises as to
the result of the work in which he took so great a
part.

In estimating the effect of missions among the
Indians there are certain things which should be
carefully considered. A rude savage race is not
raised to a high state of civilization in a day or a
generation. It took ages to civilize the ancient
Grecians and Romans. The German and English-
speaking peoples were once barbarians, and it took
a long time to bring them to their present condition,
and still there is much room for improvement. The
Indians in the Yukon Territory and in Alaska have
only come in contact with civilizing influences at a
comparatively recent date. And what are a few

T 2

years in the progress of a race? The rooting out of old customs, beliefs, the sowing of the seed, and the bringing the seed to perfection are all the work of time.

"In Europe," says Bishop Bompas, "it may appear at first sight that the Western races, such as the English, have risen from savagedom to civilization and intellectual attainment; but when the matter is investigated, it is found that each stage of improvement has been caused by a sort of inoculation with a civilization already existing further to the East. Thus in England the advent of the Romans, Saxons, and Normans were each stages of advancement to the ancient Britons, while the dispersion to the westward of learned Greeks by the Turks was a cause of advancement of learning at the time of the Reformation. All these causes of improvement were mingled with the renovating influence of Christianity."

To appreciate the work that has been done among the Indians it is well to consider their lives and mode of living before the advent of Christianity into their midst.

"A residence among a wild and untutored race yields the strong impression, that one lives there among the ruins of a bygone civilization, rather than among men in their pristine and original condition. A savage race appears in a state of decay and degeneration, nor do we see any evidence of a tendency in untutored races to rise above themselves."

MISSIONS IN THE NORTH-WEST

Though the natives have a little " knowledge of a good and evil spirit, and a confused idea of a retribution beyond the grave," yet how great is their darkness ! Completely under the spell of the medicine-men or conjurers, they are in a sad state. The sick are neglected, and often murdered, as well as the helpless and aged. At times these beg to be put to death as a release from their sufferings and miseries through neglect. Murder is nothing thought of, and when formerly a young man appeared in spring with his face streaked with vermilion, it was a sign that he had had the glory of killing a human being in winter.

When the Rev. W. W. Kirkby visited Fort Yukon in 1862, and carried the Gospel message to the Indians there, many were the tales he heard of the darkness of heathenism. Men stood up and told of the number of murders they had committed, and " no fewer than thirteen women confessed to having slain their infant girls ; some in the most cruel and heartless manner."

But with the arrival of Christianity a great change took place. " The Indians," says Bishop Bompas, " now speak of the times before the Gospel as the days of darkness. These will now seek to tend and nourish in distress those of an alien tribe, whom before they would only seek to murder as their hereditary foes. Kindness and affection and other fruits of righteousness spring up in the path of the Gospel. Even the Esquimaux promise to leave off their murders, and acknowledge the evil of these,

367

after hearing the Gospel message. Among the Indian converts bloodshed or violence is almost unknown. The knowledge of the Gospel inspires them with a thirst for instruction, and among the Tukudh tribes adults and children hasten greedily to school.

" The conjurers, when converted, often refuse to perform their old tricks even as an exhibition, confessing that while unconverted they were slaves to the devil, and professing that, since delivered from Satan's power, they have forgotten the way, and are quite unable to practise the deception, in which they formerly delighted. A female Tsimshean conjurer will exhibit the painted green wood, which by sleight of hand she had substituted for the green stone that she pretended to make float on the water. A Tukudh conjurer will relate how, at the arrival of the first missionary among his tribe, he was in immediate danger of death, through accusation of having murdered by his spells, but, on the reception of the Gospel, all the dark deeds of the medicine-man were blown to the winds and heard no more."

This is the evidence of missionaries; what do others say ?

We have seen the low condition of the Tukudh Indians at the time of Mr. Kirkby's arrival among them ; now let us bring forward the testimony of men who are not missionaries concerning their progress.

The first are the words of Mr. William Ogilvie,

The body of Chief Isaac's son brought in a boat from Dawson to Moosehide for burial, August, 1906

who was Dominion Land Surveyor in 1887, and later became Commissioner of the Yukon Territory. In his official report in 1887 he spoke of the Indians at Rampart House, and other places where Bishop Bompas, Archdeacon McDonald, and others laboured for years. These are his words :

" It is pleasant to testify that they have profited by this instruction. They hold every Sunday a service among themselves, reading from their books the prayers and lessons for the day, and singing in their own language to some old tune a simple hymn. They never go on a journey of any length without these books, and always read a portion before they go to sleep. I do not pretend that these men are faultless, or that they do not need watching, but I do believe that most of them are sincere in their profession and strive to do what they have been taught."

That was in 1887, and now let us see how they stand to-day. In August, 1907, Mr. David Cadzow, the fur-trader at Rampart House, on the Porcupine River, thus spoke of these same Indians to a newspaper reporter :

" The Loucheux live entirely by hunting, being good hunters and trappers, but will not work on Sundays. It appears that they are mostly baptized, having been for years under the influence of the English Church Missionary Society at the Mission Station on the Mackenzie River. In every way they live up to the teaching of the missionaries, and are a law-abiding, peaceful race of men."

371

MISSIONS IN THE NORTH-WEST

The same paper (the *Dawson News*) which contained this account, a year or two ago described a visit of these Indians to the city.

" The Peel River Indians, who have been visiting Dawson the last three days, selling meats which they brought from the Rocky Mountains, left to-day on a return trip to their hunting-grounds. . . . The party has had a great time in Dawson this trip. All the dainties of cheechaco foods have been indulged in lavishly, but to the credit of the visitors it must be said they have eschewed the red man's fire-water and his befuddling hootch.

" No Indians on the continent, perhaps, are better behaved, and less brought under the evils of the white man and his vices, than the Peels. Coming hundreds of miles from Dawson, they plunge out of the wilderness into the city, spend a few days selling their meats and trading, and then, without loitering or lying idly about the town, after the traditional habits of Indians, they go immediately back to their hunting-grounds.

" These Indians all belong to the Church of England. They were converted many years ago by the missionaries who pioneered the way into the Mackenzie and Yukon Valleys long before the gold-strike in the Klondyke. Joseph and Amos are native preachers in the tribe, and the Indians are devout."

Of course these Tukudh Indians are the flower of missionary enterprise. Too often, it must be sadly acknowledged, have the natives succumbed to the

THE BURIAL OF THE SON OF CHIEF ISAAC AT MOOSEHIDE

The Chief and his wife stand at Bishop Stringer's right hand

evil influences of a degenerate class of white men, the scum of civilization, who exert every effort to ruin the Indian, soul and body. Time and time again did Bishop Bompas mourn over the ravages made among his little flock by the temptations to which they were exposed.

"When the Gospel is presented to their acceptance," he says, "it is as though they were invited to eat of the tree of life. . . . But, alas ! as civilized races intermix with these barbarous and rude, there are offered also large tastes of the tree of knowledge of good and evil, and these are greedily devoured, and perhaps greatly preferred.

"It is pitiful to see the comparative simplicity of the savage imbibe the allurements to vicious pleasure, which he learns from more civilized races, without possessing that self-restraint which enables those of a higher intellectual grade to moderate their indulgence even in vice. This applies especially to the introduction of strong drink among rude races by those more civilized; but also to other irregularities."

A very marked characteristic of Bishop Bompas's work among the Indians was his wonderful faith, combined with almost complete unselfishness. He had no doubt about the final outcome, and was willing to plant the seed, and tend it carefully, and leave the increase to God. While others became discouraged at the apparent ingratitude of the natives, and at times left the work, he never seemed to look for gratitude or thanks. He found pleasure in doing the Master's service, and deemed that sufficient.

To him there was much comfort in the promises of old, and he applied them to his own field of work. Among his favourite texts in this connexion were the following :

"The wilderness and the solitary place shall be glad for them ; and the desert shall rejoice and blossom as the rose" (ISA. xxxii. 16).

"Judgment shall dwell in the wilderness" (ISA. xxxii. 16).

"They that dwell in the wilderness shall bow before Him" (Ps. lxxii. 9).

"The wilderness shall be a fruitful field" (ISA. xxxii. 15).

"He will make her wilderness like Eden, and her desert like the garden of the Lord ; joy and gladness shall be found therein, thanksgiving, and the voice of melody" (ISA. li. 3).

These and other passages show God's purposes of mercy to bless in spiritual things those who have niggard supplies of temporal blessings. Christian missions have prospered in the wilds. In the very sparse population of the far North-West, more provision is made in God's providence for the hearing of the Gospel than might seem to be the share of these countries, if compared by population only with other lands.

These memoirs are now brought to a close. We have traced the life of Bishop Bompas through many vicissitudes. With him will always be associated thoughts of mighty rivers and great inland lakes, snow-capped mountains and sweeping plains ; thoughts of heroism and devotion to duty ; but, above

376

all, thoughts of gratitude for countless unknown natives of the North on river, mountain, and plain, who have been lifted out of darkness and brought close to the Great Shepherd's side through the light of the Gospel carried by a faithful herald of salvation—this noble Apostle of the North.

INDEX

A

" ALARM BIRD," the, 45

Alexandra Falls on the Hay River, 134

Alford, Mr. Bompas's fourth curacy, 30

Anderson, Bishop, the influence of his sermon on W. C. Bompas, 19

Athabasca, Mr. Bompas consecrated first Bishop of Athabasca, 151 ; vast extent of the diocese, 167 ; mission, 182

" Aurora," 358

B

Beaver Indians, pitiable condition of the, 66

Bennett, Lake, character of, 313

" Bloody Falls," the scene of a massacre, 45

Bompas, Miss, 157

Bompas, Mrs., leaves for England, 243 ; returns to Yukon, 260

Bompas, Sergeant, 20

Bompas, William Carpenter : birth, 20; family, 21 ; brothers, 21, 22 ; characteristics of early youth, 22 ; religious nature and training, 23 ; education, 24 ; articled to solicitors, 24 ; ill-health, 24 ; confirmed, 25 ; ordained, 25 ; first curacy at Sutton, 25 ; his good work, 26 ; death of his mother, 29 ; curacy of New Radford, 29 ; curacy at Holy Trinity, South Lincolnshire, 30 ; curacy at Alford, 30 ; offers his services to the Church Missionary Society, 30 ; ordained priest by Bishop Machray, 30 ; ardour for his new work, 32 ; lands at New York, 33 ; visits Captain Palmer, 33 ; assisted by Dr. Schultz, 34 ; Indians, 35 ; reaches Red River, 35 ; journey

379

INDEX

north by boat, 36; a difficulty bravely overcome, 36; Fort
Chipewyan, 36; a severe land journey, 38; Fort Resolution,
38; crosses Great Slave Lake, 38; arrival at Fort Simpson,
39; Rev. W. W. Kirkby, 39; his stay, 40; goes to Fort
Norman, 57; return to Fort Simpson, 58; back to Fort
Norman, 61; among the Great Bear Lake Indians, 62; at
Fort Rae, 63; at Fort Resolution, 64; at Fort Chipewyan,
65; at Fort Vermilion, 77; at Fort Simpson, 80; at Fort
McPherson, 108; visits the Eskimos, 109; has snow-blind
ness, 109; plot to murder him, 123; saved by the chief, 123;
reaches Peel's River Fort with the tribe, 124; sets out for the
Peace River Valley, 126; travelling by boats, 127; reaches
Fort Vermilion, 130; visits Fort Chipewyan and Fond du Lac,
130; mining on the Peace River, 130; reaches Rocky Mountain portage, 130; while at Rocky Mountain portage he
acts as public vaccinator, 131; reaches Fort St. John, 132;
death of Mrs. Donald Ross, 132; receives instructions to proceed
to Yukon district, 133; follows Hay River to Great Slave Lake,
133; stay at Fort McPherson, 138; work among the Loucheux
Indians, 138; on the Yukon River, 140; summoned home for
consecration, 144; reaches Red River Settlement, and is entertained by Bishop Machray, 148; arrives at Montreal, and em-
barks on the *Scandinavian*, 150; arrival in Liverpool, 150; consecrated by Archbishop Tait, 151; marries Miss C. S. Cox, 153;
return to the field of labour, 156; arrival at New York, 158;
reaches Winnipeg, 158; an ordination in the cathedral at
Manitoba, 159; tedious journey by boat to Fort Simpson, 160;
the Bishop sprains his back, 162; arrival at Fort Simpson,
162; an Indian school started, 168; the first confirmation and
ordination, 168; visits Fort Rae, 170; Christmas at Fort
Simpson, 171; visits Fort Norman, 173; skill as a doctor,
174; old Martha, 174; search for Jeannie de Nord, 175; first
Synod, 179; his charge, 182; illness of Mrs. Bompas, 188;
arduous journey to Metlakahtla, 196; Mr. Duncan's objection
to confirming native Christians, 196; return to Fort Simpson,
201; famine, 201; mission farms commenced, 203; visits
the Tukudh Missions, 204; the Eskimo Mission, 208; visits

INDEX

INDEX

INDEX

INDEX

K

L

M

INDEX

N

Naas River, lava plain on the, 200

"Names," 355

Natives of the far North, 90

New Radford, near Nottingham, Mr. Bompas's second curacy, 29

"Northern Lights on the Bible," by Bishop Bompas, 339, 350

O

Owen, Rev. H., Mr. Bompas's first Rector, 25

P

Peace River Valley, Mr. Bompas sets out for, 126 ; mining on the Peace River, 130

Peel River Fort, Mr. Bompas leaves the Eskimos at, 124

Peel River Indians, the, 372

Pelly River discovered by Robert Campbell, 48

Q

Quickpak River, the, 47

R

Red River as Mr. Bompas first saw it, 35

Riel, Louis, and the North-West Rebellion, 233

Rocky Mountain portage, Mr. Bompas at, 131 ; acts as public vaccinator, 131

Ross, Mrs., death of, 132

Rowe, Bishop, on the unselfish labours of Bishop Bompas, 334

Rupert's Land, division of the Diocese of, 144

S

Schultz, Dr., assists Mr. Bompas to cross the plains, 34

"Scripture Acrostics and Texts of the Bible Reversed and Transposed," by Bishop Bompas, 343

"Scripture Analyzed ; or, Investigations in the Original Text of the Holy Bible," by Bishop Bompas, 344

Selkirk, Diocese of, 238

Sim, Rev. V. C., missionary to the Tukudh Indians, 229

INDEX

THE END

BILLING AND SONS, LTD., PRINTERS, GUILDFORD·

INDEX TO THIS EDITION

Cody's index, which usefully lists people, places, and events, as well as detailing Bompas's life chronologically, is reproduced at the end of the original text. It also should be referenced, although Cody's choice of index material is interesting in context. Under "Eskimos," for example, Cody lists not only "their habits and customs," but also their "treacherous character" and their "plot to murder Mr. Bompas." Similarly, there are only six references to "Indians," one of which is "infanticide."

Note: The index entries in capital italic Roman numerals refer to the new introduction, those in lower case Roman numerals refer to the introductory material of *An Apostle of the North*, and those in Arabic numerals refer to the body of Cody's book.

Bompas, William Carpenter
accomplishments 223–25
and Beaver Indians 66–71
and First Nations *XLIII–XLIV,*
XXVI–XXVII, L–LIV, LXVIII,
LXXIV–LXXVI, LXVIII–LXX,
61–64, 90–98, 108, 110–11,
173–78, 270–71, 329
and gold miners *LXIV–LXVII*
and H.A. Cody *XXXII*
and indigenous literacy 64
and Inuit *LIV, LV, LXII–LXIII,*
98–105, 110–22, 208
and Klondike gold rush
LXVI–LXVII, 277–88
and Loucheux Indians 138–40
and Mounted Police *LXIV–LXV*
and "Native Church" policy
LI–LII
arrives Fort Simpson 57–58
as author *L,* 337–49, 350–74
as "marginal man" *LXVII*
baptism 23
burial site *XXVIII*
character *XXVII, XXX–XXXI,*
XXXIII, XLIX–L,
LXVII–LXX,
LXXVIII–LXXIX
confirmed as Anglican 25
curate *XXXVIII–XXXIX,* 25–30
death and funeral *XIX–XX,*
LXVII, 321–35
early career *XXXVIII–XXXIX*
early life *XXXVI–XXXVII,* 20–25
internet *XXII–XXIII*
joins Church of England *XXXVII*
legacy *LXXVI–LXXIX*
lobbies Ottawa *LXII–LXV, LXIX,*
267

made Bishop *LVI,* 144–55
marriage *LVII,* 153–55
northern memorials *XXVIII*
on summer travel 126–30
on winter travel 70–77
ordination as priest *XLI,* 30
relations with wife *XII, LIX,*
187–89, 218, 242–43, 260–63,
306
resignation *LXVII,* 309
stamina *XLII, LIII–LV,* 251–52,
109–10
theology *XXXI, XXXVI–XXXVIII,*
LIII, LXXII–LXXIII, 307–9
Bonanza Creek *LXV*
Bowen, R.J. 272–74, 281–82, 285, 289,
294
Bunn, Thomas 202–3
Buxton Mission *LXXI,* 248
Buxton, T.F. 247

Campbell, Robert 47–52
Canham, T.H. *LXXI,* 119, 208, 219,
230, 237, 263, 272, 274
Carcross (Cariboo Crossing) *XIX,*
LVIII, LXVII, LVIII, LXXVI,
289–93, 299, 304–5, 313
Cariboo, Diocese of *LXIX*
Carmack, George *XX*
Carman, Bliss *IX*
Church Missionary Society *XII-XIII,*
XVI, XXXIX, XLI, LI,
LV–LVI, LXVII, LXXII, xii,
30, 32, 40, 151, 207, 247, 272,
274, 283, 317
Circle City 279
Cody, H.A. *XII, XXXII–XXXIII, LIX,*
LXXIX
as hagiographer *XXXII–XXXIII*